Somewhere Between Islam and Judaism

Somewhere Between Islam and Judaism
Critical Reflections

Aaron W. Hughes

SHEFFIELD UK   BRISTOL CT

Published by Equinox Publishing Ltd.

UK: Office 415, The Workstation, 15 Paternoster Row, Sheffield, South Yorkshire S1 2BX

USA: ISD, 70 Enterprise Drive, Bristol, CT 06010

www.equinoxpub.com

First published 2021

© Aaron W. Hughes 2021

All rights reserved. No part of this publication may be reproduced or transmitted in any form or by any means, electronic or mechanical, including photocopying, recording or any information storage or retrieval system, without prior permission in writing from the publishers.

ISBN-13	978 1 80050 055 6	(hardback)
	978 1 80050 056 3	(paperback)
	978 1 80050 057 0	(ePDF)
	978 1 80050 058 7	(ePub)

British Library Cataloguing-in-Publication Data

A catalogue record for this book is available from the British Library.

Library of Congress Cataloging-in-Publication Data

Names: Hughes, Aaron W., 1968- author.
Title: Somewhere between Islam and Judaism : critical reflections / Aaron W. Hughes.
Description: Sheffield, South Yorkshire ; Bristol, CT : Equinox Publishing Ltd, 2021. | Includes bibliographical references and index. | Summary: "Somewhere Between Islam and Judaism is of interest to scholars and students of religion concerned with comparison and those studying Islam, Judaism and Jewish–Muslim relations. The essays collected in this volume provide a set of critical reflections on what it means to study these two religious traditions within the larger context of the academic study of religion"—Provided by publisher.
Identifiers: LCCN 2021010146 (print) | LCCN 2021010147 (ebook) | ISBN 9781800500556 (hardback) | ISBN 9781800500563 (paperback) | ISBN 9781800500570 (epdf) | ISBN 9781800500587 (epub)
Subjects: LCSH: Judaism—Relations—Islam. | Islam—Relations—Judaism. | Abrahamic religions.
Classification: LCC BP173.J8 H843 2021 (print) | LCC BP173.J8 (ebook) | DDC 201/.5—dc23
LC record available at https://lccn.loc.gov/2021010146
LC ebook record available at https://lccn.loc.gov/2021010147

Typeset by JS Typesetting Ltd, Porthcawl, Mid Glamorgam

For my mum
Sadie May Hughes (née Alley)
who sent me on the journey "somewhere between"

Contents

Acknowledgments — viii

Introduction: Somewhere Between — 1

Part I Disciplinary Overviews

1 The Current State of Islamic Studies — 11
2 The Current State of Jewish Studies — 33

Part II Case Studies

3 Destabilizing "Judaism" in Late Antiquity — 55
4 *Zindīqs* and the Construction of Islamic Orthodoxy — 70
5 Modern Back-Projections and their Repercussions — 90

Part III Reboot

6 The Study of Islam in the Age of Trump — 111
7 Abrahamic Religions: The Second Generation — 127
8 The Study of Religion as a National and Nationalist Project — 147

Afterword — 165
Notes — 169
References — 181
Index — 199

Acknowledgments

Since this book is based on a series of lectures I have given over the past few years, I would like to thank a number of friends and colleagues for invitations, and the hospitality and wonderful conversations that ensued. These include Adi Bharat, Francesco Chiabotti, Farhad Daftary, Majid Daneshgar, Alon Dar, Wendy Dossett, Sami Everett, Wolfgang Fuchs, Robert Gleave, Eric L. Goldstein, Martin Goodman, Edmund Hayes, Alex Henley, Daniel Herskovitz, Reza Huseini, Carool Kersten, István Kristó-Nagy, Bruce Lawrence, Russell McCutcheon, Lauren Morrey, Jonas Otterbeck, Johanna Pink, Daryoush Mohammad Poor, Steven Ramey, Sajjad Rizvi, Alexander Samely, Marco Schöller, Matt Sheedy, Petra Sijpesteijn, Nicolai Sinai, Leif Sternberg, Alana Vincent, Elliot Wolfson, Philip Wood, and Christian Zahner.

As always, I am thankful for the advice and understanding of Janet Joyce, managing director at Equinox Publishing. For close to twenty years, Janet has provided me with the support and a venue to publish my work.

Finally I am grateful for two special ladies in my life—my mum, Sadie Hughes, to whom this volume is dedicated, and Liliana Leopardi, for the companionship and conversation.

A version of Chapter 4 appears in my forthcoming *An Anxious Inheritance: Religious Others and the Shaping of Sunnī Orthodoxy* (Oxford: Oxford University Press, 2022).

Introduction

Somewhere Between

I have spent my academic life, perhaps not unlike my personal one, occupying the uncertain terrain that exists between Islam and Judaism. The work that follows, however, is not so much about these two traditions as it is with the two subfields of study, Islamic studies and Jewish studies, that bring them into focus. These two subfields, as I conceive of them and indeed as I have plied and continue to ply my trade in them, cohabit—rather awkwardly—in the larger field of religious studies. This larger field is so fraught with its own set of structural problems that many of them have been imported into the numerous subfields housed within, including the two under discussion here.

Jewish studies and Islamic studies are certainly not confined to religious studies, however. The academic study of Islam, for example, goes back much further and indeed predates the rise of religious studies as a field of study. Indeed, the study of Islam as an academic enterprise has a lengthy tradition in Orientalism, beginning perhaps as early as the seventeenth century with the publication, in 1698, of the Latin Qurʾān by Ludovico Marracci (1612-1700). To this, one could add the subsequent work of those such as Antoine Isaac Silvestre de Sacy (1758-1838) and the foundation of the École spéciale des langues orientales in Paris in 1795.

The rise of Jewish studies in Germany in the nineteenth century, while not possessing the same lengthy and august history as Islamic studies, was nevertheless heavily influenced by this tradition of Orientalism. If European Orientalists acquired and catalogued books and manuscripts from Islamic and other lands, German Jewish scholars did the same with Jewish texts, using the methods they had learned from their colleagues working in Islam and other so-called Oriental traditions. Indeed, since

Jewish students could not take courses on Jewish history or other Jewish topics at German universities since no such courses existed, many even specialized in *Orientalistik* (see, e.g., the essays in Kraemer 1999), with some of them going on to become well-known and pioneering scholars of Islam. Jews such as Ignác Goldziher (1850–1921), Josef Horovitz (1874–1931), Heinrich Speyer (1897–1935), and Paul Kraus (1904–1944) engaged in important work, much of which is still valid to this day, and their efforts helped to create what has become the modern study of Islam.

The study of these two traditions, perhaps not unlike the traditions themselves, was thus forged under the same crucible. If medieval Hebrew grammarians and philosophers used the same tools, terms, and categories developed by their Arab and Muslim counterparts, those engaged in the modern academic study of Judaism did the same with those developed by European Orientalists who sought to understand Islam.

Given the history of these two traditions—something that stretches back to the seventh-century Arabian Peninsula—and given the history of the scholarly traditions used to study them, one would think they would be naturally affiliated. Unfortunately, this is rarely the case, at least in the current moment. Identity politics, criticism of Orientalism, Israel and the conflict in the Middle East, and a growing disinterest in textual traditions have all worked to create a barren terrain between the two scholarly traditions, just as the current political situation has done for the two religious traditions.

I know from personal experience. Though trained in Islamic studies, midway through my career I decided to take up a position in Jewish studies and, while I still have that position, my research over the last few years has, with few exceptions, gravitated back to the study of Islam. It has been a circuitous journey, meandering between the two subfields, working in one and then back to do work in the other again. But the work always felt bifurcated and, with a few exceptions, integration proved difficult. The result is that I do not feel particularly at home in either subfield. It also means that colleagues within each of these subfields imagine me as either occupying space or being entrenched firmly in the other. This occasionally leads to charges of me being a tyro or an imposter. Those in Islamic studies, for example, routinely call me a scholar of Judaism or, worse, a "Jewish scholar." Those in Jewish studies take one look at my last name, and wonder how and why I might be interested in Jewish things.

It is an unfortunate state of affairs, to be sure. It signals, for one thing, that we are completely unable to think outside of the rigid structures that the academic study of religion has bequeathed to us and that we somehow continue to impose upon ourselves. The overarching concerns of religious studies function not unlike the iron cage that makes its appearance at the end of Max Weber's *The Protestant Ethic and the Spirit of Capitalism*, as something of our own making, but that from which we inevitably cannot escape. One cannot be a scholar of hybridity or a scholar, say, of the intersectionality of diverse cultural forms. No, that cannot be. One instead has to be a "scholar of Judaism" or a "scholar of Islam." One should not be both, unless of course a department is understaffed and underfunded and needs a "twofer," two for the price of one. So stuck are we in the "world religions" paradigm that we still think with essences that can be ejected from historical contexts and then analyzed through the methodological act of comparison, all with an eye towards facilitating interfaith dialogue.[1]

One would think that the space between Islam and Judaism would prove fertile enough to engage in questions of social, religious, cultural, and intellectual interactions. And, indeed, it has functioned as such over the years, especially among scholars of medieval Judaism. One could, for example, point to the usual suspects of peaceful coexistence, such as eleventh-century al-Andalus (Muslim Spain) or sixteenth-century Ottoman Empire. But even that ground is surprisingly unfirm. Such places, especially Muslim Spain, are often examined through rose-colored glassed and then romanticized as positive exemplars of either Jewish contribution to the larger societies in which Jews found themselves (as emphasized by nineteenth-century German-Jewish scholarship) or interfaith relations (as is so common today). This latter example is indicative of where the field of religious studies finds itself at the current moment. It only wants us to focus on the "good" that religion does and when we look at intersections between so-called religions it is supposed to be positive and beneficial, especially for us in the present.

Another problem is that the elephant in the room for anyone working on some or any aspect of these two religious traditions is Israel. Since its formation in 1948, but especially after its encroachment beyond the Green Line in 1967, Israel and many Jews have had a problem with the Arab world, which they see as a source of disruption to what they imagine would otherwise be a peaceful existence. Many Muslims, both Arab and non-Arab, likewise regard Israel's existence as a threat to their own security and Israel's treatment of Palestine and Palestinians as in violation of international law.

It is, to be sure, an intractable problem. I have no intention of wading into the issues or apportioning blame, of which there is much to go around. I will instead leave that to the UN, scholars of political science, in addition to the inevitable demagogues and self-styled experts. I will say, however, that it has given rise to two subfields that are loosely related to Jewish and Islamic studies, to wit, Israel studies and Palestinian studies. Both are, needless, to say, marked by contention, resentment, and mutual grievance. To be a Jew in Islamic studies or a Muslim Arab in, say, Israel studies is not easy and one is frequently met with suspicion, despite the fact that both are working with basically the same data and questions. In spite of such similarities, however, there are scripts that must be followed when it comes to Israel. Unless a Jewish scholar of Islam assents to a set of propositions (e.g., Israel is wrong, the occupation is unjust, etc.), it is simply assumed that he or she is a closeted Zionist. Relatedly, the number of Arabs or Muslims in Jewish studies—like non-Jews, more generally—is minimal. Once we throw identity politics into the mix the situation is only exacerbated, often to the point of parody.

It is such a binary way of thinking, and the assumption is that one always has to be what one studies. This has, unfortunately, led to a decline in the humanities. Instead of intellectual freedom, we are instead shackled by the chains of our collective making. The result is that we rarely develop new and original ways to put religious traditions together except in the most essentialized and banal fashion. One would think new ways of examining Judaism and Islam in counterpoint would be easy, if for no other reason than that members of each tradition have thought a lot about the other as a way to think about themselves. Most scholars who work in medieval Jewish studies—such as the literary and intellectual traditions of Spain and North Africa—know Arabic, for example, and must also have facility in Islamic historical, literary, and intellectual traditions. This is on account of the fact that until 1948, Jews always lived in other places. However, and this is a problem, those in Islamic studies rarely learn Hebrew or even Judeo-Arabic, and rarely have even have a passing interest in things Jewish.

Despite their similarities and the historical connections between Judaism and Islam, there are many differences between them. If Islamic studies comprises one of the area studies (e.g., South Asian studies, Canadian studies), Jewish studies is part of ethnic studies (e.g., African American studies, Women's studies). There is a huge difference between area studies and ethnic studies. Most significant is the fact that the study of Islam, and I have realized this only after 20 years in both fields, is more amenable to asking difficult questions than is Jewish studies. This is most likely on account of the former's Orientalist heritage, wherein Islam has always been studied critically by non-Muslims. Jewish studies, on the contrary, and given its own unique history, is largely an insider project that has always been about defending Judaism, apologizing for it, showing how Judaism—and, by extension, Jews—are both normal and exceptional, often at one and the same time.

* * *

It is unfortunate that the field of religious studies—not unlike Islamic studies and Jewish studies—rarely engages in critical reflection on the various moves that bring data into focus. The overwhelming emphasis is on data analysis, which often involves little more than description. But these fields of study—like most others—possess countless blind spots, assumptions, and problematic assertions, all of which structure, frame, and otherwise bring data into focus or, alternatively, obscure it. It is important to note these features and, when or if possible, question what we do, ascertaining where our categories come form, and to what ends they have been and continue to be put. The work that follows seeks to ask and examine such issues.

All of the chapters below, with the exception of Chapter 4, were delivered as lectures. While I have added a scholarly apparatus to them all, I have tried to retain some of the informality and playfulness inherent to oral presentation.

What follows is divided into three interrelated parts. In Part I, I offer assessments of the current states of Islamic and Jewish studies, especially in light of my earlier critiques of these two fields.

Chapter 1, "The Current State of Islamic Studies," is based on a lecture I was invited to give at the Institute for the Study of Muslim Civilisations at the Aga Khan University in London, which I ultimately was unable to do on account of the lockdown associated with the COVID-19 pandemic. The organizers had asked me to give a presentation wherein I would reflect on the ways that my trilogy of books—*Situating Islam* (2006), *Theorizing Islam* (2012b), and *Islam and the Tyranny of Authenticity* (2015) have helped to nudge certain conversations along in the field of Islamic studies. The chapter examines the reception of my work in the field, analyses its impact, and shows what has changed and what has stayed the same.

Chapter 2, "The Current State of Jewish Studies," parts of which were delivered at the Tam Institute for Jewish Studies at Emory University, allows me—not unlike as I did in the first chapter—to reflect on the impact that my earlier critiques of Jewish studies (e.g., Hughes 2013c, 2014) have had on this subfield. To do this, I revisit some of the structural problems inherent to the field, in addition to highlighting prospects for the future.

Part II of the volume, "Case Studies," consists of a series of three "e.g.s" that, I trust, reveals some of the aforementioned problems articulated in Part I, and attempts to offer some solutions.

Chapter 3, "Destabilizing 'Judaism' in Late Antiquity," is based on lectures delivered at the Oxford Center for Hebrew and Jewish Studies, the Center for Jewish Studies at the University of Manchester, and the Department of Theology and Religious Studies at the University of Chester. It argues that, in order to avoid its apologetic and ethnocentric excesses, the field of Jewish studies needs to jettison its basic narrative that reifies something called Judaism and that tries to articulate Jewish continuity between biblical times and the modern day. Problems in that narrative are either thinly papered over or largely ignored as an examination of the Jews on the Arabian Peninsula at the time of Muhammad clearly reveals.

Chapter 4, "Zindīqs and the Construction of Islamic Orthodoxy," demonstrates how the term "zindīq" (heretic) was used to refer to individuals, though rarely communities, who were believed to be nominally Muslim, but who subscribed to what were increasingly becoming non-orthodox practices or beliefs. It was a catch-all phrase that could be used to describe everything from Manicheans to libertines, and from court secretaries to one's theological opponents. The chapter argues that zindīqs served a double role: They revealed the wages of improper belief, just as they aided in the articulation of true belief.

Chapter 5, "Modern Back-Projections and their Repercussions," based on a lecture delivered to the Institute of Arab and Islamic Studies at the University of Exeter, builds upon the previous chapter by demonstrating that despite the secular context of the Western academy, the study of Islam retains many of the assumptions and tacit presuppositions examined in our early sources. We see this acutely in how Islamic studies deals with Jews and other minoritarian groups. Not only are all of these non-Sunnī traditions marginalized in our modern academic narratives, the language used to situate them has strayed little from the categories and structures encountered in the earlier theological tradition.

Part III, "Reboot," consists of three chapters, all of which are more constructive in the sense that they attempt to nudge the field along in more productive ways.

Chapter 6, "The Study of Islam in the Age of Trump," presented initially at Aga Khan University in London and then at the Albert-Ludwigs-Universität Freiburg, argues that the critical and analytical study of Islam benefits us all. It shows us, both Muslim and non-Muslim, the heights to which historical actors have imagined their tradition. It reveals that Islam is an intricate part of western civilization, whatsoever that may be, and neither its illegitimate child nor its psychological other. Our current political moment—one of fear and distrust, of anger and xenophobia—as worrisome as it may be, cannot hold. The study of Islam has the potential to take an active role in shaping popular opinion of Islam. But this role must eschew simplistic and apologetic formulations, ones predicated simply on responding to ignorant formulations.

Chapter 7, "Abrahamic Religions: The Second Generation," originated as a lecture to the Faculty of Theology at the University of Cambridge when I interviewed for the Sultan Qaboos Professorship of Abrahamic Faiths and Shared Values. It takes as its point of departure my *Abrahamic Religions: On the Uses and Abuses of History* (2013a). Therein I argued that the term "Abrahamic religions" was extremely problematic, based on ecumenical desire as opposed to analytic rigor. The term, however, remains. It has not gone anywhere, nor been replaced by a better one. In this chapter I argue that, since the term seems to be here to stay, we need to rethink and try, to the best of our abilities, to rehabilitate it.

Chapter 8, "The Study of Religion: A National and Nationalist Project," based on a presentation delivered to the "Critical Religion" seminar at Mansfield College, University of Oxford, has a slightly different tenor than the others. It deals neither explicitly with Islam nor Judaism, but instead reflects on the study of religion at the current moment. Using Canada as my "e.g," I argue that the category "religion" is intimately caught up with the modern nation state. It is, after all, the state—with is overlapping legal, political, and social infrastructures—that is the ultimate arbiter of what gets to count as a religion and what does not, and who is religious and who is not. Religion is thus imagined, constructed, and situated in specific national frames of reference. These frames, unfortunately, are rarely examined and we instead operate as if there exists some trans-national study of religion.

* * *

Readers familiar with my work will realize that these chapters are not really about Islam and Judaism. While I trust readers who want to learn more about these two religions will find enough to pique and satisfy their interests, my main concern here, on the contrary, is about the various genealogies, lenses, terms, and narratives that scholars use to bring Islam and Judaism into what they believe to be sharper focus. There can be no knowledge without theories and methods, yet unfortunately many—whether in the field of religious studies or the subfields of Islamic and Jewish studies—operate as if that were not the case. Knowledge, they argue, is about reading more texts, engaging in the production of critical editions, and in being historical positivists who believe the facts need no interpretation as they speak for themselves.

I resist such positivism and—following a long line of thinkers who have had a big influence on me, from J. Z. Smith to Bruce Lincoln to Russell McCutcheon—instead maintain that it is we who conjure facts into existence by the often unconscious choices we make. We choose which texts are relevant and not. We choose what geographical or historical period to work on. We choose what to emphasize and what to marginalize. Unfortunately, not nearly enough attention is paid to such choices, and we instead operate as if what we are working on is as natural as can be. However, it is ultimately us who decide what terms and categories to use—terms and categories that inevitably have histories and were (and indeed still are) invested in all sorts of political and/or ideological battles. Such decisions are often overlooked and we just keep doing what we have always done: search for the sacred, define essences, and locate the experiential.

A Word on Transliteration

I always struggle with this issue. Include them and one is accused of producing a work that is too technical for the generalists found in religious studies. Do not include them and risk censure from one's colleagues, especially in Islamic studies. I have decided to retain them. I trust the non-technical reader, when coming across a word like Qurʾān will simply remove the diacritics imaginatively and see the word Quran. Likewise, when they see a word like kāfirūn (unbelievers) they will read kafirun. I apologize for this, but, at the same time, do not want to lose the attention of those in Islamic studies, whom I also want to reach with this work.

Part I

Disciplinary Overviews

Chapter 1

The Current State of Islamic Studies

I have attempted over the years to make a number of theoretical interventions in and contributions to the study of Islam, especially as carried out within the larger field of the academic study of religion.[1] I am now frequently asked two questions in the light of these interventions. The first is: Have my interventions met with any degree of success within this subfield? The second, and this primarily stems from European colleagues: Are my interventions directed solely at the North American context or can they be applicable to other, less apologetic academies?

In this opening chapter I propose to visit these two questions with the aim of assessing the current state of Islamic studies. I want to do this in a manner that, while semi-autobiographical, does not make me the focus of the narrative. On the contrary, my goal is to show how those interventions—in retrospect perhaps not always articulated as delicately as they could have been—have helped to nudge certain conversations along. These conversations, I might add, were not readily apparent when I entered the field over twenty years ago. While there still exist many theological and apologetic discourses in the subfield of Islamic studies, as indeed they do in the parent field of religious studies, it would seem fair to say that—in some ways—theoretically things are getting somewhat better.

While the 2021 me might be tempted to tell the 2001 me not to have been so angry and instead to have reached out to colleagues differently, it cannot be gainsaid that the case had to be made and that there existed—and indeed still exist—certain structural problems inherent to the field. These problems, then as now, needed to be exposed and addressed. While some might argue that these problems are solely the product of the American Academy's excesses, especially as it is increasingly hamstrung by identity politics and political correctness, as I hope to show near the end of this chapter, when I visit the second question above, such an argument is untenable.

Contexts and Frames

The study of Islam has a lengthy, if convoluted and often tortured, history in the western Academy. This history of European writing about Islam and Muslims is full of excesses that have taken place against a much broader backdrop that has included the Crusades, colonialism, and, more recently, military invasion and occupation. Running alongside these activities, both justifying and legitimizing them, are the academic discourses associated with Orientalism.[2] Though the study of Muslims and their religion has coincided with an interest in understanding "them," it has also dovetailed with the desire to vanquish and conquer. Orientalism, then, has played a key role in the subjugation and misrepresentation of both Muslims and Islam.

Within this context, non-Muslims have been writing negatively about Islam since at least the time of John of Damascus (675–749), who lived and wrote in the years following the death of Muhammad, Islam's prophet. The Nestorian author of the ninth-century Syriac *Apocalypse of Sergius Baḥīrā*, to cite another example, describes Muhammad initially as the student of Baḥīrā, an Arab Christian ascetic, but who then subsequently fell under the negative influence of a Jew by the name of Kaʿb al-Aḥbār (Roggema 2009; see also Hoyland 1997: 505–511). According to the *Apocalypse*, "Kaʿb the Scribe—cursed be his memory—passed on [faulty information] to the Ishmaelites. He confounded and corrupted everything that Sergius [i.e., Baḥīrā] had written originally. For the sons of Ishmael were uncivilized pagans, like horses without a bridle" (Roggema 2009: 298–299).

The history of western writing about Islam has thus been anything but kind. While the subsequent Orientalist tradition that picked up steam in the nineteenth century has certainly produced many useful studies, some of which are still beneficial to this day, the general tenor of that enterprise was one of hegemonic aloofness. The various iterations of Orientalism have historicized Muslims, psychologized them, and largely pathologized them.

Frames and Contexts

Ever since its emergence on the Arabian Peninsula in the seventh century, there has been a tendency to approach Islam apologetically or polemically. If the former seeks to preserve and propagate religious teachings for the faithful (e.g., Ibn Hishām 1858–1860; Ibn Taymiyya 2009), the latter seeks to undermine the tradition, often from without (e.g., the aforementioned *Apocalypse of Sergius Baḥīrā*). More recently, we have seen the emergence of a third approach, the so-called academic one, which claims to be both objective and non-partisan. This may be witnessed in classical Orientalism, briefly examined above, and in more recent attempts that resist such Orientalism and desire to create new paradigms to study Islam (see the comments in Daneshgar and Hughes 2020: 1–4). The latter usually takes the form of, what is now commonly called "engaged scholarship" or scholarly activism and is often associated—especially in North American departments of religious studies—with creating a progressive version of the religion. This often involves showing how "real" or "authentic" Islam is synonymous with feminism, ecology, gender equality, LGBTQ2S rights, and the like.[3]

Islam, in other words, has always been situated because, like everything, it only makes sense when framed and contextualized. One central theoretical question that emerges from all of this is: Why do all of the frames mentioned in the previous paragraph mistake the frame for the essence? That has been, and continues to be, a structural failure at the heart of the study of Islam, in all of its many guises. Another set of questions, again ones that are often left unasked, flow from this initial one: Where do these frames and contexts come from? Who provides them? How are they used? And, for what purposes or ends are they employed? It is questions such as these that I have been interested in over the past twenty years, and they are precisely the types of questions that I have encouraged, with varying degrees of success, other colleagues to ask of their data. Such questions, often referred to as "meta," help to show how scholars construct, describe, and analyze their data. While those who consider themselves to be interested solely in the data tend to regard such questions as too theoretical, when reflected upon they offer interesting results.

Before I set about considering the current state of Islamic studies—and, again, my interest is largely confined to the study of Islam in departments of religious studies, as opposed to, say, Near Eastern or Middle Eastern studies (though I would certainly say that many of my comments are also applicable to those contexts)—it might be worth mentioning a day that, both literally and metaphorically, changed everything. The questions that I have been asking for the past twenty years really began in earnest in the immediate aftermath of the events that transpired on September 11, 2001. Some days are so momentous that they are game changers. On that day,

19 individuals decided to fly airplanes into the twin towers of the World Trade Center in New York City and the Pentagon in Washington DC. That these individuals did so in the name of religion in general and Islam in particular posed countless problem for the field of religious studies. These problems, I would add, had been bubbling under the surface for years, and they are problems moreover that have never abated.

For years, the American Academy of Religion (AAR) had told us that religion was and is a force for all that is good, peaceful, and spiritual in the world. Religion, in the narrative they constructed for themselves, was all about social justice, gender justice, racial justice, and all other kinds of justice. Religion, to quote a theme from the AAR's 2016 Annual Meeting—fifteen years after 9/11 no less!—is about "Radical Love."[4] This dominant narrative has so many blind spots that it ultimately proved unworkable. The attackers were not really religious, we were told, but hijackers of the beautiful religion of Islam. While Islam, like any religion, may well be a beautiful religion—why should that even be an issue?—it was clear that the perpetrators of the events of 9/11 regarded themselves as the best and most pious Muslims, just as do those associated with other militant movements, such as Boko Haram, ISIS, and al-Shabaab (see Hughes 2015: xi–xvii).

Scholars of religion in general and of Islam in particular had a field day with this. Religion could never be about violence, so many argued in those uncertain days and months after 9/11. Religion, for those who had spent their lives studying it, was a force for positive change in the world. The religions of the globe, so the basic narrative goes, embody high ideals, provide inspiration for millions, and have fostered great and enduring ideas through the millennia. Though each religion may well represent its own unique genius, when taken together the world's religions share a common core in the omnipresent, if illusive and thus unanalyzable, "sacred."

If I were to sum this narrative up from the vantage point of hindsight, I might say that the constructions used by many in the general field of religious studies—both among those who specialized in Islam and those who did not—to understand the events of 9/11 were defined by confusion. A confusion of terminology. A confusion of categories. And, most significantly of all, a confusion of purpose. We failed as a guild and, in many ways, it is hard to take ourselves seriously. Religion is not just about the spiritual, the ethical, the sacred, or the high-minded. Running alongside this narrative, religion has also been used to justify and legitimate all sorts of nefarious actions, including murder and genocide, most likely because it provides the ultimate form of sublimation.

Slowly undermining our dominant narrative have been those voices that seek to show how religion is little more than a western construct that has been used to cordon off and protect a certain group of otherwise mundane activities as special.[5] This cordoning off, moreover, has been done for a host of political, social, and economic reasons. Religion is thus a category that has been invoked to privilege and deny, and to elevate and marginalize. Yet for some reason or set of reasons, many in religious studies forget this and instead focus on essences and the sacred. In claiming to take religion "seriously," we have actually failed—and failed miserably—at that task.

It has now been over twenty years since the events of 9/11. Unfortunately, with a few exceptions,[6] we have not really changed our discourses. Indeed, the "religion as peace" slogan has been expanded in recent years to include various forms of activism and justice. Religious studies is still in the business of locating in "religion" a source for positive change, with the field increasingly defined by scholarly activism as opposed to scholarship for the sake of scholarship alone. While nothing is wrong with this change of events, it is certainly worth noting as it tremendously influences how the field plays out, at which point it becomes an issue of "theory and method." In the twenty years since the 9/11 attacks a collective forgetting has taken place. There is still a tendency to think about religion with default terms such as the sacred, the experiential, and the good. Those who do bad things in the name of religion are then considered to have forfeited the right to call themselves religious.

The Aftermath of 9/11's Aftermath

Over the past two decades I have published a trilogy of books (Hughes 2006, 2012b, 2015) dealing with the various paradigms, contortions, and frames of analysis used to study Islam within the field of religious studies in the aftermath of 9/11. Some of these works, in retrospect, were more polemical than perhaps they needed to be, and my rhetoric might have been better framed so as to win over those I was trying to reach. While it appealed to the like-minded in religious studies, many who specialized in Islam recoiled from the critique. The accusations were pretty uniform: my data pool was too small, I went after soft targets, I put too much faith in rationality and the tradition of Orientalism, and so on and so forth.

Since the first volume—*Situating Islam: The Past and Future of an Academic Discipline*—came out close to twenty years ago, I thought it might be as good a time as any to examine what, if anything, has changed in the field in light of my comments and criticisms. While I certainly do not want to say that my comments and critiques are solely responsible for some of the more positive changes, I do hope that when I called attention to certain features, some colleagues felt the need to respond. The majority, however, have chosen to carry on as usual.

The first thing that has changed since the apologetic and theological excesses ushered in by 9/11 is that an old guard is slowly being replaced by a younger generation of scholars. The previous generation—the one that was most immediately impacted by the events of 9/11—sought to show North Americans (students, local communities, the media) that Islam was not a religion prone to violence and that all Muslims were not terrorists. The 2020 me now realizes that it could not have been otherwise and I give those colleagues credit for what they did. The only problem was that too many erased the line separating scholarship from public response. The erasure of this line caused all sorts of confusion as such responses—including, but not limited to, the need to show how Islam was not a violent religion—were mistaken for scholarship, and vice versa.

The other problem is the aftereffects of those responses. While it was certainly necessary to show people—both in North America *and* in Europe—that Islam was neither more nor less bellicose than other religions, the need to defend Islam from any type of critique has, in many circles, continued unabated. One should not, for instance, need to be a Muslim to study Islam academically,[2] nor should one be expected to find, let alone define, Islam's essence, or make that essence conform to one's own preconceptions of what a "good" religion should be. Again, though, a subfield can only be as good as the field in which it sits. As I recently wrote in another context:

> My concern the more I think about it over the years has never really been about the study of Islam, or Islamic studies, than it has been about religious studies. I, thus, wish to lay the blame of the paucity of theorizing (or, at least, good theorizing) squarely at the foot of the academic study of religion, particularly the American Academy of Religion (AAR), which has the unfortunate tendency of forcing many of us to contort our discourses into something ecumenical or positive for the sake of membership in the so-called guild.
>
> (Hughes 2020c: 12)

The problem, as witnessed in this quotation, is the very field of religious studies which has very definite, if strange, ideas of what religion is and should be. The field's ecumenical framework, grounded as it is in liberal Protestant assumptions about the nature of religion, has been adopted wholeheartedly among those who study Islam. Rather than study Islam "on its own terms," we largely do so through a set of Christian categories that are assumed to be universal. If reading and describing classical and other texts is what people do in Near Eastern studies departments, interpreting those texts for modern concerns drives the study of Islam among scholars of religion.

The graduate students of that generation, however, inherited a very different world. They came of age with a different set of expectations. They are the ones who will have to ask themselves tough questions as to how to proceed. It will be difficult, to be sure, as the old guard still controls the mechanisms of power. The latter include running the groups devoted to Islam at the AAR and holding the reigns to discussion groups (such as the IslamAAR listserv), wherein graduate students and un-tenured faculty have to conform to the status quo or remain silent.

When I tried to call attention to such excesses, my work was accused of reducing believers to mere data (see Schubel 2014a),[8] of being "neo-Orientalist" (Schubel 2014b),[9] of being "grossly polemical and simplistic" (Safi 2014), as having an "emotional reflex" prompted by "anxiety" (Grewal 2016: 46), and, subsequently, as lacking "profound knowledge of the history of Islamic studies" (Stewart 2018: 160). While I shall attend to some of these criticisms later on in this chapter, it suffices to say at the moment that, in some circles, my criticisms have been met with considerable suspicion and even hostility.

This hostility has been misinterpreted, perhaps on account of the way I expressed myself in some of my earlier writings. My goal was never to lash out at colleagues or tell them that what they were doing was wrong. It was only to point out and get them to reflect on some of the structural problems inherent to the study of Islam. These structural problems, as I have said time and again, are not confined to this subfield, but they emerge from the way the academic study of religion is carried out. Contrary to Schubel, my interest was not in having us return to some form of Orientalism, but it was to say that what currently passes for the study of Islam in many departments of religious studies across North America is oftentimes very much a response to Orientalism—and that we need to understand that. If some forms of Orientalism went too far in certain political and ideological aspects, the responses to it do exactly the same thing. Just because I argued that the field could stand to be a little more historical, a little more language-based, and a little more theoretical does not make me an Orientalist. Far from it. Orientalists are, after all, largely averse to the types of theorizing I have encouraged (see Stewart 2018: 191).

Increasingly younger scholars who study Islam in the context of religious studies are looking for new venues in which to write and express themselves. Rather than be part of insider conversations, many are interested in using their data to illumine larger questions. As a co-editor of *Method and Theory in the Study of Religion* (MTSR), a journal devoted solely to—as the title suggests—issues of method and theory we have witnessed in recent years a pleasant and welcome increase in submissions dealing with Islam: with Islam and the cognitive science of religion (CSR) (e.g., Nakissa 2021), with some of the structural problems in Islamic studies, with differences between the study of Islam in the Muslim world and in Europe. All of this makes for very fascinating reading. Most importantly, it means that (parts of) Islamic studies is slowly coming of age in entering conversations with the larger field of (critical) religious studies. Increasingly we witness scholars treat Islam as a set of rhetorical moves, authenticity narratives, or legitimating myths which function in the creation, maintenance, and contestation of social formations (e.g., Ahmed 2016; Daneshgar 2020).

What the Work is About

Though my criticisms struck a nerve with several colleagues working in Islamic studies, they fortunately found favor with those in the larger field of religious studies, but who do not work with Islamic data. The paradox, then, was that my work which tried to intervene in Islamic studies became tied to a larger trend within religious studies called "critical religion," "theory and method," or the like. I thus became the "Islam person" in that group.

Nickolas Roubekas, a scholar of religion and specialist in early Christianity, for example, noted of my *Theorizing Islam* (Hughes 2012b) that "those interested in Islam and Muslim life around the world should look elsewhere. This volume is about meta-questions on the redescriptive level, that is, a study of how Islam is studied rather than a volume on what Islam *is*, i.e., its beliefs, practices, institutions, etc. The highly critical nature of the book denotes the still existing theological and apologetical language within the academia, which remains a serious and yet formidable issue in the academic study of religion" (Roubekas 2016: 121).

Roubekas, who, to repeat, is not in Islamic studies, seems to get what the book is about unlike, say, many colleagues in Islamic studies. Writing in an afterword to a series of attempts to work though the exchange between Omid Safi and myself on the future of Islamic studies, Russell T. McCutcheon writes:

> And that's what sets Hughes's work apart, in my reading, from that of many of his peers—e.g., that technical, social theory terminology, such as the category myth (defined as something other than a lie, of course), social formation, inheritance, innovation, anachronism, not to mention origins and authenticity (both seen as contestable claims made by situated social actors rather than as descriptive realities), along with the names of such theorists as Benedict Anderson, Jean-François Bayart, Pierre Bourdieu and Bruce Lincoln, regularly appear in his work, nearly as frequently as do an insider discourse of transliterated Arabic terms and the names of various theologians thought by many to be important to this thing called "the tradition." And it is the fact that both are present—not just a recapitulation of the emic discourse but also an accompanying etic, comparative and explanatory analysis—that, although making Hughes provocative to some, ensures that, from where I sit, his work is essential reading.
> (McCutcheon 2018: 210)

Again, McCutcheon gets what the critique is and what it is meant to accomplish. It is meant to nudge colleagues working with Islamic data in the larger field of religious studies to enter a bigger conversation, one that critical scholars working with other data partake of. I am not, *pace* some of my critics from within Islamic studies, trying to transform everyone into "theory heads." Rather, my work has sought to offer a critical intervention to get colleagues to address a broader set of questions supplied by the critical wing of the academic study of religion. In this regard, I would like to think that my project has been—at least to some extent—successful. Even those who vehemently disagree with me, as we shall see in the following section, have to situate themselves to my work.

What the Work is Not About

Matt Sheedy (2018) has edited a volume that contextualized a debate between Omid Safi and myself (see Safi 2014; Hughes 2014b) with the aim of showing that the issues raised by the debate were not confined solely to the subfield of Islamic studies. According to him, the debate offers "a glimpse into some of the overarching concerns that have troubled the institutional study of religion since its formal beginnings in late nineteenth-century Europe, including the lines between insiders and outsiders, between critique and identity politics, theology and Wissenschaft, along with the search for historical-critical and comparative theories and methods that can offer a model for the study of religions as a whole" (Sheedy 2018: 8). While I certainly have no intention of revisiting my debate with Safi, as revelatory as it (and the responses to it) was, my contention is that the field has moved on—for the most part positively—on account of it.

In Sheedy's volume a rather surprising chapter, written by Devin J. Stewart, appeared. Seemingly impervious to the tenor of the volume, including the theoretical issues it was designed to raise, Stewart opted to critique my own critique, particularly that found within *Theorizing Islam* (Hughes 2012b). Despite the fact that all of the other chapters in the collection get at what their respective authors thought were the theoretical issues raised by the debate, Stewart argues that my aforementioned work "is 132 pages, contains a handful of Arabic words, has a tiny number of footnotes, refers only to sources in English, is fairly accessible, and does not show evidence of profound knowledge of the history of Islamic studies" (Stewart 2018: 160).

Stewart misunderstood—unlike, say, Roubekas, McCutcheon, and even Sheedy—the nature of the work. The fact that he has no training in religious studies, and instead comes out of the field of Middle Eastern and Islamic studies, is certainly on clear display. If you want to understand Islam, he goes onto say, "read *Iḥyāʾ ʿulūm al-dīn* (The Revival of the Religious Sciences) by al-Ghazālī (d. 505/1111). ... Reading this single book would do more to raise the bar in Islamic studies scholarship than fifty Bruce Lincolns and J. Z. Smiths put together" (191). While I certainly agree with him that reading al-Ghazālī will tell us more about Islam than will reading Smith or Lincoln, the point is lost on Stewart that in the context of *Theorizing Islam* I am not interested in learning, let alone teaching, about Islam. I am instead interested in exposing some of the paradigmatic structures—their genealogies, their assumptions, their investment in ideologies—that are used in the modern academic study of religion using Islam as my datum. Rather than "raise the bar in Islamic studies," I sought to raise the bar when it comes to asking theoretical questions of our data.

Stewart thinks that the solution for the integration of Islamic studies into the humanities' curriculum is to read more texts. According to him:

> Do not make secondary literature the basis of your scholarship ... In most cases, original ideas do not come from reading someone else's summary that filters out the odd details and includes only those points that support a particular argument. Original ideas most often come from making an unexpected connection, and this occurs when one is reading the raw, unfiltered data.
>
> (Stewart 2018: 195–196)

Yet, I would contend, scholarship is not just about making connections or sets of connections between premodern texts. It begins with the acknowledgement, to quote Bruce Lincoln, someone that Stewart is not at all interested in, that all texts—so-called primary and secondary—are human products. In his fourth thesis on method, Lincoln states:

> The same destabilizing and irreverent questions one might ask of any speech act ought be posed of religious discourse. The first of these is "Who speaks here?", i.e., what person, group, or institution is responsible for a text, whatever its putative or apparent author. Beyond that, "To what audience? In what immediate and broader context? Through what system of mediations? With what interests?" And further, "Of what would the speaker(s) persuade the audience? What are the consequences if this project of persuasion should happen to succeed? Who wins what, and how much? Who, conversely, loses?"
>
> (Lincoln 1996: 226)

According to this statement, texts are the products of ideologies that demand theoretical apparatuses to understand them.

Moreover, Stewart argues that it is okay to write apologetically because, in his own words, "in many fields scholars end up saying nice things about the traditions they study; professors who study Islam do not have a monopoly in this regard. Professors of Christianity, Judaism, Hinduism and Buddhism often write laudatory comments about these religious traditions, the high ideals they embody, the inspiration they can provide, the great ideas they have fostered and their unique genius" (Stewart 2018: 160). Once again, he misunderstands that the point of my critique is to examine some of the discourses created in the contemporary study of Islam to think about the larger issue of reverence in the academic study of religion.

Obviously, Stewart raises some very important issues for the study of Islam in his critique. I would certainly agree with him, for example, that the reading of primary sources—in their original languages—are central to the field. There is no way to get around this fact. However, to such knowledge, I would also add that a healthy dose of self-reflexivity and attunement to theoretical questions is equally essential, especially for those working within the larger field of religious studies, of which Stewart does not. Without the latter knowledge, we risk two issues. The first, the most obvious, is that it is precisely these theoretical questions that unite those of us who work in religious studies, thereby allowing for a common vocabulary with which we can talk meaningfully to one another. How else can individuals studying everything from Taoism to the United Church of Canada engage one another in meaningful and productive ways?

Secondly, and more importantly, is that if we simply assume that data exists naturally in the world, awaiting our ability to uncover it, we do not reflect on how we make data. What rhetorical moves do we use—and have others used—to bring data to light? Why do we choose this text, for example, and not that one? Why do we focus on that set of rituals and not others? Why do we do fieldwork in this country, but not others. All of these questions create our data—yet, surprisingly, we rarely, if ever, reflect upon them.

Within this latter context, it is also extremely important that our analyses are only as good as the terms and categories that are in our possession. We have to remember that the secular and academic study of religion is, at most, 150 years old, and it was preceded by two thousand years of theological speculation.[10] There is, then, much potential for terminological and taxonomical slippage. This is why we must be vigilant. Engaging in theory is anything but indulgent. It is absolutely necessary. Terms like "religion," "myth," "ritual," "comparison," "origins," and "extremism"—to name only a few—are neither objective nor value neutral. They are all terms with histories, genealogies, and investments. They are terms, moreover, that have structured the modern academic study of religion in general and Islam in particular. If we do not reflect upon them, and simply use them as if they named real things in the world, problems inevitably ensue.

Beyond Normativity

The field of Islamic studies—again, to reiterate, my concerns are largely confined to the study of Islam as carried out within the context of departments of religious studies—is slowly becoming more interested in issues of theory. Allow me to illustrate with a few examples from recent years.

At the 2013 Annual Meeting of the American Academy of Religion there was a roundtable devoted to the topic of "Normativity in Islamic Studies." Three years later, the proceedings of that roundtable were published in the *Journal of the American Academy of Religion*. Though I had been asked to respond to the initial roundtable in Baltimore, I was unable for a variety of reasons to attend the session. While issues of "normativity" are not necessarily the type of theorizing I have encouraged over the years, since I maintain that we ought to be more interested in the discourses and moves that manufacture something called "normativity," the very fact that a set of reflections on the idea was occurring was only good for the health of the field. In his review of the published set of papers, McCutcheon notes that "despite his absence from this set of papers, what's curious is that almost all of the contributors at least implicitly situate themselves in relation to Hughes's work—so it's not only that without his unremitting critique I doubt such a panel would have been organized" (McCutcheon 2018: 211).

In her introduction to the set of published papers, Juliane Hammer notes that "the history of Islamic studies within the American Academy of Religion (AAR), beginning in the early 1970s, can be read as a history of sometimes rather passionate debates about the place of religious normativity and prescription on one end of the spectrum, and detached as well as supposedly more critical scholarship on the other. This is a debate about method as well as about purpose" (Hammer 2016: 25). While there is an acknowledgement that we need to reflect on what exactly we are doing in Islamic studies, her bifurcation between "religious normativity and prescription" on the one hand and "*supposedly* more critical scholarship on the other" is problematic (my italics; see also McCutcheon 2018: 212). The term "supposedly" would seem to indicate that, for Hammer, critical scholarship is not that critical, but—perhaps, as I cannot speak for her—somehow invested in various wills to power. While I would certainly concur with such a statement, I would quickly add that surely normativity is also "supposed," in addition to noting that this is the reason we engage in theory: to try to make critical scholarship more critical. Hammer's reasoning is binary, and like all binary constructions, too neat and artificial.

It soon becomes readily apparent, however, that this is not what Hammer has in mind. She goes on to note what she calls "the elusive boundary between theology and the study of religion" (Hammer 2016: 26). Though I might be tempted to argue that there is nothing "elusive" about this boundary. Many have, for instance, argued that it ought to be firm,[11] and if we cannot make it so, then something is surely amiss or, perhaps better, disingenuous. The boundary is about being clear on just what it is we are doing. Theology is one thing; and the secular and academic study of religion is something quite different. It only becomes elusive when individuals or groups desire to see it as elusive, *viz.*, for their own purposes. Hammer also contends that eschewing "supposedly more critical scholarship" and further erasing the "elusive boundary between theology and the study of religion" is, again in her words, "an important step in reclaiming the humanities as a tool for change in contemporary society (ibid.: 26–27).

This is an odd turn of phrase. Have the humanities been coopted? And, if so, by whom and for what purposes? It would seem that Hammer—and this is certainly indicative of a certain strand within contemporary discourses within religious studies—is trying to use theory to carve out a safe space wherein the humanities can be selectively used to address certain pressing problems (e.g., racial injustice, gender injustice, and the like). While there is certainly nothing wrong with doing that, why not just say that this is what one wants to do? To say that more critical work is only *supposedly* more critical calls into question the entire intellectual tradition that we are all ostensibly a part of, and thus strikes me as unfair. The humanities, in other words, is much larger than many increasingly want to give it credit for, and cannot simply and categorically be reduced to making the world a better place for the disenfranchised. While certainly we, as humanists, can call out injustice, we also need to, *à la* Devin Stewart, read texts and, to that I would add, be vigilant of the terms, categories, and narrative we employ.

While I may have certain problems with the roundtable on "Normativity in Islamic Studies," that the authors engage in theoretical reflection—even if ultimately to undermine their ostensible utility—is a surely a sign of progress. However, if the invocation of "theory and method" is just a sleight of hand to keep on doing scholarly activism, which it just may well be, then it is potentially problematic.

As another example, allow me to cite the work of Shahab Ahmed. His *What is Islam?* (2016) is a wide-ranging book that is learned, informed, and informative.[12] Ahmed is well-read, eloquent, and impressively engaged with numerous fields and subfields. One of these fields is, thankfully, religious studies. On one level, the premise behind the book is very simple. Can one, Ahmed cheekily asks us near its beginning, be a "Muslim wine-drinker" (Ahmed 2016: 3)? It is an interesting question, to be sure. We all know about Islam's prohibition against alcohol, but Ahmed asks us to suspend that knowledge and instead imagine how the act of imbibing wine can be "positively valued in non-legal discourse" (ibid.: 66). Islam, on his reading, becomes more than simply a "religion" and more than just a set of interlocking cultural forms. In this, his analysis upends a particular history of looking at or framing Islam. Instead, for him, "a valid concept of 'Islam' must denote and connote all possible 'Islams' whether abstract or 'real', mental or social" (ibid.: 104). Or, as he states in his conclusion, "this book has sought to locate the logic of difference and contradiction as coherent with and internal to Islam—that is, to provide a coherent account of contradiction in and as Islam" (ibid.: 542).

To be sure, this is not a book fixated on the use and enjoyment of alcohol in Islam. As Ahmed clearly states, alcohol serves as but a metaphor for other types of ideas and discourses (e.g., philosophy, Sufism, iconism) that have been marginalized over the years as somehow being "un-Islamic." I find myself returning time and again to this formulation. Religions qua social forms are balls of confusion and self-contradiction. In this assessment, he is certainly correct. But, and for me this is a big but, surely all of this should be obvious to the well-informed and critical scholar of religion. Who posits tidiness, consistency or essentialism in 2021? It would seem that many dealing with Islam, and that is who. However, that he has to spell all this out, and the fact that many seem to find this to be one of the novel aspects of the book, is surely telling of the state of the field.

What is the theoretical payoff of all of this? Has he succeeded, as some have argued, of extricating Islam from European categories of analysis? Is this the natural telos of the Saidian project? I do not think so. He has problematized terms like "religion" and "culture" in ways that, while important, are certainly not novel and, indeed, their critique has emerged out of Euro-American analysis.

The third example I wish to focus on is the work of my friend and colleague Majid Daneshgar. In his recent *Studying the Qur'an in the Muslim Academy* (2020), Daneshgar—who was trained in Iran, Malaysia, and now works in Europe—provides an examination of what it is like to study and teach the Qurʾān at academic institutions in the Muslim world, and how politics effect scholarly interpretations of the text. The tensions between the study of Islam within the Muslim world and that in the West, he argues, are great, bound as they are by centuries of mistrust and deceit, including the history of Orientalism. In a set of criticisms that could also be levelled at the likes of Hammer and the other individuals involved in the roundtable on "Normativity in Islamic Studies," Daneshgar writes:

> Islamic apologetics allows an author to censor a text, misrepresent it, and be selective in choosing various types of sources. Islamic apologetics is a specific method of studying Islam that is not and, from an insiders' perspective, *should not* be compatible with modern (Western) scholarship. In Islamic apologetics, a "relentlessly erudite researcher" is not to be an archaeologist of knowledge, aiming to "dig up [different] documents, raiding archives, rereading and demystifying texts"; instead, he is forced to trust, follow, study, and live with his past and tradition. Islamic apologetics both is and is not an indigenous approach toward teaching and studying the Qurʾān in Muslim academic contexts, one which is tied in with reformism, nationalism, and sectarianism.
>
> (Daneshgar 2020: 22)

Here, he shows how certain aspects of the Muslim world elide with certain trends in North American circles of Islamic studies to create a situation wherein scholarship on Islam has been used for a host of non-scholarly engagements, including to usher in a host of political and religious reforms. Daneshgar instead calls for an approach that is more attentive to its genealogies, honest about its motivations, and historical in its concerns.

It is a provocative work, to be sure. In many ways, he lays the blame at the feet of Edward Said, showing how his *Orientalism* has provided a convenient mechanism to question the credibility of contemporary Western-produced scholarship on Islam and the Qurʾān. It is not simply a deconstructive project, however. Daneshgar also seeks to rebuild by demonstrating how Islamic studies could benefit from a cross-pollination of Western and Islamic or more indigenous approaches. This involves, for him, bringing theories developed in the West into Muslim contexts in such a manner that the former can inform, shape, and be shaped by the latter. Furthermore, the close attention to philology and textual work as carried out in Muslim academic contexts has much to offer western scholarly traditions devoted to Islam. The payoff is to encourage a greater theoretical and critical engagement with the Qurʾān and the Islamic tradition more generally.

In so doing, Daneshgar goes far beyond the likes of W. C. Smith and others, who sought—among other things—to study Muslims only using the language and categories to which Muslims themselves could assent. Though, of course, Smith's mode of analysis rarely entertains the questions of which "Muslims." Daneshgar not only argues for importing and adapting certain western theories of religion into the Islamic academic context, but also makes room for both Sunni and Shīʿī scholarship.

What I appreciate about Daneshgar's analysis is the manner in which it demonstrates that insider approaches to the Qurʾān need not necessarily be uncritical. To this end, he and I recently edited a volume, *Deconstructing Islamic Studies* (2020), with the following aim (as we wrote in our introduction to the work):

> in order to illumine these diverse approaches to the study of Islam regardless of context, and to demonstrate how they have influenced one another into the present, our volume explores how classical Muslim scholarship has structured (and, indeed, continues to structure) the modern academic study of Islam. We have established as our goal an examination of the organizing frames and taxonomic rubrics through which Islam has been and continues to be approached in indigenous scholarship, and then to show how Western scholarship appropriates, adopts, and otherwise adapts these frames/rubrics. This will permit us (a) to understand how these classical subjects have been approached traditionally, theologically, and secularly, and (b) to examine some of the tensions inherent to and across these approaches.
>
> (Daneshgar and Hughes 2020: 4)

The volume then asks a talented group of young and international scholars—all working within the context of Islamic studies—to address a set of theoretical questions. These include: Are external and scholarly approaches different, for example, from internal and indigenous approaches? If so, how and why? How does the so-called insider/outsider tension manifest itself or play out in the study of each of these topics? And, how might said topics be approached using different and non-indigenous analytical frames of reference? Each chapter takes a particular indigenous term (e.g., Qurʾān, ḥadīth, kalām, adab) and shows how it has been treated in classic Islamic scholarship and, then, how it might be reframed or retooled using the language and categories of western scholarship. The tensions that abound in this create interesting space—both theoretical and methodological—to begin the process of thinking about the study of Islam's place in the modern Academy, whether in the so-called West or the so-called Islamic world.

The examples considered in this section all show what tremendous strides theorizing data has taken in the study of Islam over the last 15 years. When I first published *Situating Islam* (2006) very little was done. Now we witness approaches that either seek to refute what I have tried to do or that try to build on it. I think both options are healthy, and I imagine they will only aid the vibrancy of the subfield. There have even been seminars as far away as Tehran, in Persian, devoted to the issue of theory and method in Islam, using the debate between Omid Safi and myself. Again, these are all positive signs.

A Tale of Two MTSR Roundtables

Another telling aspect of this greater attunement to theory and method on the part of scholars of Islam may be found in the terms of debate witnessed in two roundtables from a leading journal, *Method and Theory in the Study of Religion* (*MTSR*), one that I co-edit with my colleague Steven Ramey.[13] In 2012, then editor, Matthew Day published a special issue devoted to the topic of Islamic studies within the context of the academic study of religion. He invited me to write the lead article in that issue (Hughes 2012a), wherein I tried to reflect upon what is often referred to as "theory and method" in religious studies and its apparent paucity within the study of Islam.

In particular, I tried to argue that the integration of the latter into the former was neither easy nor particularly successful. The article was deliberately meant to be provocative (even using the term in the subtitle), trying to account for some of the reasons behind the complicated and contorted relationship between Islamic studies and religious studies. In particular, I argued that a large part of the problem was the apologetics—found among both Muslim and non-Muslim scholars—inherent to the study of Islam. I located this tendency, as I continue to do (see above), in the aftermath of the attacks of September 11, 2001, which forced many to defend Islam as opposed to studying it critically and in a manner that was disengaged. This confessionalism, as I called it, was the result of a complex amalgam of academic and non-academic forces.[14] While the responses in the same volume agreed with some of my points, they were for the most part rather critical. John Kelsey, for example, argued that I unduly limit my sample pool to "the AAR and its journal" (Kelsey 2012: 358). Richard Martin responded that my prose was too full of "rhetorical jabs" (Martin 2012: 382). Perhaps the harshest criticism came from the late Andrew Rippin. He accused my provocation of having "personal aspects to them" (Rippin 2012: 409). I must admit that I am still rather confused by this charge. Regardless, I do note that all the respondents to that provocation were non-Muslims and, with one exception (Ruth Mas), all were males. Moreover, all were written from within the context of the North American academy.

That was ten years ago. Much has changed since then. In 2020 I was contacted by Mohsen Feyzbakhsh of the University of Tehran wondering if *MTSR* would be interested in publishing a roundtable on Majid Daneshgar's aforementioned *Studying the Qurʾan in the Muslim Academy* (2020), especially as the book reflected on issues of "theory and method." What is significant from my perspective is that the responses to Daneshgar's monograph are all written by Muslim scholars, half of whom were writing in the context of the Islamic world. They are all critical, engaged, and self-aware of the theoretical issues involved and the problems that are at stake. This, to me, is exciting. Though, it might be worth pointing out, and this is surely telling, that only one of the respondents was trained in or works within North American departments of religious studies. This example shows that the entire debate has changed—and changed for the better—over the past decade. It also demonstrates that some of the more critical and theoretical engagement with Islam from a scholarly perspective occurs outside of religious studies. I might go so far as to say that Muslim scholars of Islam would seem to be more amenable to the types of issues and questions raised in the critical academic study of religion than are many non-Muslim scholars of Islamic religious studies in the West.

All of the responses are fully aware of issues endemic to the study of religion, such as the tensions between "insiders" and "outsiders," not to mention "critics" and "caretakers." Such issues moreover are analyzed from outside of the traditional confines of the apologetically inclined AAR and its journal, the *JAAR*. It also shows to just what an extent some of the critical discourses on religion produced in the West have been received in the Islamic world, and how scholars within that context have wrestled with some of the more critical discourses as produced by scholars in Europe and North America. I would go so far as to argue that it is now up to us to be part of this conversation and engage critically with the fruit of these scholars' labors.

Is the Critique Valid Beyond North America?

This brings me to the second question that I wish to address in this chapter. Frequently I am asked if my critique is at all applicable outside of North America. This question tends to come from colleagues working within European contexts. The short answer is I think that it does. In the time that remains, allow me to explain why I think this to be the case.

Virtually all European countries have a "Muslim Question" (Norton 2020: 1–7; and also see the general discussion in Fernando 2014: 1–28). This question revolves around what to do with Muslims, and whether or not they can be integrated within the modern European nation state. And, if so, how do *they* change or what do *they* have to give up for such integration to take place? Such a question—not unlike the "Jewish Question" that modern European nation states faced in the nineteenth century—reveals more about Europe and its perceived values than it does anything about Islam and Muslims (or Jews and Judaism for that matter).[15] Such "questions," to invoke Said, say more about those who ask them than those to whom they are directed. Such questions also allow those who ask them to better define their own values by creating an "other" to bring such definitions into clearer focus.

It is also not a coincidence that most Orientalist writings emerged out of a European context. Europeans—from scholars in the nineteenth century to populist politicians today—have long thought with Muslims and Islam as a way to think about themselves. Anti-immigration parties, on the rise today in so many European countries, focus almost exclusively on Muslims, both immigrants and refugees. This means that many European scholars of Islam seek, albeit in somewhat different ways than their North American colleagues, to portray Muslims in a favorable light. This may be seen, for example, in the massive edited volume edited by two French scholars—Abdelwahab Meddeb and Benjamin Stora, Muslim and Jew respectively—to show the history of largely positive Jewish–Muslim relations, and that was published jointly in France and the Anglophone world, by Albin Michel and Princeton University Press respectively (2013). It was an attempt, scholarly to be sure, to show how, since Jews and Muslims have had such a lengthy period of coexistence, they should surely be able to do the same in the context of modern France. Such features are also on display in how some German scholars of Islam deal with the ways in which Islam is portrayed in German schoolbooks (e.g., Spielhaus 2018; Johansen and Spielhaus 2019).

A crucial difference between the North American and European contexts is the institutional space wherein apologetics is carried out. In Germany, for example, much work on Islam is carried out in the context of Islamic theological colleges. These university-based Centers for Islamic Theology are funded by the Federal Ministry of Education and Research, and they have subsequently been replicated in Austria and Switzerland.[16] They often consist of professorships in Qurʾān, Islamic history, in addition to professorships in Islamic Religious Education and Didactics.[17] Though there can be—dependent upon the college—an emphasis on history and scripture, such appointments have very little or nothing to do with more entrenched and traditional departments of Oriental studies (*Orientalistik*) in German and other European universities. Indeed, whereas traditional German Islamic studies seeks to examine Islam from a non-confessional perspective, and are usually associated with faculties of philosophy or philology, the Centers of Islamic Theology are in the business of developing a normative Islam.[18] In fact, many Orientalists in Germany want nothing to do with these theological colleges, despite the fact that they are often well-funded. In other centers, future chaplains are trained under this structure to work at German prisons, hospitals, and mosques. Such endeavors, of course, are attempts by the German government, aided by faculty in these centers, to create a "German (i.e., good) Islam."

Other countries have done something similar. Not unlike the United States after 9/11, France witnessed a number of new positions—all funded by the state—in Islamic studies after the terrorist attacks of 2015 and 2016, with the aim of diffusing tensions and encouraging integration. Moreover, the Oxford Center for Islamic Studies, to use another example, is also comprised of scholars and offers courses in various aspects of Islam, in addition to a host of pedagogical programs, such as the Young Muslim Leadership Programme (YMLP) that seeks to encourage greater participation by British Muslims in public life. The Center, a beautiful campus with a large mosque within, however has a minimal relationship to the main university and its Faculty of Oriental Studies.

New faculty, centers, or institutes—such as those found in Germany, Austria, Switzerland, France, and England—are all engaged in creating a palatable Islam, one that attempts to integrate Muslims into the larger body politic by making them compatible with a common set of societal values and norms. While structurally different from the type of theologizing that goes on in Islamic studies circles as carried out within departments of religious studies in North America, all share the need to manufacture a good Islam, one that can then be held up to be the most authentic, and against which others can be found wanting.

Conclusions

This chapter has offered an admittedly idiosyncratic set of reflections on the current state of the field of Islamic studies. I have framed it around a number of the issues that I tried to raise in my previous publications on this topic with the aim of seeing what has changed and what has stayed the same. It would seem that, while much of the field is still dominated by a set of theological and liberal Protestant assumptions about the nature of religion—not surprising given the fact that this takes place against the backdrop supplied by the AAR—there are certainly some promising features.

Most significant is the growing trend among scholars of Islam—both Muslim and non-Muslim—to engage more theoretical works and, in the process, to try to show how their data illumines larger questions in the (critical) study of religion. I hope that as more and more of these scholars find positions on editorial boards, search committees, journal editorships, and leaders of professional organization we will see an even greater paradigm shift.

The chapter also tried to show how the critiques that I levelled at the field close to twenty years ago is not confined solely to the North American context. I would instead argue that within any secular (read: Christian) country with a sizeable Muslim minority, there is a need to try to make that minority conform to the values of the dominant group. The place where this is usually done is in institutions of higher learning. While in North American this may well be grass roots, in Europe it is often state-sponsored. The results, while not identical, certainly overlap.

Chapter 2

The Current State of Jewish Studies

If the previous chapter examined the current state of Islamic studies, in the present chapter I wish to do the same for Jewish studies, the other subfield in which I work.[1] As with the former, I have also tried to make a number of interventions at the subfield level over the years. Much like in Islamic studies, these interventions have primarily been directed at the field as it tends to take place within departments of religious studies (e.g., Hughes 2013c, 2014a, 2016a), though I do think that my criticisms certainly apply to other subfields of Jewish studies (e.g., history, literature). Islamic studies and Jewish studies, in other words, have tended to function as my data to get at some of the critical issues facing the academic study of religion. My argument in these works was—and remains—that the study of Judaism, for a host of political reasons, is largely an apologetic affair that is in the business of reifying Jews and Jewishness at the expense of the larger contexts in which Jews happened and continue to find themselves.

Much of these problems emerge from the rather awkward position in which Jewish studies finds itself in the modern academy, caught as it is between a set of centripetal and centrifugal forces. The centrifugal force insulates Judaism, reveling in the particular, often coinciding with an unwillingness to explain the tradition using the terms and categories provided by larger disciplinary frameworks, and instead prefers to use a set of terms that are internal to the tradition. This means that Jewish data largely become untranslatable within the context of larger humanistic conversations and risks being inaccessible to anyone but those born or initiated into a particular ethnos or tradition.

The centripetal forces are no less insidious, representing the other side of the same coin. Such forces emerge from the desire either to subsume the particular into the so-called universal—which, of course, is little more than a Euro-Christian hegemon sublimated—or, if it will not be subsumed, then to marginalize or excise it. So, just as there is a tendency in Jewish studies to navel-gaze, the opposite tendency exists in fields like religious studies or history wherein Jewish data can be completely ignored as somehow too insular, as too parochial, or as too insignificant to be exemplary. This is the paradox in which the academic study of Judaism currently finds itself in the present moment. This situation hamstrings the field and unfortunately prevents full integration of Jewish studies into the humanities curriculum.

While more theoretically sophisticated than their cohort in Islamic studies, theory only goes so far. When theoretical concerns bump up against ethnicity, the latter always takes precedence. Or, perhaps framed somewhat differently, theoretical insights can be used to show how Jews and Judaism are different from other social groups, including those in whose cultures they dwell. Perhaps this is a natural state of affairs given that Jews from the destruction of the Second Temple in 70 CE to the formation of the State of Israel in 1948—with some, often ignored exceptions (see, for example, the following chapter)—have been diasporic. The result is that Jews, say, in medieval Islam have to be shown to be different from their Muslim neighbors. Recent trends in the field—particularly the study of Jews and American popular culture—have only exacerbated these structural problems as some vague notion of cultural Judaism has replaced previous generations' emphasis on Judaism as a religion encountered in traditional texts such as the *Talmud* or classical biblical commentaries. While Judaism is clearly different from other religions—just as Hinduism, Buddhism, or any other religion is different from other religions—when the focus shifts to some amorphous notion of "Jewish culture," such difference becomes much more difficult to maintain.

Whenever Judaism is reduced to culture, there is an overwhelming tendency to essentialize something called "Jewishness." This is analogous to those trends in the parent field of religious studies that talk about equally amorphous concepts such as "the sacred" or "religious experience." While Jews are imagined to fit into larger cultural contexts, this is accompanied by a simultaneous desire to show how they are unique in their cultural expression within those larger contexts. This often means examining how Jews have absorbed or adopted non-Jewish forms (e.g., humor, film, food) and then somehow "judaized" them. The latter then coincides with a celebration of Jewishness. The movement from reading rabbinic and other texts to how Jews form an intricate part of American culture, not unlike what we witness in the more apologetical wing associated with the study of Islam, is certainly a direct response to larger political forces—in this case an increase in anti-Semitism—and is meant to show that Jews are normal, if just a little different.

From Wissenschaft des Judentums to Jewish Studies

There are real historical and intellectual reasons for Jewish studies' propensity for introversion, which take us back to the origins of the secular study of Jewish texts at the end of the nineteenth century. The field, for all intents and purposes, took shape on the margins, functioning as a pariah academy that was deprived of full integration into the institutional frameworks of nineteenth-century German higher education.[2] Like their non-Jewish colleagues, Jewish scholars developed models of nationalist history predicated on imagined past greatness, something that would contribute positively to future renewal. If German historians could produce multi-volume works devoted to the greatness of "*the* German People" (*das deutsche Volk*), German Jewish scholars did the same thing, but focused their attention on *the* Jews. However, since they were forbidden from teaching at German universities, they were forced to do so from within the parochial context of newly created seminaries, where they quickly became implicated in sectarian battles that were then in the process of shaping modern Jewish life (see Schorsch 1994). This Jewish scholarship was directed at two distinct constituencies. On the one hand, it was directed at a Jewish readership, showing them what was essential to Judaism (e.g., ethical monotheism) and what was not (e.g., rabbinic legalism). For those historians associated with the new Reform movement, traditional Jewish law was not imagined to be essential so it could be jettisoned, but ethics and monotheism—which they believed formed the core of Judaism—had to be retained. On the other hand, this scholarship was also intended to get the attention of non-Jews in order to show them that Jews were just as normal as they were, in possession of as glorious a history, and thus deserving of full emancipation in German society.

Wissenschaft des Judentums ("The Science of Judaism"), the intellectual forbearer of Jewish studies, thus inauspiciously began as an insular and largely apologetic project. Wissenschaft scholars, hearkening back to the previous chapter on the state of Islamic studies, used academic tools to adjudicate what counted as true Judaism (and what did not), and was also intended to show non-Jews that Jews, too, were in possession of a noble pedigree with a rich history. This raises a set of questions that all who ply their trade in Jewish studies ought to ask themselves, but of course rarely do: Can Jewish studies overcome its apologetic past? If so, at what cost? Rethinking the gaze of Jewish studies will, it seems to me, ultimately mean rethinking the very ethnonym that ostensibly gives the field meaning, to wit, "Jewish."

It is worth noting that many of the founding fathers of the academic study of Judaism—Leopold Zunz (1794–1886), Abraham Geiger (1810–1874), and Moritz Steinschneider (1867–1907), to name but a few—would have been more that content to have joined their non-Jewish peers in the non-Jewish academic world. They were, however, refused entry. If they had been allowed in, perhaps things would have looked considerably different. Without getting into counterfactual arguments, of which I am never particularly fond, such an opportunity was denied them. This denial would have far reaching consequences. Indeed, the current introspection within Jewish studies is the direct result of such external forces. Geiger, whose pioneering work on the Jewish stratum of the Qurʾān I will revisit and challenge in the following chapter (Geiger 1970 [1833]), had to make due as a pulpit rabbi, first in Wiesbaden and then in Breslau, Frankfurt am Main, and Berlin (Koltun-Fromm 2006: 1–11; Heschel 1998: 1–22). Though he continued to publish, in addition to founding and editing many journals that were important vehicles of dissemination for the new Wissenschaft movement, Geiger conceived of the task of Jewish studies in what we might today call distinctly apologetic terms. It was to accomplish at least three goals: (1) to show Judaism as the most original monotheism that subsequently bequeathed itself to the world by giving birth to more epigonic forms, such as Christianity and Islam;[3] (2) to show what was important in Judaism (e.g., ethical or prophetic monotheism) and what was not (e.g., *halakhah* or Jewish law); and (3) to create a new Judaism for the modern age. This triangulation was at the heart of Reform Judaism, many of whose early architects were scholars of Judaism.

It was only when the centers of Jewish learning transferred from central Europe to the United States—first as Jewish semitics, then as Jewish studies, and sometimes to the more Latinized (and thus respectable-sounding) Judaic studies—that more centripetal forces began to set in (e.g., funding of chairs by local donors and community appointments). This was despite, or perhaps because of, the fact that the study of Judaism was now beginning to be taught in the secular context of the modern university.[4] Communal support for Jewish studies, a feature of the field that is still largely in place, had and indeed continues to have connotations and repercussions for how the field is structured. The primary role of Jewish studies, originally in Central Europe and then in North America, has been to construct "good" Jews and "good" Judaism.

Jewish studies has thus functioned as the primary theatre to normalize Jews to the outside world. Within this context, the academic study of Judaism has historicized Jews, sociologized them, psychologized them, and philosophized them. It has shown, simultaneously, how Jews are normal and how they are special, how they are a social group just like any other and how they are also an ethnos deserving their own modes of scholarly analysis. Comparison has always been a central method of this articulation with its purported ability to show what is uniquely "Jewish" and what is not. This has created a tension at the heart of Jewish studies in the sense that some have tried to integrate the study of Judaism into the non-Jewish curricula of the modern university, whereas others have resisted this integration on account of the fact that Judaism and Jewish texts must be understood on their own terms of reference.

The study of Jews and Judaism, like the study of anything, however, does not occur in an intellectual vacuum. As in Germany in the middle of the nineteenth century, we must also be aware of a host of other, non-academic, trajectories that have contributed to the internal gaze of Jewish studies. In this regard, the field has certainly been complicated by a host of such factors: by anti-Semitism; by 1967 when Israel defeated its Arab enemies in the Six Day War; by the rise of special interest programs defined along the lines of identity politics in the 1970s; by Israel's treatment of its Arab minority and Palestinians; and now increasingly by the Boycott, Divestment, and Sanctions (BDS) movement, including the reaction to it by Israeli and American Jewish leadership, and so on. All of these features have contributed to a certain reification of Jews and of Judaism, including a need to apologize and defend. Needless to say, such features have also exerted strong institutional pressures—from donors, from local Jewish organizations—about how Judaism should be taught.

Full Circle: Before and After Jacob Neusner

A defining character in shaping Jewish studies in North America and beyond was the indefatigable, if difficult, Jacob Neusner (for authorized biography, see Hughes 2016a). Before Neusner came on the scene in the 1950s and 1960s, the study of Judaism was either confined to the study of the Old Testament and taught by Christian clergy or it was shuttered away in a variety of Jewish seminaries. The latter included places like the Jewish Theological Seminary (JTS) in New York City or Hebrew Union College-Jewish Institute of Religion (HUC-JIR) in Cincinnati. In such places, Jewish texts were studied as they had been for centuries and with very little engagement with external methodologies.

Neusner, trained as a rabbi at JTS, while simultaneously receiving a PhD in religious studies from Columbia, began to connect Jewish data to questions asked by those in the academic study of religion. In so doing, not only did Neusner redefine the academic study of Judaism, he changed the larger frame of religious studies by forcing that field's categories to expand to include postbiblical Judaism. Even those who disagreed with his interpretation of rabbinic texts had to engage his pioneering methods. Neusner's vision was motivated by the desire to make the study of Judaism respectable in the secular academy and inclusive so that even non-Jews might be interested in its study. It was not to be an insider's club, as it was in the traditional Jewish seminary, but an academic and intellectual endeavor that simultaneously informed and was informed by rigorous theoretical and methodological frameworks that were external to the tradition. Many, both Jew and non-Jew, objected to this. More traditional Jews believed that the study of Judaism's timeless and sacred texts belonged in the yeshiva. Such texts, they argued, were significant on account of the fact that Jews wrote them, and they maintained that there was no reason to engage critical historical or methodological questions that might minimize these texts' intrinsic sacrality.

Others in the secular academy also objected, but for different reasons. Many, reflecting the Christian biases of the field, had very little interest in Judaism after the time of Jesus. Because of this, the study of rabbinic texts was largely unheard of on account of being either too technical or too irrelevant. As divinity schools gave way to departments of religious studies beginning in the 1960s after the Schempp ruling, the study of other religious traditions—Buddhism, Hinduism, Islam—entered the academy to be studied alongside Christianity. This is essentially the story of the academic study of Judaism—and indeed the academic study of religion—in the United States.[5]

Neusner's attempt to normalize the study of Judaism was in many ways effective. It is, after all, hard to believe today that any self-respecting department of religious studies would not have a scholar of Judaism in their ranks. This is all thanks to Neusner. However, that scholar of Judaism is inevitably Jewish. The field has, despite rhetoric from organizations like the Association for Jewish Studies (AJS), proven completely impervious to non-Jews and, thus, I would argue to connecting Jewish data to larger fields of study. Despite Neusner's advances, the field has regressed. When a point of pride is "Hey, so-and-so is interested in Jewish stuff, and she's not even Jewish" it is clear that problems exists at the heart of this subfield. Or, when, at a scholarship dinner for undergraduates, Jewish donors for an essay prize in Jewish studies, upon learning that it will be awarded to a non-Jew, ask "Couldn't you find a nice Jewish kid to give the prize to?"

There are just too many institutional pressures that have an impact on how Judaism is taught. These pressures include mollifying donors, many of whom are ardent supporters of Israel, and the desire for faculty to pursue community engagement, which in the context of Jewish studies means speaking in synagogues and other such Jewish communal institutions, and which often means speaking about Muslim-Jewish—or Arab-Israeli—relations in the most reductionist and unnuanced ways. These pressures, as we shall see in a subsequent section, are only getting worse. It might also be worth pointing out that, at present, this is unlike anything faced in Islamic studies. However, as more and more donors begin to fund positions in Islam, such pressures and tensions might very well emerge.

Judaism's emphasis on the particular translates into Jewish studies emphasis on the particular. While Neusner had tried to transform Jewish studies' parochialism, the "cultural turn" has returned us to the state of affairs before he came on the scene. As I wrote earlier: when one studied Jewish texts, there were real issues at stake. For example, the work of the towering Jewish thinker Maimonides (1138–1204) clearly engages with and adapts the writings of earlier Muslim thinkers and philosophers to a Jewish context. We can see this clearly and are able to demonstrate the changes undertaken. Such adoptions and adaptations unfortunately are rarely of interest to those working with Muslim thinkers. However, when one studies an amorphous concept like American "Jewishness" and does so culturally, analysis proceeds on hunches and feelings. What is similar to both textual and cultural approaches to Judaism, however, is the fact that anything that Jews have done is significant by virtue of the fact that Jews did it. Now, one can point to and take pride in, as is inevitably done, the "Jewish" comedy of Jerry Seinfeld or Larry David or the "Jewish" spouse of a non-Jewish actor/actress or famous politician. The main difference between today and then, however, is that now a theoretical apparatus—and at times a rather sophisticated one at that—is used. The results, however, are the same: some sense of Jewishness is reified and then can be located and discovered in the data. The results are usually of only parochial interest, and rarely of concern to those working outside the narrow confines of Jewish studies.

Some might argue that this is a two-way street. Namely, that Jewish studies is so parochial because those in other fields have historically marginalized—and indeed continue to marginalize—Jewish data as insignificant and to be of little broader significance. There is certainly much merit to this argument. The universal rarely is interested in the particular on account of the fact that the particular resists the universal's overtures to become like it. To this we could even add that the categories of the universal—despite the fact that they are imagined to be catholic in scope—are, more often than not, those of Christianity. The only way to get out of this paradox is to write for those outside of Jewish studies. Or, as I am doing here, to engage in a set of theoretical reflections on, say, how data is produced and manufactured in the first place. This, it seems to me, is the only way to move forward.

Comparison

Rarely acknowledged or even analyzed with any degree of clarity, the study of Judaism is predicated on the method of comparison. Though the excesses of comparison are widely known to the more critically minded within the field of religious studies, where the method has been used to make egregiously superficial connections between highly reified concepts (i.e., discrete religions), often with little or no regard to temporal and/or geographical coordinates, Jewish studies has rarely reflected on what comparison means to illumine and elucidate Jewish data. It is often used implicitly and with the sole intention of showing how "Gentiles do 'x,' but we do 'y.'" This, of course, maintains Jewish distinctiveness and difference.

Comparison is frequently based on hunches (i.e., "that reminds me of ...") as opposed to a well thought-out and systematic mode of analysis with the result that one rarely "shows one's work." Too often comparison is invoked for apologetic purposes: either to show how two things are the same (e.g., prayer in Hinduism is the same as prayer in Judaism, therefore they both represent manifestations of the "sacred") or that they bear no resemblance to one another (e.g., the Christ event is unique in the annals of world history).

In Jewish studies, by contrast, comparison has tended to be employed as a way to articulate some intangible or unquantifiable special trait (e.g., monotheism, chosenness, genius, continuity, or the like) or to isolate what is ostensibly "Jewish" from what is ostensibly "non-Jewish." Comparison, then, largely functions as a way to mark Jewish difference even in the face of no compelling evidence. The question we have to ask is, Why do we insist on doing this? Does it have something to do with the history of the field and its emergence from a largely apologetic framework as I described above? Such questions take us to the heart of the enterprise of Jewish studies. What is our goal? Is it to define Judaism and/or Jewishness in an essentialized fashion and then locate it retroactively in the historical record? Is it to justify or give historical legitimation to a series of truth claims manufactured in the present?

Let me take up an example, one I have used elsewhere (indeed, the next three paragraphs draw on Hughes 2017b: 24–27), from my own area of research. In his *Jews and Muslims* (1955), Shlomo Dov Gotein (1900–1985), one of the pioneering figures involved with research into the Cairo Geniza, coined the term "symbiosis" to refer to the historical interaction between Jews and Muslims, and, by extension, Judaism and Islam.[6] The basic narrative that "symbiosis" structures goes something like the following: Judaism helped to give birth to Islam in the late sixth century before Islam returned the favor in the tenth to twelfth centuries by facilitating the rise and florescence of, among other things, "Golden Age" Hebrew belles-lettres and Jewish philosophy. Informing this dominant narrative is the fiction of a creative and stable Jewish essence that gives life to Islam (as it had to Christianity several centuries earlier) and that later borrows from a now equally creative and stable Islam what it needs. Judaism's essence is assumed to remain untouched by this encounter. While others have tried to modify this somewhat (e.g., Laskier and Lev 2011a, 2011b), "symbiosis" still largely remains as our default metaphor (see, e.g., Wasserstrom 1995: 224).

Goitein, someone who functions as a conduit between old-world Wissenschaft des Judentums and North American Jewish studies, seems to have been attracted to "symbiosis" because it facilitated a conceptual framework that preserved Judaism's unique features, its ahistorical essence, within a dominant culture while still enabling Jews to be full participants within it. Islam, for him, was "from the very flesh and bone of Judaism" (Goitein 1955: 130). Or, again: "Judaism could draw freely and copiously from Muslim civilization and, at the same time, preserve its independence and integrity far more completely than it was able to do in the modern world or in the Hellenistic society of Alexandria" (ibid.).

In this one example we clearly witness the traditional deployment of comparison in Jewish studies. Comparison is here used to protect, to assign value, and to envisage normativity. It is used moreover in such a manner that neatly removes a reified essence of what Judaism is imagined to be and then differentiates it from a set of related—and most likely identical—cultural forms. Religions, envisaged as species or organisms, interact with one another and in such a manner that one of them, Judaism, is stable and this stability permits it to transfer its essence of monotheism to the framers of Islam. Judaism gives, Islam receives. A couple of centuries later, Islam returns the favor, but this return in no way impacts Judaism's eternal core. Changes in the latter context are superficial or cosmetic at best, and in no way transform what Judaism is or is meant to be.

This type of comparison is one of the primary methods used to understand Jews in the distant past, and it has more recently been employed, once again, as the primary method to show the uniqueness of Jews in contemporary America. Jewish cultural practices now take on religious forms so that, for example, eating traditional "Jewish" food—without attendant Jewish practices—provides a way of being Jewish and of maintaining Jewish continuity (see, e.g., Gross 2021). Or, how Jewish mobility in nineteenth-century America looks different from non-Jewish mobility (e.g., Rabin 2017).

Do not get me wrong, such studies are learned, illuminative, and informed by a set of often interesting theoretical interests. My concern, however, is that, like Goitein and indeed like so much else in Jewish studies, there is an implicit reification going on of something called Jewishness. It is no longer religious Judaism, as it was in the past, but something much more opaque that goes by the name of "Jewish culture." Such a term remains in the ether, largely undefined, but we are somehow supposed to know what it is. What, for example, is "Jewish" food—gefilte fish? brisket? Israeli couscous? And by eating it, just how is one transported into religiously Jewish space or world?

Community Engagement

In December of 1984, Jacob Neusner interviewed for the Koshland Chair in Jewish Studies, a newly created position at Stanford.[7] He was invited to campus for an interview and was told that, in addition to the usual deans and other administrators, he would have to meet with both Hillel and faculty members involved in the local Jewish fund-raising effort. When he returned home, Neusner wrote the following to the chair of the search committee. I quote from his archives:

> While I personally share the goals of Hillel, on the one side, and the UJA and Jewish community organizations, on the other, I do not believe that it is appropriate to join these activities to a candidacy for an academic professorship. Perhaps in your context I take too strict a view of the severely academic definition of the work of a professor of Judaic studies, and, on that account, I believe I would not be a suitable candidate for your consideration. In any event I have to conclude that the interests of those involved in defining the chair involve matters inappropriate, in my view, to the tasks of an ordinary professor and scholar, and that my goals in building Judaic studies as an academic field do not entirely cohere with the goals of yourself and your colleagues for the position at hand.[8]

I would, in 2020, only add to Neusner's comments by arguing that the situation has actually gotten worse. Much worse. Whereas Neusner was only asked to meet with members of Hillel, the Jewish students' group on campus, and members of the federation, we now have a situation in which such groups take an active role in the hiring process, vetting candidates, and serving on search committees.

Allow me to illumine with a few select examples. A recent job announcement came out for an endowed position at Christopher Newport University, a private university in Virginia. "The University," so the advertisement begins, "seeks a passionate and engaged teacher and productive scholar who will lead the department's efforts in broadening its course offerings in the Jewish tradition and in developing a Jewish Studies minor." This is fine and one would think would be part of any call for a position in a department of religious studies, no matter the religion in question. A chair in Islamic studies, for example, should "seek a passionate and engaged teacher and productive scholar who will lead the department's efforts in broadening its course offerings in the Islamic tradition and in developing an Islamic Studies minor." However, to return to the advertisement in question, we subsequently read that "the professor will support the University's related programs and organizations that promote a hospitable environment for Jewish religious and social life on campus. The successful candidate will also provide outreach to the vibrant and active

Jewish community of the [local] peninsula, with whom an open presentation will be scheduled as part of the interview process."

This university is not looking for a colleague, I would venture, but a teacher, researcher, rabbi, and a facilitator of Jewish life, both inside and outside the university. What are we to make of such a posting? Well, at least it is honest, and while I do not have a problem—in theory—with people engaging in such non-academic activities in their private lives, it should not be part of a job description. Moreover, the line that I have the most problem with is the following: "The successful candidate will also provide outreach to the vibrant and active Jewish community of the [local] peninsula, with whom an open presentation will be scheduled as part of the interview process."

What if the local community does not like a particular candidate? This, of course, means, that the leaders of the local Jewish community have a say—perhaps the defining say—in who does or does not get the position. It also means that a non-Jew would, by virtue of the announcement, be ineligible. Even if the university hires a perfectly good scholar, which they ultimately did, the fact remains that the position has somehow been undermined by virtue of the fact that it was not open to all qualified scholars, as every position should ultimately be. However, because the operative structures within Jewish studies largely make the study of Judaism unavailable to non-Jews beyond the undergraduate level, it would seem that every position in Jewish studies in North America goes to a Jewish scholar of Judaism.

While local communities can, and should, benefit from the expertise of local faculty members, they have absolutely no business being part of their actual hiring process. Lest we dismiss this as a one-off or as the machinations of what a small private university can get away with, another announcement came out just a few weeks after the aforementioned one from the State University of New York (SUNY) at Buffalo, a large state university that, in theory, works with a model of separation between "synagogue" and "state" (this is the reason, for example, why the University has no Department of Religious Studies). Perhaps because of this, its description is more measured, nevertheless the language is again worth quoting. It reads as follows:

> The Visiting Professor will also participate in department programing to build knowledge and awareness of Judaism tradition [sic], culture and history for both Jewish and non-Jewish students and community members,

and will work directly with Hillel and the Jewish Federation of Greater Buffalo to create connections that serve the community, the region, and the university.[2]

At least this ad keeps Hillel and the Federation out of the Search Committee, but it does mention that the hired candidate will "work directly" with them. This begs the question, however: for what? For the betterment of the local Jewish community? Now, to be fair, I worked at SUNY Buffalo for three years and only have nice things to say about the local Jewish community and Jewish Federation there. However, I will add that, when I interviewed for the position, I had to give part of my job talk at the local synagogue, and there was a non-academic, who was Jewish, on the search committee.

Both of these positions, I hope readers will agree, potentially put the academic candidate under the control of non-academic groups, which often promote certain ideologies. Federations and Hillels, for example, are slavishly pro-Zionist, and both seek to control the discourse on Israel both in the community and on campus. This means that left-leaning speakers—from B'Tselem, Ta'ayush, Breaking the Silence, Jewish Voices for Peace, and so on—are never invited to speak on college campuses, at least under their auspices. Instead, we get an endless supply of former IDF (Israeli Defense Forces) soldiers and generals or members of the Druze community who served in the IDF and who speak about how fair and inclusive Israel is. Local Jewish Federations and Hillels thus seek to control a particular discourse about Israel (and by extension, Palestinians) on campus.

The development of Jewish studies in universities ought not, as Neusner so acutely recognized, be shaped to meet the parochial interests of the Jewish community, which often has very conservative ideas about what Judaism is or should be and which patrols the discourse on Israel. When Jewish studies gets too close to the local community, its faculty may well be expected to continue in the classroom the advocacy of Judaism and of Israel that begins in the Sunday school and continues into the synagogue pulpit. This risks transforming Jewish studies scholars into Federation employees, which, I am sure, is something that the Federation would more than prefer, and something they seem to be actively willing to procure. However, the scholar of Judaism ought, by definition, to be a critic, a personality trait that necessarily removes him or her from the community, or that at least makes the relationship somewhat uncomfortable. Were this not the case, Jewish studies ceases to be intellectually rigorous or responsible, and would be little more than the extension of what local Jewish organizations do.

My final example comes by way of a personal experience that further illumines some of the inherent problems that beset Jewish studies. A couple of years ago, I was "long shortlisted" for an endowed position in Jewish studies at Case Western University. Before the Skype interview, I did my homework: looked at people's pictures, bios, and publications to make sure I could put names and ideas to faces on the screen. When I showed up for the Skype interview, I looked around the screen and could recognize most of them. But there was one middle-aged man in a suit who stuck out like a sore thumb. He introduced himself as "so-and-so" from the local Jewish Federation. I raised my eyebrow and did a double-take, and was subsequently informed by the head of the Search Committee that he was indeed on said committee, along with another non-academic from the Federation who could not be present for my interview. Two non-academics on five-person Search Committee? I was truly astounded.

Just to be clear: Jewish Federations seek to define discourses when it comes to Israel. Most Federations in the US are obsessed with BDS and the ways in which Israel is treated on college campuses. They also assume that every campus is like the University of California at Berkeley, where uber-left leaning professors are imagined to proselytize and brainwash naïve and unsuspecting students. This is why my campus, for example, like many other campuses with sizeable Jewish student populations, has an Israeli-funded and Federation-backed teaching fellow associated with their Hillel. They are paid, in other words, to undo the "damage" we are imagined to inflict, and they do so moreover by administering a healthy dose of *hasbara* (pro-Israeli propaganda). When I first taught my Israel-Palestine course at my present institution, I received a call from the president of the local Jewish Federation, asking how I could name the course as such, since there is no "Palestine." I joked back, saying that I had just received a phone call from a local Palestinian group, asking the same question but that they replaced the name "Palestine" for "Israel."

Indeed, as it says on the Jewish Federations of North America homepage, "We stand by Israel's side. Always." Always? So, again, why are these people on search committees? Most members of Jewish Federations that I have known over the years, and this is certainly relevant to the point I wish to make here, know very little when it comes to Judaism as a religion, let alone its historical development. They are fundraisers. They are major backers of Israel. Yet, rarely do they know anything about the study of Judaism as an academic enterprise. So why put such individuals on a search committee? I subsequently found out that "the suit" on the computer screen was the president of the Jewish Federation of Cleveland and that he had made disparaging comments about Muslims in print and on screen.[10] What, then, was this guy doing on a search committee and, most importantly, what kind of ideological litmus test was he imposing on short-listed candidates? The fact that two members of the search committee—roughly 40 percent—were non-academics from the local Federation should cry out for investigation. If that had been two imams from the local Muslim community on a five-member search committee for a position in Islam there would be headlines in the local and probably national media.

I was curious how the non-Jewish scholars on this search committee could sit there with a straight face as a pro-Israel, anti-Muslim/Arab, and non-academic (one of two) was introduced in their midst. I wondered if, when they hired their scholar of Islam, they invited (anti-Israel or anti-Semitic) representatives from the local Muslim community to adjudicate the candidates' credentials? If they had not, and I somehow doubt they had, then I would like to ask them what was the difference with Jewish studies? Was it the terms of reference of this particular chair? The paradox was that the department to which I was interviewing had actually prided itself on being one that was attuned to theory in the academic study of religion. Indeed, they have, according to their website, a two-year M.A. program that, in their own words, "concentrates on method and theory in the study of religion." What, I am curious, do these colleagues think "method and theory in the study of religion" means? Surely, they would be aware that one of the major issues in that larger field was the difference and tensions between religious "insiders" (i.e., believers) and "outsiders" (i.e., scholars). If aware of it, they certainly showed no signs of discomfort with the situation in which they found themselves.

Now, many of my colleagues in Jewish studies have very few problems with these kinds of positions. When I complain to them at conferences about the state of affairs, some are sympathetic, but nothing ever changes. Such positions, I would suggest, make a mockery not only of Jewish studies, but of religious studies and the humanities more generally. These examples, I would suggest, are instances of community interference and attempts to derail the freedom of speech in general and of academic speech in particular. The future of Jewish studies, at least for me, is at stake. Do we really want to be perceived as little more than rabbis or as employees of campus Hillels or local Jewish Federations? Do we not want

Jewish studies to be a critical field, one wherein we are not afraid to test out various cutting-edge ideas and theories? Do we not want to pave the way for younger scholars? And, do we not want to open the field of study to non-Jews? Whenever I raise these and related issues with the top brass of the Association for Jewish Studies (AJS), the main body dealing with Jewish studies in North America, I am met with silence. I have asked previous presidents and executive directors of that organization that they review the criteria for search committees, to wit, who can or cannot be on such committees. But, again, I am rebuffed and told that everything is fine the way it is, so why fix that which is not broken.

The issues that I have raised in this section are not anecdotal or the result of idiosyncratic job announcements. Rather, they represent particular instantiations of a set of systemic problems that threaten not just the subfield of Jewish studies, but also the academic study of religion more generally. When we let local communities fund chairs or positions in departments of religious studies we risk letting those communities have a say on who can and cannot, should or should not, be hired. This means that certain things can be said in the classroom and certain things cannot. What if a funded chair in Islamic studies taught about Islamic origins and the redaction of the Qurʾān? Would the community threaten to pull their money? What if the funders of a chair in Jewish studies heard or read something from the faculty member holding "their" chair that she was supportive of BDS and critical of Israel? Or what happens when the government of China finds out that their paid faculty member in the Confucius Institute is critical of them or supportive of Tibetan rights?

All of these are sites wherein we witness the ways in which knowledge about religions, about social groups, are manufactured and structured. Religious philanthropy in the Academy may, thus, be less about philanthropy and more about selfishness. Jewish studies, given its history, is however more prone than other traditions to these sorts of pressures. It has, from the beginning, been supported by community largesse. Such largesse was the only way that courses at universities could be offered. If Jews wanted courses on their tradition, so the unfortunate narrative of university administrators went, they would have to pay for them. While this worked for generations, and those donors are to be recognized for what they did, recent years have seen more pressure put on Jewish studies faculty. This problem needs to be addressed, but it never is on account of colleagues and organizations that are willing to turn a blind eye to it on account of personal gain and prestige in the field.

Israel

Israel is always the elephant in the room. No matter what one's area of study within Jewish studies, one can rarely avoid the topic. Israel structures conversations, determines collegiality, and even professional mobility. I have no intention here of wading into the legality or illegality, the rightness or wrongness, of Israel's actions against Palestinians, other than to point out some aspects of how it plays out theoretically in the field of Jewish studies. As witnessed in the previous section, it is increasingly becoming common to witness the presence of non-academics, who work for local Jewish organizations, on Jewish studies' search committees. These include the likes of leaders of local Jewish Federations who, as I noted above, make the explicit point to "stand with Israel."

Again, a few examples are in order to make a point. In 2019, H-Judaic—an online forum for Jewish studies—published a review of an Israeli scholar, Ronit Lentin's *Traces of Racial Exception: Racializing Israeli Settler Colonialism* (2018), a book which argued that Israel is a settler-colonial state, not unlike the United States, and one that maintains white supremacy by mistreating Indigenous populations. The reviewer, Eric B. Morgenson, a graduate student at SUNY Albany, reviewed the book favorably, showing how Lentin—a proponent of the BDS (Boycott, Divestment, and Sanctions) Movement—is critical of Israel (Morgenson 2019). The review flew under my radar until the next day when Jonathan Sarna, the chair of H-Judaic, issued a statement:

> Since 1996, when I joined as Chair, H-Judaic has dispassionately focused upon providing scholarly assistance, accurate information, responses to queries, and book reviews in the field of Jewish Studies. We have studiously sought to avoid politics and to steer clear of all advocacy. Behind the scenes, we have refused or rewritten posts that departed from these standards. Unfortunately, a book review published on our list on Tuesday failed to adhere to these standards. It should not have been published by H-Judaic. We have, in response, strengthened our procedures. Our hard-working editors—all of them volunteers—have rededicated themselves to upholding the standards that you have come to expect. Many thanks to those readers who contacted us concerning the review. We appreciate your interest in H-Judaic.
>
> (Sarna 2019)

Sarna's response was strange. Rather than be critical of the contents of the book—which seems to have been the real issue—he seems to focus his outrage on an unsuspecting graduate student who had volunteered to review the book. I suspect that Sarna was critical that the book in question had been sent out in the first place for review. Rather than censure the author or the commissioning book review editor, Sarna—a senior scholar with an endowed chair at Brandeis—chooses to focus his attentions on a young and powerless graduate student. Though Sarna claims that "we have studiously sought to avoid politics and to steer clear of all advocacy," he fails to acknowledge that not reviewing books critical of Israel—by an Israeli, no less—amounts to another form of advocacy, to wit, that of advocacy in support of Israel. Couching that support in terms of what he considered to be a bad—or in his words "political"—review is disingenuous.

Another *exemplum gratia*, if in fact one is needed, is some of the work of Harvard's Ruth Wisse, one of the most respected scholars of Yiddish in the world. Now retired, she currently works for the neo-conservative Tikvah Fund, which publishes, among other things, the *Jewish Review of Books* and the Library of Jewish Ideas at Princeton University Press, both of which share a similar agenda. Speakers at Tikvah events include the likes of John Bolton, Elliott Abrams, and Michael Oren.

In her *Jews and Power* (2007), Wisse is critical of the accommodation wing of Judaism, and argues that Zionism and the formation of the State of Israel in 1948 should have put an end to it. Instead, she argues, any concessions—such as surrendering the Sinai Peninsula to Anwar Sadat and the signing of the Oslo Accords in 1993—are dangerous because *the* Muslims, who she argues are inherently anti-Semitic and anti-Jewish, cannot be trusted (135). Jews must, according to her, finally learn to wield power. Indeed, Wisse goes so far as to imply that Palestinians have no place in Israel, since they "share the language, religions, customs, and territory of the Arab majority. They form a majority in Jordan, which they consider a natural repository of their national aspirations" (159). She also excoriates Palestinian leaders: "had they prepared themselves to build their own societies rather than destroying someone else's" (158). Though, of course, no mention is made of Israeli intransigence or malfeasance. Instead, as the only democracy in a region hostile to the values of the West, she continues, Israel must defeat its enemies (e.g., 131, 181–184). It is a tendentious argument, to be sure, but it reveals clearly just how Israel structures many conversations within Jewish studies.

Israel also creates mistrust for Jews who happen to work within Islamic studies. it is usually assumed that such scholars support Israel by virtue of some sort of genetic or biological affiliation. It is an unfortunate situation, but Islamic studies' mistrust of Jews on the one hand and Jewish studies' mistrust of Muslims and Arabs on the other often makes meaningful and productive dialogue between these two related subfields extremely difficult. It means, to return to my Introduction, two subfields with a great deal in common rarely talk to one another.

Conclusions

This chapter, like the previous one, has tried to take stock of a subfield at the current moment. Providing a snapshot in time, it has examined some of the current trends, issues, and problems of Jewish studies. Not unlike the study of Islam, a number of genealogies, political forces, and tacit assumptions have governed knowledge production, but are rarely the focus of scholarly attention. Rather than examine these issues, we simply replicate them. This was the main reason behind my decision to write Neusner's biography: to show that the battles between insidership and outsidership, on the one hand, and universalism and particularism, on the other, have already been fought, indeed fought fiercely. If we ignore this, we not only forget what was at stake—and I do think that is where we are at the current moment, in a general malaise of forgetfulness—we will have to fight them all over again ...and then again ...

While Jewish studies and Islamic studies rarely talk to one another, the problems that beset them are remarkably similar. If Islamic studies began as a way to understand the Oriental "other," Jewish studies emerged as way to show that Jews were not other. Both subfields were thus born in sets of misrepresentations. While both were apologetic enterprises, they were always framed in the guise of "Wissenschaft" or scientific objectivity. Though recent trends in both subfields have now changed the terms of those origins, transformed them in light of identity politics and the need to feel heard by the larger academy, the end results are similar. This largely involves the reification of one's object of study and the need to protect or defend it from criticism.

It is time to begin to reflect on these issues. As argued in the previous chapter, this ought to involve attention to the genealogies of the terms, categories, and narratives that have structured our fields of study and taken us from there to here. In the following set of chapters, I use three case studies to try to do precisely this.

Part II

Case Studies

Chapter 3

Destabilizing "Judaism" in Late Antiquity

In the previous chapter I argued that one of the most used, yet undertheorized, methods in Jewish studies is that of comparison.[1] Jews are imagined as different from non-Jews, and much intellectual effort goes into elucidating the contexts and contours of such difference. What I want to do in the present context is begin the process of using comparison to problematize, if not actually subvert, the dominant narrative that was created in the ateliers associated with Wissenschaft des Judentums, one that I would argue still largely structures our thinking about Judaism.[2] That narrative reifies something called Judaism and articulates—indeed, affirms—something called Jewish continuity between biblical times and the modern day. Problems in that narrative, as we shall soon see, are either thinly papered over or largely ignored.[3] To demonstrate this, I wish to focus on the "Jews" present on the Arabian Peninsula before and at the time of Muhammad (d. ca. 632), Islam's prophet. These Jews are often assumed to be kosher and their Judaism is perceived to function as the midwife to the birth of Islam.[4] We do not want to ask too many questions of these Jews—like querying the complexity of their identity or talking about Arab converts, let alone the types of Judaism present—lest the narrative collapses in on itself. What, after all, do we do with "Jewish Arabs" or "Arab Jews" in a post-1948 world? Instead, they are simply imagined as Jews who, like those reified by the likes of Wissenschaft des Judentums, gave Muhammad the raw materials to imagine a new religion of monotheism. This is in keeping with our basic narrative in Jewish studies that has tended to focus on centers as opposed to margins, on normativity as opposed to heterodoxy, and on the consolidation of rabbinic Judaism at the expense of those groups that were responsible for such consolidation in the first place. Indeed, Bernard Lewis (1984) says of these "Arabian Jews" that they "were of no great importance in Jewish history and are virtually unknown to Jewish historiography" (74). While I might agree with his latter assessment, the former is based less on fact than political expediency. Moreover, the latter lacuna would seem to be the reason for the former assessment.

Implicit in the inherited narrative of Jewish studies, predicated as it is on the notion of Jewish continuity, is that Jews were present in the Arabian Peninsula at the time of Muhammad, and that Judaism functioned as the catalyst for the formation of Islam, just as it had done for Christianity at the other end of the late antique period. While there can be no doubt that late antique Arabia witnessed a plethora of religious forms, the latter narrative assumes a stability that is difficult to support. It also works with a number of problematic assumptions, such as: we know who these Arabian Jews actually were and just what type of Judaism they practiced; that we understand the nature of the contact between these so-called Jews and the earliest Muslims; and that we can somehow show the interconnection between the Qurʾān and the religious ideas that circulated among these Arabian Jews. Despite the assurances of many, our understanding of this period is hindered by a paucity of sources on the one hand, and a desire to conflate salvation history with history, on the other.

That is it. We then proceed to assume they were Jewish because our Wissenschaft forebearers told us they were. We do not bother to learn the languages of their inscriptions (e.g., Nabatean, Sabaic), of which there are a great many, and instead focus on either the biblical period (the period prior to the one in question) or the rabbinic period (the one immediately thereafter), leaving Arabian Jews marginal—reflecting Lewis' assessment—to the narrative of Jewish history. This leads to necessary, but perhaps uncomfortable, disciplinary questions. Why is Hebrew and Aramaic—the latter, the language of the Talmud—considered to be a language of Jewish studies, but not, say, Sabaic? Why are seminars on the Mishnah or Talmud offered in graduate schools across the country, but not on, say, South Arabian epigraphy? And, even more poignantly: Why are some Jews deemed more worthy of study than others? Answers to such questions take us to the heart of what we do. I would go so far as to argue that there exists an unquestioned normativity—again, one derived from our Wissenschaft ancestors, and that we have simply taken over willy-nilly—built into our field.

For some strange reason, and I am not sure why, the topic of the Jews of Arabia is perceived to be an Islamic studies problem as opposed to a Jewish studies one. This seems to be how the two subfields have decided—by unwritten agreement? by default position?, it is not entirely clear—to divvy up the topic. It would seem that the thinking is that Arabian Jews should be of interest to those who work on Islamic origins, who by necessity work in Islamic studies, but the period immediately before (Second Temple) and after (rabbinic) are then set aside for Jewish studies.[5] Just imagine the interesting crosspollinations if the two subfields could, among other things, collaborate on such topics.

The result is that these Jews and the Jewish communities on the Arabian Peninsula of which they were a part pose a number of intractable problems to the researcher. Despite the fact that they had political autonomy, evident in the Ḥimyar kingdom of South Arabia, they rarely figure in our narratives documenting the history of late antique Jews and Judaism. What, after all, are we to do with Jews who had political autonomy between 70 and 1948? Our master narrative is that Jews were, to recall Wisse's argument at the end of the previous chapter, powerless—thus these Jews and others, like the Khazars, tend to be neatly overlooked and understudied. Despite the proximity of the Arabian Peninsula to Palestine, both at the time of the Second Temple period and to centers of Jewish life and learning there after its destruction, these Arabian Jews remain an enigma. Basic and fundamental questions remain. Who were they? Where did they come from? And, perhaps most importantly, what kind of Judaism did they believe in or practice? While their rulers seem to have regarded themselves as Jewish and external sources (both coeval and subsequent) refer to the kingdom using this term, what exactly Judaism meant on the Arabian Peninsula in the fourth to sixth centuries, the period of the Ḥimyarite kingdom and its control over most of Arabia, is anything but clear.

Despite the fact that we should know better, scholars of religion love monoliths and are attracted to essences. These Jews, however, were anything but monolithic, and to try to ascertain what defined them "essentially" is well-nigh impossible. There seems to have existed *at least* two different groups on the Peninsula. Whether or not these two groups represent two different types or strains of Judaism present there is, again, impossible to ascertain—this, despite the fact that the tendency has simply been to call them "Arabian Jews." It also seems pretty clear that, historically, they could not have been rabbinic Jews (*pace* Mazuz 2014) on account of the simple fact that rabbinic Judaism was neither normative there nor anywhere else in the third and fourth centuries CE (see Cohen 2006). At any rate, these two communities possessed different languages, scripts, and social organizations. The one group lived in the Ḥijāz, that is the western part of the Peninsula (and that would have included the oases of Mecca and Medina). According to tradition—both later Jewish and

Muslim—many of these Jews were believed to be the descendants of those who fled Jerusalem after the destruction of the Second Temple in 70 CE. However, many north Arabian inscriptions associated with these Jews lack any Jewish liturgical formulae or even explicit symbols.

The other significant Jewish community dwelt in South Arabia, modern-day Yemen, and seems to have formed the nucleus of the Ḥimyarite kingdom there. Their Jewish bona fides—if this is even the correct term or even question to ask—are equally difficult to ascertain. Like those Jews to the North and West of them, some claim that they, too, derived from Jewish exiles who made their way there from Jerusalem; others argue that they might have been autochthonous South Arabian clans who had converted to some form of Judaism (Bowersock 2013); or, that they professed some form of monotheism that to others only resembled Judaism or what they thought Judaism was supposed to be (Beeston 1984). Evidence for the latter derives from the fact that there exist numerous inscriptions and graffiti (in Hebrew, Arabic, Nabatean, and Sabaic) in the area that refer, for example, to Jews, but with non-Jewish sounding patronyms. Once again, however, we have very little idea of the contents or contours of this "Judaism." On the one hand we can proclaim, along with David Ben-Gurion, Israel's first prime minister, that it ought to suffice that they imagined themselves as Jewish. While I have no problem with this, left uninterrogated is the diversity and fluidity of Judaism as a marker of identity in this period.

There are, to be sure, a number of problems that beset those trying to reconstruct Jewish life on the Arabian Peninsula in Late Antiquity. What we know about these Jews is based, as we have seen, on epigraphical evidence, graffiti, contemporaneous external sources, and later Muslim sources, all of which are potentially problematic. Also significant is the fact that neither the Mishnah nor the Talmud mentions them.

While most of the ancient north Arabian inscriptions are difficult to date, ancient South Arabian inscriptions seem to have been written until at least the sixth century, when all these languages were gradually replaced by Arabic, the language associated with the rise of Islam. While we also possess Muslim sources that deal with these social groups, they are also problematic given the notorious issues involved in accurately dating early Islamic literature, much of which comes from later periods than are implied by their authors. Within this context, such literature may offer us more back-projected literary tropes than historical accounts. The "Jew" often functions in this literature—not unlike "Pharisee" in early Christian literature—as a metaphor for stubbornness or resistance to

Muhammad's prophetic call. While such back-projections may well tell us what later Muslims thought about Jews and Judaism, they provide little contemporaneous information as to their actual lives and beliefs. The history of Arabian Judaism, unlike the history of most other types of Judaism, derives from reading inscriptions as opposed to more traditional and more normative sources. This may well be the reason that scholars of Islam are more interested in these so-called Jews than scholars of Judaism are.

It seems to me, however, that Jewish studies ignores them at their own peril since these Jewish communities stand at the intersection of two much larger sets of issues. In terms of Jewish studies, we need to try to figure out how they relate to other communities of late antique Jewry. How, in other words, did various types of Judaism make inroads into places like the Arabian Peninsula? Did such groups proselytize local inhabitants? And, relatedly, how did Judaism fit within the larger political struggles between the Byzantine and Sasanian Empires, both of which sought vassal tribes among the Arabs. Did Jews do the same? The second major issue and importance for these Jews involves figuring out their role within the larger context of the rise of Islam. Arabian Jews are thus also a potentially important group for Islamic studies. Did the Ḥimyarites, for example, represent an amalgamation of local autochthonous monotheistic claims that could have been legitimated by some kind of proximity to (some type) of Judaism? Did Islam emerge as some local Arabizing version of Judaism or some Judaizing version of Arabian monotheism? These are major questions, and Arabian Jews are situated wonderfully between Jewish and Islamic studies. Yet, rather than ask questions of them, our dominant narratives have preferred to find in them an "authentic" Jewish identity that stretches out from the destruction of the Second Temple and moves directly through to the codifiers of the Babylonian Talmud (and beyond). Within this context, these Arabian Jews, imagined as true rabbinic Jews, form a missing piece of the puzzle.

If anything, these Arabian Jews teach us to be cautious of assuming an orthodoxy of stable Jewish identity and practice based upon what the rabbinic academies of Babylonia were producing at this time. What "Arab Jewishness" consisted of, in other words, might have looked considerably different than other forms of Jewishness in the larger context of the Mediterranean basin and beyond.

The view from the center, which has functioned as our operative one, portrays Jewish history as an outgrowth from a single nucleus, a spreading inkblot that we label "the rabbinate."[6] But what other than this political label held Judaism together at this point? How did it establish cohesion and what happened to those who departed from it? The view from the margins offers the possibility of addressing questions like these. It starts from the fact that doctrinal cohesion and theological normativity emerge gradually and are the direct result of the tensions between center and margins.

The Jews of Late Antique Arabia

In order to put some of the above statements into relief, allow me to focus on the problems associated with trying to define Judaism in late antique Arabia.[2] Comparison has traditionally been the model used to think about some of these issues. Whereas non-Jews did "x," Jews did "y" or "z." This was a method developed by those associated with Wissenschaft des Judentums, as explained in Chapter 2 above. In terms of the Jews of Arabia, it was—and I would still say is—assumed that there existed "Jews" (and, by virtue of that, "Judaism") on the Arabian Peninsula who, while seemingly indistinct physically and culturally from their neighbors, were somehow imagined as distinct from them religiously. I say imagined because, other than rock inscriptions, we possess very little information about them. Jews, it is assumed, wrote great books and thought deep monotheistic thoughts, they did not write on rocks, especially in the fifth century CE.

Heinrich Graetz (1817–1891), the great historian of the "*the* Jews," could, for example, write of these Arabian Jews:

> in consequence of their Semitic descent, the Jews of Arabia possessed many points of similarity with the primitive inhabitants of the country. Their language was closely related to Arabic, and their customs, except those that had been produced by their religion, were not different from those of the sons of Arabia. The Jews became, therefore, so thoroughly Arabic that they were distinguished from the natives of the country only by their religious belief.
>
> (Graetz 1955: 56)

Graetz's analysis turns on the notion that these Jews were somehow religiously and, by extension, ethnically normative. They may have appeared as Arabs on the outside, but they remained pure Jews on the inside. Physically indistinct from their Arab neighbors, he is then forced to explain how they were Jewish. According to him:

> In the form in which it was transmitted to them, that is to say, with the character impressed upon it by the Tanaim and Amoraim, Judaism was most holy to the Arabian Jews. They strictly observed the dietary laws, and solemnized the festivals, and the fast of Yom Kippur, which they called Ashura. They celebrated the Sabbath with such rigor that in spite of their delight in war, and the opportunity for enjoying it, their sword remained in its scabbard on that day. Although they had nothing to complain of in this hospitable country ... they yearned nevertheless to return to the holy land of their fathers, and daily awaited the coming of the Messiah.
>
> (Graetz 1955: 58)

Like Geiger before him and like countless others after him, including Goitein, Graetz contorts these Arabian Jews in his imagination so that they now become pious individuals who otherwise shared in the manly, poetic culture of the Arabs. He further relates—in good Orientalist fashion—that on account of "the Arab mind, [which was] susceptible to intellectual promptings, [and which] was delighted with the simple," these Jews were able to instruct them in the meanings of monotheism (ibid.). It is a comparative enterprise that is self-serving: smart and pious Jews help jump-start other monotheisms.

We must be cautious, however, of retroactively projecting the stability of later centuries back onto the period in question and then using such projections to compare imagined identities. In terms of Judaism, our dominant narrative is indebted to the fiction of a creative and stable Jewish essence that gives life to Islam (as it had to Christianity several centuries earlier). Often marginalized in that narrative are a series of difficult questions. While we know of the existence of Jews on the Arabian Peninsula in the pre-Islamic period, we have no idea what kind of Jews they actually were. There exists, as witnessed above, very little material or other archaeological remains that tell us how they lived. There is, as already mentioned, no mention of them in contemporaneous rabbinic literature.

There is a tendency to assume that "Jew" or "Judaism" (or "Arab" or "Arabness" etc.) meant in the fifth century what they meant in cosmopolitan Baghdad in the ninth century, and that both meant the same as they do in our post-1948 world.[8] We thus think that we know much more than we actually do, and the comparative schema aids and abets this assumption. If we do not know who the Arabs were and we do not know who the Jews were, we also have to admit that we also do not know what kind of Christians existed in the area. It seems, and again much of this is gleaned from external sources and numismatic evidence, that they would have been Christians who would have been deemed heretical after the Council of Chalcedon (451) issued its famous decree that Jesus was both fully human *and* fully divine (Bowersock 2013: 63–77).

Jews and Others: Comparison or Fluidity?

Despite the confidence of both (later) primary and secondary (including scholarly) sources that use them unproblematically into the present, we have absolutely no idea what Judaism looked like in these various regions on the Arabian Peninsula in the third or fourth century, let alone in the sixth when Muhammad and his followers come on the scene of world history. Just to put this into perspective: this former date coincides with the period just around the time of the codification of the Mishnah in the Galilee. It is difficult to imagine that there was a normative Judaism at this period, let alone a normative Judaism on the Arabian Peninsula that existed far removed from what was simultaneously emerging as tannaitic Judaism in rabbinic centers such as Yavneh and Usha. One thing that does seem possible to say is that how we imagine difference in late antiquity or even the early medieval period rarely falls along modernist lines. Different social groups—groups we may today conveniently label using anachronistic concepts such as "ethnicity" or even "religion"—certainly interacted and overlapped with one another (Gruen 2011: 5). Yet charting the contours of these interactions is the difficult part. Was the identity of such groups stable or fluid? Was it fixed or uncertain? We have tended to assume the former term in each of these dyads with the result that comparison has been imagined as the useful model, to wit, "x" can be neatly understood as Jewish, "y" as Muslim (and, oftentimes "z" as Christian). However, it is more than likely that the interactions between these manifold and overlapping social groups may well be better accounted for using other schemas that can appreciate this complexity as opposed to simplistic comparative ones that have historically overlooked it.

Who Were the Jews of Arabia?

In order to move the analysis forward, I wish to examine a set of data that I have already examined in other contexts (Hughes 2020a, 2021b). This is not the place to bring in new data, as my concerns are largely theoretical in the present study, but to show how what I have examined in those others contexts reveal, once again, the social and religious fluidity examined above. Tradition tells us, for example, that a Jewish presence existed on the Arabian Peninsula as early as the first century CE, prior to the destruction of the Second Temple.[9] There exists in Dedan, an oasis in central Arabia not far from Yathrib (which would subsequently be renamed Medina, after Muhammed moved there to become its lawgiver in 622), for example, a tombstone erected by one Yaḥya bar Shim'un for his father that dates to 307 CE (e.g., Juasson and Savignac 1909-1922: no. 386). There also exist numerous graffiti in the area that would, again, appear to denote Jewish names and, one would assume, Jews. However these graffiti are written in Nabataean (a dialect of Aramaic) or Arabic, and not Hebrew.[10] Then there is what later Muslim traditions tells us is the Jewish community at Yathrib. It is these Jews, to invoke once again the dominant narrative, who were believed to play a "formative" role in the emergence of Islam and they are the ones to whom the most attention is paid. Tradition has it, as we saw above, that these Jews were the descendants of those who fled Jerusalem after the destruction of the Second Temple in 70 CE (Donner 2010: 35; see also Bausi and Gori 2006: 121). But, why should we accept tradition? Many of the north Arabian inscriptions associated with these Jews, as Robin notes, lack any Jewish liturgical formulae or explicit symbols (Robin 2004: 842). Yet, for some reason, based on this dearth of firm evidence, we want to make these "Jews" normative and then have them be responsible for the birth of Islam. Robin, who has probably worked more on these inscriptions than anyone, claims that "dans le judaïsme aux multiples variants des siècles qui précèdent l'islam, il est difficile d'établir à quel courant se rattachent les juifs d'Arabie" (2004: 863). The genealogist Ibn Kalbī (737-819)—again note he is writing at least two centuries after the time in question—mentions, for example, that Jews of Yathrib married polytheists from the tribe of Quraysh in Mecca, the tribe from which Muhammad came (Robin 2004: 865). This would seem to contradict the notion, based on other later sources, that the Jews of Yathrib represented a priestly oasis where Jewish elites assembled in the aftermath of the destruction of the Second Temple.[11]

The "Jews" of Ḥimyar

As a way to further problematize both the ethnonym "Jewish" and the comparative method that brings it into existence, I wish to focus on those Jews based in the South Arabian kingdom of Ḥimyar, which corresponds roughly to modern day Yemen (see Newby 1988: 33–48). What we know about them largely derives from local inscriptions (see, especially, Robin 2004: 831–908), in addition to external inscriptions (e.g., the *Monumentum Adulitanum*),[12] Christian hagiographies (e.g., the early sixth-century Syriac *Book of the Ḥimyarites*), and other works (such as the fifth-century Anomean Philostorgius's *Ecclesiastical History*). Such sources inform us that, at some point in the fourth century, the kingdom of Ḥimyar seems to have converted to Judaism, perhaps not coincidentally about half a century after the conversion of the Ethiopian kingdom of Axum (just cross the Red Sea) to a Monophysite version of Christianity.[13] This Jewish kingdom lasted for roughly two centuries until it was taken over by its Axumite rivals in the sixth century (Nebes 2010: 48–52; see also Gajda 2009: ch. 5). While our dominant narrative will say that these South Arabian Jews, like those Jews in the Ḥijāz (including Yathrib/Medina), provided the raw materials for the birth of Islam in the seventh century, the situation seems to be much murkier on the ground.

South Arabia was home to, depending on the narrative, Jewish communities derived from Jewish exiles of Jerusalem and environs (Ahroni 1986: 47–48), or autochthonous South Arabian clans professing some form of monotheism/Judaism. Rather than subscribe to or endorse either narrative, I prefer to use these communities as a mechanism to problematize "Judaism" in the late antique period and to reveal how these Ḥimyarite Jews show with some degree of clarity just how difficult it is to neatly disentangle Judaism, the so-called religion, from other markers of identity, such as ethnicity, tribalism or other political configurations.

While it is clear that the Ḥimyarite kingdom converted to some form of Judaism based on numerous Sabaic inscriptions in the area, we have very little idea of the contents or contours of this "Judaism." Robin notes that around 380 CE inscriptions cease to reference the polytheistic deities of South Arabia, and begin to refer solely to *Raḥmānān* ("the Merciful One") (see Robin 2004: 833). Though these "post-conversion" inscriptions refer to a monotheistic deity, it is worth noting that they nonetheless remain in the Sabaic language of South Arabia. Some have argued that *Raḥmānān* might be related to the Hebrew *raḥamim* or be a precursor to Allah, the high god of the North. But it is not at all clear if these, to use Nebes's locution, "Ḥimyarite Rahamanists" in South Arabia are synonymous with "Jews," or indeed what monotheism even meant in this particular time and place.[14] Perhaps also significant is the fact that this presumably widespread conversion elicited no changes in the script, calendar, or language of the Ḥimyarites.

Both the internal and external manuscript traditions—including from the later Islamic tradition—verify the existence of this Jewish kingdom (Robin 2004: 833-835). Surprisingly, Jewish sources, particularly rabbinic ones, ignore them. There is no mention, for example, of any Ḥimyarite king in either the Mishnah or the Talmud (Nebes 2010: 39n56). Likewise, according to Robin, "Seules les sources juives détonnent dans cet ensemble. De manière étonnante, elles sont totalement muettes sur l'existence d'importantes communautés juives en Arabie" (Robin 2004: 834). Despite the absence of these Jews from canonical and normative sources, we possess inscriptions informing us of their identity as far away as Beth Sheʿarim in the Galilee. A Hebrew inscription from Ṣuʿar (modern day Jordan) from roughly 470 CE, for example, notes the burial of one Yosi b Awfa:

> This is the resting place of Yoseh b. Awfa, who died in the city of Tafar in the land of the Ḥimyarites, leaving for the land of Israel and who was buried the day of the eve of Sabbath, the 29th day of month of Tammuz ... equal to the year [400] of the destruction of Temple. Peace [Shalom] ...[15]

While the name Yosi is certainly attested in Jewish sources, the patronym Awfa is not and would seem to be of "Arab" derivation. So, who is this Yosi b. Awfa? An Arab Jew or a Jewish Arab? Or something entirely different? But even this raises as many questions as it answers, however. Was he, like many of the Ḥimyarite Jews, a "convert"? If so, to which type of Judaism was he a convert? A later heterodox form of Judaism—if so, does this account for the relative silence in later Jewish sources? Presumably he was not a convert to what was slowly becoming normative rabbinic Judaism since, once again, there is no mention of these Arab Jews in either of the two Talmuds (Yerushalmi completed in ca. 400CE and the Bavli in ca. 500).[16] Another burial inscription, this time in both Aramaic and Sabaic:

> Aramaic: Here lies Leah, daughter of Judah. May her soul [rest] for the life eternal and may she be [ready] for the resurrection at the end of days. Amen and amen. Shalom.

Sabaic: Here lies Leah, daughter of Yawdah. May Raḥmānān allow her rest. Amen. Shalom.[17]

As Robin notes this inscription is interesting in the sense that the Aramaic inscription denotes the afterlife and gives no name of the deity, whereas the Sabaic inscription mentions the deity's name (the aforementioned *Raḥmānān*), it fails to make any mention of the afterlife (Robin 2004: 840).

I have mentioned these two inscriptions because, like other ones from this time and place, they push us to rethink just what we know (and do not) about Judaism and Jewish history. Such inscriptions, and the questions to which they give rise, would seem to complicate the operative model of Goitein and all those others who subscribe to the narrative of symbiosis. What are we to make of these Jews? Our tendency in Jewish studies is to ask, "are they *pure laine* or real Jews?" Even Robin, who as far as I can tell is neither Jewish nor in Jewish studies, has to ask: "La Première [question] est de savoir si ces juifs d'Arabie sont véritablement juifs" (Robin 2004: 865). Yet, I hope we can appreciate just how problematic such an utterance is. What do "real" Jews look like in the fourth century, a period prior to the codification and dissemination of the Babylonian Talmud? Why should we assume that what is going on in Amoraic academies is normative and binding on all Jews at this point in time? G. W. Bowersock, who has also spent considerable time working on these materials, has no doubts that these Ḥimyarite Jews "were authentically Jewish" (Bowersock 2013: 83) and that "it has become absolutely certain that the Arabs of Ḥimyar genuinely embraced Judaism as converts" (ibid.: 84). But there are problems with such assessments. What does "authentically Jewish" mean in the context of the fourth century? What does an "Arab-Jew" or "Jewish Arab" mean? What does it mean to embrace Judaism as a convert? And, just as importantly, did more normative centers of Jewish learning embrace them as converts? The answer to the latter question would seem to be negative since, as noted, neither the Mishnah nor the Talmuds makes reference to them. Since we possess no material remains—no mikvahs, no synagogues, no Hebrew inscriptions—Bowersock's confidence is difficult to maintain. Bowersock can also boldly claim, against the evidence, that "an entire nation of ethnic Arabs in southwestern Arabia had converted to Judaism and imposed it as the state religion" (ibid.: 4). Though he does not, for reasons mentioned, I think we can safely put many of the above nouns in scare quotes: "nation," ethnic," "Arabs," "conversion," "Judaism," and "state religion."

Violent Jews?

The Ḥimyarite Jews were, by all accounts, rather bellicose and persecuted Christians and those who did not convert to their version of Judaism. They were perhaps most famous for their destruction of the Christian population at Najrān, including the inhabitants of its monastery.[18] What do we do, as Newby well notes, with such Jews, who ostensibly fit neither rabbinic nor our own narrative of Jewish passiveness or political quiescence (Newby 2013: 44)? We can question their bona fides—how Jewish were they? Or, failing that, we can argue that their conversion to Judaism might have been for other than spiritual reasons. Again, we see this default position as one that argues that if we do not like a certain religious expression, we transform it into "political" or "cultural" realms. Some, for example, have suggested that the Ḥimyarite emperors had sought to control the lucrative spice trade and route to India. Whereas the Byzantine Empire had sought to control the area in Northern Arabia by converting the local inhabitants to Christianity, the Ḥimyarites instead converted to Judaism.

Regardless of how "Jewish" they were, the question remains: What do we do with a "Jewish kingdom" with political autonomy that existed between the destruction of the Second Temple in 70 CE and the formation of the State of Israel in 1948? Why do we ignore them along with, say, the Khazars? How, framed somewhat differently, do we contextualize or place the Jewish kingdom of Ḥimyar, especially when our normative Jewish sources completely ignore it? Robin suggests that the silence is the result of the rabbis' distrust of political power in the aftermath of the Bar Kokhba Revolt (132–135 CE) and their desire to wait for messianic as opposed to political fulfillment (Robin 2004: 855). Perhaps. Or, perhaps, they were not seen as Jewish enough—both in the past and in the present? This, then, says a lot about how we construct Judaism, Jews, and Jewish history.

It seems to me that we are content to call these Ḥimyarite (or, alternatively, Ḥijāzī) kingdoms "Jewish" when it suits our narrative of Judaism present at the birth of Islam—to show, paraphrasing Geiger's title, what Muhammad took, or stole, from the Jews. Yet, we dare not probe too deeply into the Jewish bona fides of Ḥimyarite Jews or other Jews on the Arabian Peninsula for fear of unintended consequences.

This is where traditional models of comparison used in Jewish studies fail. This model, to recapitulate, is to isolate Jewish ideas and to show Jewish difference. To what can we compare Judaism? Instead of learning the relevant languages (Sabaic, Nabataean, Arabic, etc.) to read these inscriptions and to help understand the complexity of Judaism on the Arabian Peninsula, we repeat the simple narrative that Judaism—not which Judaism, but just plain old Judaism—functioned as the "midwife" to Islam at the time of Muhammad. Such narratives imply stability—in doctrine, in form, in identity—that flies in the face of what we know about late antique social formation.

Conclusions

Why do we persist in the assumption that we know who these Arabian Jews were and then proceed simply to perpetuate a fiction that was manufactured in the nineteenth century and that was premised on "the gift of the Jews"? Like a bad undergraduate paper, we assume that if we say something enough times then it must, by virtue of the repetition, be true. It would seem that we tend to bypass these Jews rather quickly either because they are simply assumed to fit within our basic narrative of Judaism and its perceived ethnic continuity or because they uncomfortably problematize it. In the former case, we simply presume that a stable and normative Judaism existed and, while we may not know that much about it, we know that it inevitably helped to produce Islam—after all, where do those biblical stories in the Qurʾān come from? In the latter case, their ethnic bona fides are not so easy to establish so that they might not really be Jewish or Jewish enough. In which case, we do not know what to do with these Jews so, until further evidence comes to light, let us not worry too much about them.

The question that I frequently ask myself is: Why are not dissertations written on such Jews and on trying to figure out the contours of this Jewish kingdom in South Arabia? We are content to learn the languages (both literal and metaphorical) to study Christian origins and the "parting of the ways" between Christianity and rabbinic Judaism, to study rabbinic texts, to study medieval Jewish philosophy, to study kabbalah, and to study—ad nauseum—Jews in American popular culture. Why, then, do we ignore roughly five hundred years of Jewish settlement in late antique Arabia? Is it because we assume we know the narrative? Is it because we do not want to know the narrative? Or, do we make these Jews a problem for those working in other fields, such as that of Islamic origins?

If Jewish studies is going to look outward, as I think it must, then it needs to rethink at least two things:

1. ascertain its relationship to the disciplines, which will broaden the scope of analysis; and
2. rethink the very term, "Jewish," that sustains the field.

We think we know what Jewish languages, Jewish texts, Jewish history, and so on are. But do we? We also think we know who, what, when, and where *the* Jews were. But, again, do we? Rather than use comparison to maintain Jewish difference, we need to think about comparison as a method that facilitates similarities between social groups that may not be as different as we are accustomed to believe.

Chapter 4

Zindīqs and the Construction of Islamic Orthodoxy

The early framers of Islam were relentlessly self-conscious of the fact that their new religion existed within a world of entrenched and rival religions.[1] This manifested itself, for example, in the Qurʾān's often ambiguous relationship to other religions, especially those of Judaism and Christianity. Offering words of acknowledgement and praise on the one hand, other passages are often highly disparaging of them on the other. This ambiguity was a direct result of the anxiety that these religious others produced at a formative moment in Islam's emergence. Although these religious others powered the theological articulation of Islam in subsequent centuries, they were rarely flesh-and-blood individuals or groups. Rather, they represented a set of textual foils that could be conveniently orchestrated, and ultimately controlled to facilitate self-definition.

If we situate Islam as a continuation of the late antique period, a practice that is becoming increasingly common,[2] this means that its early framers inherited a social world that had been largely defined by previous empires in the region (i.e., Roman, Byzantine, Sasanian). Of especial significance was the *Theodosian Code,* commissioned by the Emperor Theodosius and composed between 429 and 438, which represented a compilation of all the laws of the Roman Empire under Christian emperors since 312.[3] Among other things, this *Code* successfully created a society where communal divisions based on religion was the predominant means of identifying individuals and their loyalties.[4] This is particularly clear in its sixteenth and final book, dealing specifically with the matter of religion. Therein, we witness the increased political necessity of defining and establishing one orthodoxy at the expense of what could now, at least through back-projection, be defined as a variety of heterodoxies and heresies. In so doing, the *Code* further reinforces the notion that orthodoxy and heterodoxy are intimately connected in the religious imagination.[5] They feed off of one another, with each requiring the perceived negative traits of the other for its existence. The definition of one, in other words, is necessarily contingent upon the definition and subsequent elucidation of the other.

Since Islam entered a world that was in large part defined by the *Code*'s desire to create communal divisions based on religion, the new tradition, perhaps not surprisingly, took religion for granted as a way to imagine social differences between communities.[6] As the conquering armies made their way into places like Iraq, Syria, and Egypt, Muslims—very much a minority at this point[7]—everywhere encountered the spiritual and physical traces of these other religions.[8] As a new religion lacking such an ancient pedigree, inevitable questions arose: What were those responsible for articulating Islam to do with these other religious traditions? How, for example, could older religions be situated within a much broader narrative that naturally culminated in Islam's rise and florescence? The interpretive acts used to address Islam's relationship to these other religious traditions were necessarily fraught with tensions as a set of deep-rooted connections between the old and the new needed to be mined and ascertained with the aim of using the former to make sense of the latter. While the early framers of Islam could tap into these previous narratives, both positively and negatively, the last thing they could do was ignore them since religious others were, especially in the early period, quite literally everywhere.[9]

From its beginning, then, the framers of Islam struggled with religious others, both external and internal, and this struggle was ultimately responsible for the creation of what would eventually emerge as (Sunnī) orthodoxy. While the latter would appear as the natural outgrowth of Muhammad's preaching to those doing the framing, it was ultimately little more than a subsequent development accompanied by a retroactive projection onto the earliest period. Non-Muslims (among them Christians, Jews, Zoroastrians) and the "wrong" kinds of Muslims (e.g., Shīʿa) became integral—by virtue of their perceived stubbornness, infidelity, heresy, or the like—to understand what true religion was not and, just as importantly, what it should be. Without such religious others proper belief could not be articulated and orthodoxy would simply have remained adrift in its own inchoateness.

Yet if Jews, Christians, and Shīʿa represented real, if often highly reified and textualized, others in early Muslim literature, I wish to focus here on an even more amorphous group, that of so-called "heretics." Despite their amorphousness, they played just as important a role as these others in defining the contours of orthodoxy.

Qurʾānic Scripts: Creating Religious Others

The *zindīq* (pl. *zanādiqa*, though in what follows I shall use the anglicized plural "*zindīqs*") were those individuals who were believed to be nominally Muslim, but who subscribed to what were increasingly becoming non-orthodox practices or beliefs. As such, they were charged with *zandaqa*, to wit, "heresy." Though it is certainly worth pointing out that it is virtually impossible to identify any commonly held belief or set of beliefs that held all of these individuals—and they tended to be individuals as opposed to communities—together. It was a term, as van Ess remarks, that could be used to designate everything from dualists to libertines, and virtually everything in between (1991–1997, vol. 1: 416). Manicheans, poets, philosophers, court secretaries, rival theologians, homosexuals, and many others were frequently labeled and even charged with the crime of *zandaqa*. It was an extremely useful and open-ended category to attack and disparage one's enemies, theological or otherwise, and of course to define better one's own beliefs and doctrines in the process.

Religious others tended to be understood by reducing them to the script that the Qurʾān had developed for them. Once reduced, they were rarely able to escape their textual fates. It was the initial qurʾānic encounter, or what was at least imagined to be this initial encounter, that ultimately made others comprehensible to later generations of Muslims, and that also produced a certain inevitability to their interactions. Unlike Jews and Christians—who could be made sense of on account of the script of rise-and-fall provided to them by the qurʾānic narrative—*zindīqs* possessed no such precedent since the term was non-qurʾānic (de Blois 1960–2005: 510; see further Gillot 2009: 32–33). *Zindīqs*, in other words, lacked a foundational script, and perhaps because of this were, in equal parts, everywhere and nowhere.

Like "the Jew" and "the Christian," "the *zindīq*" allows us to mine further the outer edges of orthodoxy by focusing on the fuzzy—and increasingly anxiety-producing—border between Islam and non-Islam, the place where differences between the two categories were coming into sharper focus. Within this context, the *zindīq* provided yet another foil to construct what was considered to be a pure and authentic Islam at a formative moment (Chokr 1993: 12). Defining the characteristics of what a "heretic" was, both what he believed in and what he practiced, enabled the creation of what a Muslim was or should be. But if Jews and Christians represented communities who had at least initially possessed some form of truth, the *zindīq* was someone who had never been in possession of such a revelation and who prima facie represented a revolt against all that was increasingly becoming defined as orthodox. *Zindīqs*, then, conveniently personified the negation of all that was Islam: *tawḥīd* (monotheism), revelation, the creation of the world, prophecy, and corporeal resurrection.

The *zindīq* was also dangerous because he functioned as a quasi-converso. While ostensibly a Muslim on the outside, underneath his exterior was imagined to surge that which undermined the spiritual and theological health of the Muslim *umma* ("community"). Precisely because it was such a fuzzy category, any number of competing and contradictory characteristics could be assigned to the *zindīq*. They were blasphemers; they were dualists; they were poets who threatened the pure language and message of the Qurʾān, and who actively sought to parody it (*muʿāraḍa al-Qurʾān*); and they were the ones who endangered the sexual (and other) mores of Islam. On account of this, the crime at least in theory for being a *zindīq* was death (Tirmidhī 1978 [1398], vol. 4: 59). And, unlike those religious others who were tolerated, the Caliph al-Mahdī (r. 158/775–169/785),[10] set up an office and a magistrate—the *ṣāḥib al-zanādiqa* or alternatively the *ʿarīf al-zanādiqa* (literally, the "overseer of the *zindīqs*" or sometimes translated simply as "inquisitor")—to begin the process of weeding them out. The *zindīq* thus allowed the Caliph, at a time when they still styled themselves as the spiritual head (*amīr al-muʾminīn*) of the community,[11] to put an end to perceived religious anarchy in the burgeoning empire (Turner 2013: 7–8; Chokr 1993: 11–12). The *zindīq*, in other words, facilitated the creation of two important distinctions: (1) who was and was not a Muslim; and, since they were not imagined as part of *ahl al-kitāb* ("people of the book") (2) who did and did not count as a member of the *ahl al-dhimma*, that is, legally protected minorities.

Clarifying the Term: Zindīqs as Manicheans and the Account of Ibn al-Nadīm

The term *zindīq* is not qurʾānic, but a Persian loanword that seems to have emerged in the eighth century, initially in the narrow sense of a "Manichean" (de Blois 1960–2005: 10). In the first part of the ninth chapter of his *Fihrist* ("Catalogue"), the tenth-century Ibn al-Nadīm (d. 380/990) presents us with one of the most extensive accounts of the Manicheans by a Muslim author, and shows us the early overlap between "Manichean" and "zindīq."[12] His lengthy and detailed account includes not only a description of Mani's birth and early life, but often very elaborate descriptions of Manichean beliefs and practices. Again, since my interest here is in the *zindīq* as an amorphous textual character as opposed to real flesh-and-blood Manicheans, allow me to focus briefly on some of Ibn al-Nadīm's comments that illumine my point. According to him, when the Caliph al-Maʾmūn journeyed through the region of Ḥarran, he was met by a group of them. According to Ibn al-Nadīm's description, the caliph subsequently asked them, "Which of the *dhimmī* [legally recognized minorities] are you?"

> They replied, "We are the Ḥarnāniyya." He asked further, "Are you Christians?" They replied, "No." "Are you Jews?" "No," they said. He inquired further, "Are you Magians?" They answered, "No." So [al-Maʾmūn] said to them, "Have you a book or a prophet [*kitāb aw nabī*]? They were hesitant in replying to him, so he said, "Then you are unbelievers [*kāfirūn*], the slaves of idols, Aṣḥāb al-Raʾs, who lived during the days of my father [Hārūn] al-Rashīd. As far as you are concerned, it is legitimate [for me] to shed your blood since there is no contract that establishes you as *dhimmī*." They replied, "we will pay the poll tax [*jizya*]." To which he responded, "The poll tax is accepted only from those who do not contradict Islam [*min khālif al-islām*] from among those people of religion [*ahl al-diyān*] that God, exalted and magnified, mentioned in his Book, and who have a book of their own, assuring them of good relations with Muslims. Since you do not belong to one or other of these groups, you must choose one of two alternatives. Either embrace the religion of Islam, or else that of one of the religions mentioned in the Book of God. Otherwise I will kill you all. I will grant you a delay until I return from my journey; then, unless you have become Muslims or members of religions mentioned in God's Book, I will order your death and extermination."
>
> (Ibn al-Nadīm 1872: 320; 1970: 751)

Ibn al-Nadīm continues the story by remarking that they all decided to change their distinctive dress and appearances, and that some became Christians, some Muslims, and others remained as they were. One of the latter's leaders said that rather than convert to Islam or one of the other religions, they should simply say they were "Sabians" (*al-Ṣābiʿūn*), a religion mentioned in the Qurʾān, but of unclear provenance, and thus in possession of a script as a "people of the book."

With this story we clearly witness the overlap between individuals and/or groups variously identified as *zindīq*s, unbelievers, idolaters, and the like. We should not be surprised to witness qurʾānic terms employed as the primary way to make sense of them. As implied above, if a group is not mentioned explicitly in the Qurʾān, like the *zindīq*s, it and its members must be fitted into one of the rubrics used therein to designate "unbelievers" (*kāfirūn*) or "idolaters" (*mushrikūn*). If they need to be fitted positively therein, then the equally amorphous qurʾānic term "Sabians" can be invoked. Indeed, al-Bīrūnī (d. 441/1050) makes mention of a thriving Manichaean community in Samarqand, where they were, significantly, referred to as Sabians (al-Bīrūnī 1879: 209). If anything, the story recounted above reflects the confusion and taxonomic fluidity that undoubtedly confronted early Muslims as they encountered groups such as Arameans, Manicheans, Mandaeans, and the like.

All of these latter groups were no longer recognizable as Christians, and were for the most part completely repudiated by Christian orthodoxy. Muslims thus classified them as "dualists," making such communities ineligible for the status of *ahl al-kitāb*. If any of them converted to Islam, they were perceived to be insincere and, even worst, as threats to the faith of simple believers. It seems that from here, the category "*zindīq*" could be expanded or contracted at will to include any or all that threatened the nature of what was becoming "true" and "authentic" Muslim teaching. *Zindīq*s thus served a double role: They revealed the wages of improper belief, just as they aided in the articulation of true belief.

From the earliest introduction of the term into Arabic and Muslim theologizing, *zindīq*s are presented as the antithesis to Muslims and, by extension, other peoples of the book (*ahl al-kitāb*). For example, and once again using the phrasing of Ibn al-Nadīm, but now put into the mouth of Mani:

> He who would enter the religion [of Manicheanism; literally *al-dīn*] must examine his soul. If he finds that he can subdue lust and covetousness, refrain from eating meat, drinking wine, as well as from marriage, and if he can also avoid causing injury to water, fire, trees, and living beings, then let him enter. But if he is unable to do all of these things, he shall not enter the religion. If however he loves the religion, but is unable to subdue his lust and craving, let him seize upon guarding the religion and its Elect

[*al-ṣiddīqūn*] that there may be an offsetting of his unworthy actions, and times in which he devotes himself to work and righteousness, nighttime prayer, intercession, and pious humility.

(Ibn al-Nadīm 1872: 332; 1970: 788)

On the level of belief and doctrine, Manichaeans went against those tenets of Islam that were currently under construction. They did not eat meat, for example, and were not supposed to marry, or have sexual relations. In addition, the *ṣiddīqūn*, those select members who performed all the rights of the religion and who were dependent upon the lay members, would have been anathema to what was coalescing as Sunnī orthodoxy.

Unlike Jews and Christians who, for the most part, remained within their ancestral religions, *zindīqs* were imagined to have only pretended to convert to Islam, whence they could subvert it from within. Within this context, they resembled those hated figures from Judaism, such as the arch heretic ʿAbdāllah Ibn Sabaʾ,[13] who personified more than anyone the discord and dissent in the young community by perfidiously entering the community through conversion. It would seem, and Ibn al-Nadīm's detailed descriptions attest to this, that Muslims knew that Manicheans had books. Yet, as the story recounted above concerning al-Maʾmūn reveals, they did not possess the proper books in the sense that they were not mentioned in the Qurʾān—unlike the books of the Jews and the Christians.

Ibn al-Nadīm's description of the contents and practices of Manicheans—including their books and sectarian divisions—leads him into a discussion of *zandaqa*. He informs his reader that in the days of Muʿizz al-Dawlah (r. 334–356/945–967), the first of the Būyid emirs of Iraq, he was personally acquainted with over three hundred Manichaeans in Baghdad, but at the time of writing there were not more than five (Ibn al-Nadīm 1872: 337; 1970: 803). His discussion of those charged with *zandaqa* however is relatively short in comparison, listing only a few names of theologians—whose books, he informs us, were destroyed (Ibn al-Nadīm 1872: 338; 1970: 804). His main concern in this short section is to show how issues of "dualism" made their way into the heart of Islamic theology. The brevity of the section however would seem to mean that the "threat" of the *zindīqs* had largely passed by his time.

Zindīq: Towards a Typology

As the term *zindīq* became increasingly synonymous with heretic, it became interchangeable with related terms such as *mulḥid* ("apostate," or "heretic"), *murtad* (also "apostate"), and *kāfir* ("unbeliever"; "infidel") (de Blois 1960–2005: 510; see also Chokr 1993: 43–45; Josephson 2006: 175–178). Before I discuss these more generic senses of the term, it is worth noting that Manicheans—unlike Zoroastrians—were never granted the legal status of an *ahl al-kitāb* (Stroumsa and Stroumsa 1988: 38; see also Vajda 1937–1939: 179–182). This may well be the result of the fact that *The Theodosian Code*, which played a significant role in shaping the Islamic religious worldview, outlawed Manicheanism as heretical. Moreover, as Stroumsa and Stroumsa note, the first century of Islam seems to have witnessed a renaissance of sorts of the religion (Stroumsa and Stroumsa 1988; see also Gabrieli 1961: 23–25). This, according to Lieu, seems to have been the direct result of the relative tolerance witnessed under the Umayyad caliphs.[14]

Manicheans imagined themselves as the true Christians, accused other Christians of being "judaizers," and they imagined their prophet, Mani, as the last prophet who had brought the true Gospel. Such features would certainly have contributed to their harsh treatment in *The Theodosian Code*. According to Ibn al-Nadīm, "Mani asserted that he was the paraclete [*al-fāraqlīṭ*] about whom Jesus, for whom may there be peace, preached" (Ibn al-Nadīm 1872: 328; 1970: 776). While Manicheans never imagined themselves as representing the true or even the most authentic Muslims, there was nevertheless fear on the part of Muslim theologians that Manichaeans would surreptitiously infiltrate the Muslim community with the aim of undermining it from within by, among other things, sowing confusion among the simple-minded (Chokr 1993: 61–62; see also Stroumsa and Stroumsa 1988: 39).

Since Muslim law denied Manichaeans the status of *ahl al-dhimma*, they were ultimately put in the same legal position as all those believed to be hostile to Islam and who were imagined to desire its dissolution. For this reason, according to de Blois, the words *zindīq* became dislodged from "Manichean" and began to be used interchangeably with *mulḥid* (de Blois 1960–2005: 510). The semantics of the term were now expanded to include anyone that denied the basic principles of what was slowly coalescing into orthodoxy. Though an individual Jew, for example, could be accused of being a *zindīq*, the Jewish community writ large was rarely or never accused of *zandaqa*. On account of the amorphousness of the term, *zindīqs*—especially in their new rôle as "heretics"—played a crucial role in the shaping of orthodoxy because they became synonymous, especially under the reign of al-Mahdī (to be discussed in greater detail presently), with the possession of all those characteristics imagined to represent the opposite of Islam (see, for example, Chokr 1993: 62; see further Fück 1935: 95–100). This caliph was the one who initiated their repression under the guise of "returning" to Islamic purity, something that was becoming associated with the *ahl al-sunna* and the ḥadīth folk, two groups beginning to take shape at the exact same time, not coincidentally, as their opposite (Chokr 1993: 14).

Within this context, so many of the theological features associated with *zindīqs*—dualism, the denial of God's existence, that the world was eternal as opposed to created, determinism, denial of revelation—could now be conveniently labelled as the opposite of what would only emerge at the end of this process as normative Muslim belief and practice. It is certainly no coincidence that Wāṣil b. ʿAṭāʾ (d. 131/748), the founder of the first school of Islamic theology, the Muʿtazila, was said to have written over a thousand refutations against the Manichaeans, showing the need to refute their principles.[15] In this the Manichean/*zindīq* played a crucial role in the beginning and subsequent articulation of Islamic theology (Nyberg 1929: 430–431; see also Vajda 1937–1939: 173; more recently, see Badawi 1993: 27–33). According to Patricia Crone, the existence—perceived as real or otherwise—of *zindīqs* (and their cognates *dahrīs* and *mulḥids*) played a formative role in the development and subsequent articulation of Muslim theology, forcing those tasked with its elaboration to provide alternatives to the perceived "ungodly cosmologies" of the latter (Crone 2016: 118–150). Once again we witness just how religious others—reified, textualized, and easily manipulated—became a convenient foil for the process of the clarification of Islamic doctrine and practice, and its differentiation from others.

It is also worth mentioning that into the category of "*zindīq*" could also be folded so-called freethinkers. These individuals, in the words of Sarah Stroumsa, "embodied the idea that one can wish to establish a personal ethical system, organize a human society, or even worship God without relying on the authority of revealed scriptures" (Stroumsa 1999: 6; see further van Ess 1968: 1–5). Within this context, it is certainly worth noting that one of the most important "freethinkers," Ibn al-Rawāndī, was a student of the Manichean Abū ʿĪsā al-Warrāq (Stroumsa 1999: 40–46). What they shared with more classic zindīqs, *qua* dualists, was an alternative worldview to that which was shaping into orthodoxy.

Zindīqs and the Accusation of Falsifying Prophetic Traditions

The second/eighth and third/ninth centuries would prove instrumental in the creation of what would eventually emerge as Islamic orthodoxy. It was a period that witnessed, among other things, the appearance of those who tried to preserve—if not actively create—the *sunna* of the prophet through the collection of reports (*aḥādīth*; sg. *ḥadīth*) of things that he was purported to have said or done. Such reports would soon take their place, along with the Qurʾān, as the foundation of what would crystallize as the Islamic tradition. Various legal schools (*madhāhib*) subsequently arose that were predicated on how best to interpret such sources based on, among other things, local custom and tradition.[16] It is certainly worth pausing to appreciate that at this period we quite literally witness the formation of Islam as the end product of such forces. It should come as no surprise, then, that Islam, like all religions, does not appear fully formed, but rather emerges slowly through a complex process of concentration and rejection.

Alterity played a crucial role in this process because others, whether real or perceived, provided one of the most basic and convenient ways to construct and subsequently test the bounds of community. This can be framed as simply and matter-of-factly as the locution "us/not-us." Whether real or imagined—or perhaps better both real *and* imagined—religious others functioned as the catalyst responsible for drawing the boundaries around what was slowly emerging as Islam. For this reason, the identification and subsequent definition of religious others—including listing their incorrect beliefs, their incorrect practices, and so on and so forth—would become a regular activity in the quest to ascertain authority and to delineate orthodoxy.

Those tasked with such boundary maintenance included legal scholars, *ḥadīth* collectors, doxographers, and others, and they began to coalesce into what Hodgson called "*ḥadīth* folk" (*ahl al-ḥadīth*) (Hodgson 1974: 315–409, esp. 385–392). These individuals, he argues, "combined with a keen concern for conservation of what had been achieved a moral rigorism more emotional than intellectual, which led them into an opposition to the actual current conditions among Muslims, in the name of an ideal past. Their triumphant yet populistic piety won them a large popular following, notably at Baghdad" (ibid.: 385). Indeed, Christopher Melchert, in trying to give greater definition to the term, argues that "two salient features of traditionalist piety were unremitting seriousness and an overwhelmingly moralistic conception of the Islamic community" (Melchert 2002: 427). The latter in particular, in Melchert's words, meant that "voluntary membership and equality flow from a stress on morality, which continually makes the individual choose to do one thing and not another; it also tends to demand the same choices from all individuals" (ibid.: 429). This growing sense of a unified moral community, the *umma*, enabled the *ḥadīth* folk to put their own community in increasingly sharp juxtaposition with others—in particular, other communities—which could now be constructed as not-moralistic. Religious others increasingly functioned as religious competitors, and it was incumbent upon the *ḥadīth* folk to show just how, when, and where these others entered into theological error, all the while simultaneously bringing themselves and their own beliefs and doctrines into sharper focus.

Perhaps on account of the imprecision and fluidity inherent to the category, *zindīqs* could be—and frequently were—imagined as everywhere and nowhere at the same time. As orthodoxy was taking shape and coming into clearer epistemological focus with religious others playing their part in the necessity for self-definition, as just witnessed, the need arose to supplement the qurʾānic narrative with other sources to develop what would become the Islamic legal tradition. It is important to be clear that at this point—just prior to the creation of the *miḥna* ("inquisition") to deal with *zindīqs*—all of this was in a flux. *Ḥadīth* reports were being collected, but not yet in their authoritative collections, and Muhammad's *sunna* ("way" or "example") was slowly being articulated (see, for example, Melchert 2003: 310). In order to ascertain the latter—that is, the body of literature used to prescribe the traditional customs and practices of the community, both social and legal—one needed the former, namely, the verbally transmitted record of the teachings, deeds and sayings of the prophet and his companions.

While all of this would be taken for granted over the course of the ensuing centuries, it is important to note that at this time, the time of the early ʿAbbāsid caliphate, none of this was clear. As prophetic reports were being collected there was a growing fear on the part of "ḥadīth folk" that their work on constructing a particular vision of Islam was being corrupted.[17] We now begin to see the charge levelled at *zindīqs* that accuses them of actively attempting to do this through their falsification of prophetic traditions.[18] "The zindīq" thus played a crucial role in defining what should and should not be included in what was emerging as orthodoxy.

Famous zindīqs like Ibn al-Muqaffaʿ (executed in 139/756 or 142/759; see the important study in Kristó-Nagy 2013), ʿAbd al-Karīm b. Abī al-ʿAwgha (executed sometime between 152/769 and 155/772), and Salih b. ʿAbd al-Quddūs (executed in 167/783) were all accused of falsifying ḥadīth reports and thereby spreading heresies within Islam. Al-ʿAwgha, for example, was said to have forged over 4000 ḥadīth reports before his execution.[19] Chokr argues that such charges were the direct result of the widespread ideological antagonism between the ḥadīth folk on the one hand, and rationalist theologians who were beginning to coalesce as the Muʿtazila on the other (Chokr 1993: 131–133; see further Hurvitz 2002: 115–144). Such debates revolved around the nature of reason, metaphorical language and the Qurʾān, whether or not the Qurʾān was created, the nature of divine attributes, and free-will v. determinism. Charging one's opponents of being "heretics" became a convenient way both to discredit their ideas and to further sharpen one's own. Rival or dissenting theologians could now be accused of being zindīqs, who had taken foreign ideas learned from, for example, the pagan Greeks or Persians, and who subsequently tried to apply them to both an articulation and an understanding of Islam.

The accusation of being a zindīq further allowed the ḥadīth folk and those others responsible for the construction of Islam to excise anything they disagreed with as "heretical." If a ḥadīth report did not coincide with emerging orthodoxy it could be written off as the forgery of a zindīq. Most significantly, though, the zindīq enabled the ḥadīth folk to define themselves and their beliefs as normative and as orthodox by staking out a position for themselves in a manner that was imagined as the polar opposite of heresy.

Not only were zindīqs such as the aforementioned accused of forging ḥadīths, another charge levelled against them was parodying the Qurʾān (muʿāraḍa al-Qurʾān) (see Chokr 1993: 152–170). In this, and returning to the idea of a qurʾānic script, they were imagined to have been the spiritual descendants of the Meccan kāfirūn mentioned in the Qurʾān, who were informed that they would never be able to produce a text as perfect as that of Muslim holy scripture. Showing the deep-rooted and structural connections between qurʾānic unbelief and contemporaneous heresy, the zindīqs were imagined as actively taking up the challenge. Engagement in such activity, whether real or imagined is not the point, further contributed to the suspicion that *zindīq*s denied the divine nature and nobility of the Qurʾān, while simultaneously undermining the perfection of its messenger, Muhammad. In particular, *zindīq*s were accused of parodying the Qurʾān," a charge that further invoked the qurʾānic trope of the deceit and trickery of unbelievers.[20] Once again, we see the fluidity between earlier qurʾānic terms, on the one hand, and contemporary nonbelievers on the other. *Zindīq*s thus stand charged of actively subverting what would become the two major sources of Islamic law, namely, the Qurʾān and the ḥadīth.[21]

Within this context, one of the most famous *zindīq*s was the aforementioned Ibn Muqaffaʿ (d. 139/757 or 142/759). A Persian, he served as a secretary under the ʿUmayyad governors. He was by all accounts a belletrist, a translator between Persian and Arabic (most notably of *Kalīla wa-dimna*), and a denizen of the courtly culture of the ʿUmayyad and subsequent ʿAbbāsid empires (see Vajda 1937–1939: 181–183; Chokr 1993: 189–196; Kristó-Nagy 2013: 49–62). When the ʿAbbāsids overthrew that dynasty, he—unlike many others—was able to maintain his courtly position, serving in Basra as a secretary under the uncles of the second ʿAbbāsid caliph al-Manṣūr (r. 136/754–178/775). He thus personifies the transition between the two caliphal dynasties and, wherever such a transition exists, we not surprisingly witness a source of potential anxiety. Because of this, though himself a Muslim, his enemies accused him of writing a defense of Manicheanism *and* of writing a parody of the qurʾānic text, thereby coupling the danger (Chokr 1993: 166–170).

We have already seen how a number of court secretaries were accused of being *zindīq*s. The great majority of those tried and executed during the reign of al-Mahdī, to be discussed in the following section, existed within this class, which seems to have functioned as the epicenter of late ʿUmayyad Basran literary culture (see the comments in Arjomand 1994: 20–21). Ibn al-Muqaffaʿ was firmly entrenched in this culture and seems, according to Arjomand, to have won over important members of the Arab aristocracy (ibid.: 20). Again, whether or not there existed an actual culture of *zandaqa* in Basra is less my concern here so much as it that a Persian intellectual class of secretaries and courtiers were responsible for generating a number of political accusations on the part of their Arab rivals. Again, we see a complimentary set of tensions—this time, for lack of a better word, "ethnic" or "nationalist" ones—folded into the complex and amorphous criteria of "the *zindīq*" (Chokr 1993: 175–186). It is Ibn al-Muqaffaʿ, one of the main figures associated with the *zindīq*s, who is charged with a host of offences: he is a Persian; a poet; a holdover from the ʿUmayyad dynasty; one who undermines the Qurʾān; and someone who is believed to secretly harbor Manichaean beliefs and practices. He thus becomes the *zindīq* personified. This seems to have been one of the main reasons why he was believed to be the leading figure in the group of four intellectuals who reportedly conceived of the project to undermine the Qurʾān, and the only name agreed upon in all of the sources.[22] The continued charge of *zandaqa* and a change in political climate that meant the withdrawal of his political protection meant that Ibn Muqaffaʿ was executed in 139/756 or 142/759 (Chokr 1993: 189–196; Kristó-Nagy 2013: 49–74; Cassarino 2000: 35–46).

Caliphal Authority, Deviancy, and the Shaping of Orthodoxy

We would do well to remember that heretics were never deemed heretical on account of the fact that they believed differently from the majority. Rather, such an accusation more often than not conveniently served the needs of those levelling the charge. In the present case this was no less a person than the Caliph himself. Abū ʿAbd Allāh Muḥammad, better known by his regnal name al-Mahdī (r. 159/775–169/785) was the third caliph of the ʿAbbāsid caliphate. Without a routinized system of succession, according to John P. Turner, "each Caliph needed to demonstrate from the outset of his reign and at regular intervals that he was indeed the Commander of the Faithful" (Turner 2013: 35). Every caliph, in other words, was upon his succession immediately faced with a crisis of legitimation that had to be dealt with. Since the ʿAbbāsids had come to a power on a tide of messianic hopes, much of which drew upon popular support of ʿAlīd loyalists, it is perhaps fitting that al-Mahdī took the title he did since, according to ʿAlīd tradition, the Mahdī was the rightly "guided one," an eschatological redeemer who would usher in the day of judgment (*yawm al-qiyamah*) and rid the world of evil and corruption (Haider 2014: 96–100; Halm 1988: 21–26; Amir-Moezzi 1994: 65–68). The Mahdī, in other words, is synonymous with a just and protective rule over the *umma*. Since the "parting of the ways" between Sunnism and Shīʿism had yet to occur, al-Mahdī certainly drew upon such sentiment to help legitimate his rule.

That Abū ʿAbd Allāh Muḥammad chose this name signals to just what an extent he imagined himself as reaffirming the divine origin of his office and as functioning as the guarantor of true guidance to the Muslim community (Lapidus 1988: 87; see further Hodgson 1974: 289–291; and, more generally, Kennedy 1981: 96–114). Al-Mahdī, more than his predecessors, stressed his role as champion of Islam. For example, he ordered the *al-Aqṣā* mosque in Jerusalem to be remodeled, in addition to overseeing an extension to the mosque in Mecca (al-Ṭabarī 1879–1901: 483. English translation: Kennedy 1985: 194; more generally, see Kennedy 1981: 97). Such displays were undoubtedly meant to show to just what an extent he needed to legitimize his acquisition and subsequent exercise of political *and* religious authority, given the fact that the two were not entirely separate from one another in the manner that they increasingly would become among his successors. In the first year of his reign (160/776), for example, al-Ṭabarī relates the following letter that al-Mahdī wrote to his governor in Baṣra:

> In the name of God, the Merciful, the Compassionate, the most just thing that the governors of the Muslims, their couriers, and the general public is that they must undertake their affairs and their judgement in accordance with the Book of God [*kitāb Allāh*]. They should synchronize their desires with it. They should persevere with it and take pleasure in it, in both their likes and dislikes because [this book] establishes the legal punishments of God, the knowledge of His Law, the following of His wishes, and the obtaining of His rewards, and his good recompense. Whatever goes in conflict with it, in rejecting it and in surrendering to desires other than it, leads to all sorts of going astray, and depravity in this world and the next.
> (al-Ṭabarī 1879–1901: 479–480; English translation: Kennedy 1985: 190, with modification)

Since the Caliphate, with the Caliph at its head, ostensibly embodied the unity of the community, at least in this very early period, the Caliph was necessarily responsible for trying to provide limits to the boundaries of orthodoxy by defining the correct position on any number of doctrinal and legal issues. This is why, once again, the early ʿAbbāsid caliphs sought to intervene in religious matters—which were, by definition also political—by establishing what counted as normative Muslim belief and practice. Perhaps nowhere is this clearer than in the respective *miḥnas* (inquisitions) of al-Mahdī and al-Maʾmūn. This caliphal policy to set proper belief, according to Lapidus, was not uncommon in the late antique environment with Byzantine and Sasanian emperors doing the same. According to him:

the Byzantine imperial view was that the emperor influenced the formulation of religious doctrines so that they were in accord with political interests of the state. Byzantine emperors took the utmost interest in the regulation of church doctrine. They called and presided over church councils and suggested formulas for the creed ... The emperors also appointed the leading patriarchs, archbishops, and bishops.
(Lapidus 1988: 88)

Ascertaining correct religious doctrine necessarily meant defining deviancy therefrom. Only by engaging in the latter activity, and its subsequent back-projection, could a path be ascertained, and from which others were now shown to have strayed. Within this larger context, caliphs and those who worked in their service sought to define themselves and their positions as normative and as existing at the time of Muhammad, all the while juxtaposing that normativity with religious deviants, whom as we have seen time and again could also be projected onto the earliest period. If we continue with the aforementioned passage from al-Ṭabarī, we witness just how al-Mahdī seeks to differentiate his own rule from that of his predecessors. Of particular concern was his desire to distance himself from Muʿāwiya (the founder of the Umayyad caliphate), whom, we are informed, did not rule according to "piety, good guidance, or by observing the *sunna*, or the example of the past Imāms of truth. Rather [he ruled] on account of his desire for the destruction of his faith and his afterlife, and his determination to contradict both the *sunna* and the Book" (al-Ṭabarī 1879–1901: 480; English translation: Kennedy 1985: 191, with modification). Juxtaposed against Muʿāwiya, we are informed that al-Mahdī

> is following the words of the Prophet of God and what truthful people and the rightly guided Imāms have agreed upon. He does not hold permissible what Muʿāwiya has ventured that contradicts the Book of God and the *sunna* of His prophet. The Commander of the Faithful is the person most entitled to do that and to apply it because of his kinship with the Prophet of God and his following in his tracks, his keeping alive his *sunna*, and his rejection of the *sunan* of others that deviate and outrage truth and good guidance.
> (al-Ṭabarī 1879–1901: 481; English translation: Kennedy 1985: 192, with modification)

With such claims, according to Turner, al-Mahdī "was making a legitimating claim for his social role as Commander of the Faithful. He clearly asserted his right to determine the correct response to a legal problem and his ability to make authoritative pronouncements about the meaning of the Qur'ān and which Sunna to apply" (Turner 2013: 7–8). Indeed, in stressing his kinship to the prophet, al-Mahdī was in effect proclaiming that he was Muhammad's true heir, that he personified the true practice (*sunna*) of the Prophet, and that he alone was in a unique position to define what Islam was and what it was not.

Within this context, al-Mahdī presents us with one of the earliest attempts at dogmatic enforcement of doctrine and practice with his establishment of a *mihna*, "inquisition," to enforce correct belief. The problem, of course, is that some want to see a sharp distinction between the "religious" and the "political" in late eighth- and early ninth-century Islam (perhaps most dramatically and artificially in Ibrahim 1994: 55–56). The *zindīqs* figured highly in this process since they were, after all, isolated as the main antagonists to what was coalescing into normative practice and belief. They may well have been singled out on account of their inchoateness. Indeed, the very fluidity of the term—inclusive of everyone from dualists, materialists, libertines, and essentially anyone who went against the mores of the community—seems to have led to an active and repressive campaign to weed them out of the *umma*. Both everywhere and nowhere in equal measure, they threatened by their very amorphousness since anyone, in theory, could have been one. This campaign was conducted, according to Chokr, under the guise of returning to Islamic purity (Chokr 1993: 12). In this respect, the practice of signaling out heretics helped, among other things, to publicize membership in a unified moral community, to invoke Melchert's conception of the piety of the *ḥadīth* folk mentioned above.

The campaign against the *zindīqs* officially began in 160/776, when according to al-Ṭabarī, al-Mahdī had a dream in which al-ʿAbbās, the paternal uncle of the Prophet, and the eponymous founder of the ʿAbbāsid caliphate, appeared to him and told him to kill anyone who worshipped two gods (ibid.: 62). Despite the dream, however, the initial repression of *zindīqs* did not occur until 163/779 when al-Mahdī commenced his campaign against the Byzantines, and while in Aleppo he ordered his *muhtasib*, ʿAbd al-Jabbār, to arrest *zindīqs* in the region.[23] The arrested were subsequently brought before the caliph, who ordered the execution of some of them, and the proclamation was then issued that their heretical books were to be, both symbolically and literally, lacerated with knives (al-Ṭabarī

1879–1901: 499; English translation: Kennedy 1985: 214; see further Chokr 1993: 63).

This seems to have been the only systematic Muslim persecution of *zindīqs* that we know about in the early Islamic period.[24] *Zindīqs* were now arrested and either given the chance to recant or, if unwilling to or on account of political expediency, were executed (al-Ṭabarī 1879–1901: 499, 519, 522; English translation: Kennedy 1985: 214, 237, 241). By 167/783, the inquisition changed focus from weeding out "obvious" *zindīqs* to focusing on Muslims who were now suspected of being *zindīqs*, which of course functioned as a type of code for all those not holding beliefs deemed "orthodox" or "normative." Even after al-Mahdī's death, the *miḥna* was continued by his sons, al-Hādī (r. 169/785–170/786) and perhaps even by Hārūn al-Rashīd (r. 170/786–194/809) (Kennedy 1981: 97–98).

Before I finish this section, it is worth pointing out that al-Mahdī's *miḥna* served as an important precursor to the more famous one by his subsequent successor, al-Ma'mūn (r. 198/813–218/833).[25] In the latter's, also at stake was the perceived need to establish God's absolute unity (*tawḥīd*) by denying to Him all that might be regarded as co-eternal. The particular source of confusion seems to have been over the exact nature of the Qur'ān, namely, was it eternal or created. If eternal, this would imply that there existed two eternal concepts, both God and the Qur'ān.[26] Under the influence of Muʿtazila theologians, al-Ma'mūn forced judges, witnesses, and *ḥadīth* transmitters to swear an oath that they believed the Qur'ān was eternal.[27]

Both al-Mahdī and al-Ma'mūn, in other words, imagined the institution of the caliphate as divinely given and they took it as their responsibility to be the supreme custodian and guardian of Muhammad's religion and its laws on earth. The caliph's duty, and this notion would cease quite quickly in the decades after al-Ma'mūn's death, was to combat unbelievers, excise heretics, and clearly define Islam, thereby protecting the unity of the state and fostering the maintenance of public order and security. The caliph, in sum, was accountable to God, and God alone, for his actions, and was thus regarded by his subjects as the executor of the emerging prophetic *sunna* and divine *sharīʿa*.[28] As with his predecessor, al-Mahdī, al-Ma'mūn's *miḥna* fits the patterns of defining the borders of orthodoxy by articulating proper belief against those imagined to be opposed to it.

Conclusions: The *Zindīq* and the Shaping of Orthodoxy

Religious others—both external (e.g., Jews and Christians) and internal (e.g., the Shīʿa)—possessed distinct teachings that could either be recycled or repudiated. *Zindīqs* however had very little specific teachings ascribed to them with the result that they, more than anyone, could be conveniently imagined as everything that Islam was not. They could be made into dualists, they could be become atheists, they could be lustful or lascivious, or they could simply be those with whom one disagreed politically or theologically. *Zandaqa* was, on account of its inclusivity, a fairly popular charge to be levelled. If the period prior to al-Mahdī had seen a great deal of fragmentation—including Arab clients who were believed to be only minimally Muslim, in addition to the need to ascertain the status of non-Muslims in Islamic lands—there was the growing desire to "return" to a pristine Islam imagined to have been practiced at the time of Muhammad. The *zindīq* played a crucial role in all of this (see the comments in Chokr 1993: 12-14).

Al-Mahdī inherited a diverse empire full of political instability and many diverse religions. This inheritance, more than anything, led to the rise of Islamic theology (*kalām*) and the need to refute other religions while simultaneously clarifying Islamic doctrines and beliefs. Those tasked with the framing of Islam came to define *zandaqa* as the negation of the basic principles (e.g., *tawḥīd*, the creation of the world, prophecy) of what they imagined to define orthodoxy. Anyone who did not fit the criteria of what a "good" or "authentic" Muslim was could thus potentially be accused of *zandaqa*.

At least Jews and Christians were connected—no matter how loosely or inchoately in the minds of Islam's framers—to certain essentialized ideas that were deemed to define them. In this, they represented religions that, while once in possession of the truth, had gone astray. The Qurʾān at least was able to explain to Muslims why that had happened by pointing to the sources of their errors. Jews and Christians, Judaism and Christianity, were originally pristine religions—like Islam, if not actually Islam—that had been corrupted and tampered with. They stood as witnesses to what could happen if believers were not careful.

Although not explicitly mentioned in the Qurʾān, the Shīʿa could also be plotted within the same narrative of a pure and originary message, and a subsequent fall from grace. They were the group, in other words, that were unable to recognize the Islam that the *ahl al-sunna* was creating in their own image and back-projecting onto the earliest period. The Shīʿa, then, were those Muslims—necessary, but unfortunate—who went astray and threatened the pristine character of the early *umma*.

As a non-qurʾānic term and thus category, however, the *zindīqs* posed eighth- and ninth-century Muslim thinkers with considerable problems. They had no script and therefore no explicable past. If others represented non-Muslims, *zindīqs* represented "anti-Muslims." So many of the theological features that they were charged with—their views on God, creation, determinism, revelation, and the nature of prophecy, among others—became the opposite of what Muslim theologians constructed. But in functioning as the opposite, they played a crucial and necessary role in that construction.

In terms of the tenor of the present volume, we return once again to the issue of naming and the employment of categories to understand oneself, one's history, and, just as importantly, all those who are different. In this chapter, we witness how this is not just a problem unique to contemporary scholarship, but rather that it is a basic way that others—in different times, and places—have constructed their worlds. Problems arise, as the following chapter will reveal in greater detail, when we use these earlier constructions as if they were simply natural markers employed by those we study.

Chapter 5

Modern Back-Projections and their Repercussions

Despite the secular context of the Western academy,[1] the study of Islam retains many of the assumptions and tacit presuppositions examined in our early sources.[2] We see this acutely in how Islamic studies deals with the Shīʿa and other minoritarian groups on the one hand, and rival religions such as Judaism and Christianity on the other. Not only are all of these non-Sunnī traditions marginalized in our modern academic narratives, the language used to situate them has strayed little from the categories and structures encountered in the earlier theological tradition.[3]

Within this context of privilege and denial, stereotypes and misinformation, the present chapter argues that Sunnī Islam, with few exceptions, continues to serve as the main prism through which we organize the messiness of Islamic history, providing the thread that permits many to impose retroactive order on a disparate set of individuals, ideas, and texts (see the informative comments in Lauzière 2016: 3). The overwhelming majority of our narratives employed to understand Islamic pasts emerge from Sunnī-centric perspectives that are, by definition, impartial and faulty. Our blind acceptance of such narratives means that that past continues to be predicated on what is, for all intents and purposes, a set of polemical tropes arranged to replicate the heresiographical traditions of times past. A good majority of the terms and categories that structure these narratives have been simply accepted, as opposed to interrogated, in the western scholarly traditions dealing with Islam.

To put this in comparative perspective, it would be akin to modern secondary scholarship on ancient Judaism recycling anti-Semitic tropes and imagery lifted from the Gospels as scholarly categories of analysis. Or, it would be similar to employing blindly and without hesitation the terms of late antique Christian heresiologists to describe "accurately" all those groups that that tradition has labelled as heretical. While this might strike us as odd and leading to hopelessly inaccurate results, when it comes to the study of Islam in the earliest centuries we have no problem transferring later Sunnī terminology and categories into our frameworks of analysis. Like our sources, we then back-project a self-styled normativity onto the earliest period. How we write the history of Islam, in other words, often involves using certain select sources—sources written from a particular perspective of what Islam is or should be—and not others. The field's focus on normativity leads to anachronism and a set of self-fulfilling beliefs about the nature of Islamic history including what groups count as significant, and what groups do not. The result, as this chapter seeks to show in greater detail, is but a partial understanding of Islam, an understanding that tends to take only one set of sources at face value and that confuses the polemical for the universal.

Heresiography as History

We see these oversights most acutely in how Sunnī Islam is constantly privileged at the expense of other forms of the tradition. More often than not, this involves defining Sunnism based on later texts and then searching for its emergence and development in earlier ones. This, of course, is not unlike what Sunnī sources themselves do, and when we repeat such claims we—wittingly or unwittingly is not entirely clear—take sides in early and medieval theological debates about the nature of orthodoxy and what gets to count as the most authentic version of the tradition. We then write the history of Islam from a largely Sunnī-centric position—a position that frequently has very negative things to say about religious others. These others are then either ignored or marginalized in the case of Jews and Christians on the one hand, or implied to represent later developments in the case of the Shīʿa, on the other.

The result is that we in Islamic studies have largely conflated pre-modern theological constructions for historical reality. We witness this, for example, in all those accounts, so prevalent in Islamic religious studies, that assume later sources to provide historically accurate descriptions of what really happened.[4] Yet the history of the treatment of others tells us much more about Sunnī Islam and those doing the writing/constructing than it does about actual religious others. While we should in theory know and recognize this, we rarely do.[5] And while such marginalization is a common theme within the history of religions, where at least it is often historicized and contextualized, for some reason when it comes to Islam we simply reinscribe the heresiographical tradition.

The question becomes, at least for me, how does this normative Islam, along with its artificially constructed despisers witnessed in our sources, become similar to the type of Islam disseminated in Islamic studies? Why, in other words, does the modern academic study of Islam simply, with obvious minor variations, mirror the medieval heresiographical tradition when it comes to dealing with religious others? That which does not fit a narrowly constructed Sunnī perspective or that which is imagined to be non-normative is cordoned off as "the strange," "the antinomian," or, in the case of Christianity and Judaism simply as "irrelevant" and, by implication, that which has been "superseded." Yet, the point I wish to underscore here is that the minute we enter into discussions of normativity/non-normativity or orthodoxy/heterodoxy we construct an Islam no less artificial than that manufactured in the theological ateliers of centuries past.

Islamic studies, not unlike medieval Islamic theology, reduces others—be it Shīʿīs, Jews, Christians, or other traditions—into caricatures that can then be used for a host of reasons, but mainly to clarify how (Sunnī) Islam differs from them. How many times, for example, have we read or hear statements in contemporary scholarship such as "Christians do 'x,' whereas Muslims do 'y.'" Such religious reifications are decidedly unhelpful, and problems inevitably arise the moment we, in the present, mistake premodern caricatures and other textual stereotypes for real historical actors. We see this, for example, whenever an introductory textbook presents—as they inevitably do—the Sunnī narrative as somehow the "proper" or most "authentic" one and then proceeds to present the Shīʿī position as, at best, an afterthought.

At this point it might be worthwhile to examine the contents and structures of some of these introductory textbooks with an eye towards understanding how earlier discourses structure modern assumptions. In his *Islam: The Essentials* (2017), for example, Tariq Ramadan waits until over half way through the book to mention, albeit briefly, that there are some *slight* differences among Muslims. In downplaying such "differences," however, he elides over them politically and makes the history of Islam conform to his own Sunnī worldview. His Islam is as timeless as any we have encountered in this study, and rather than historicize the tradition, he chooses to reaffirm its ethereal qualities. He informs us, for example, that "Islam's unity arises from the fact that Muslims, be they Sunni, Shiʿa or Ibadi, and of whatever culture—Arab, African, Asiatic or Western—or trend of thought—literalist, traditionalist, reformer, mystic—agree on the fundamental principles of their religion" (ibid.: 123). He then goes on to list those principals: the centrality of monotheism, the Qurʾān, faith (īmān), and so on. Yet, implicit in such a statement is that all Muslims are essentially the same—and this sameness would seem to mean conformity to what he imagines to be Sunnī normativity—when it is quite clear that, historically, the imposition of such conformity masks real and important differences. The Shīʿa, not infrequently, are imagined as outliers to that which was slowly and naturally coalescing into orthodoxy. It was the *ahl al-sunna*, according to Ramadan, that functioned from the earliest period as the "majority," those who would "ultimately prevail," and who based their notion of authority on the caliph's "moral pre-eminence, his integrity and his competence" (ibid.: 16).

In like manner, Reza Aslan, in his *No god but God* (2005), waits until chapter 7 to introduce his readers to the Shīʿa. In that chapter, titled "In the Footsteps of Martyrs: From Shiʿism to Khomaneism," he informs us that the rise and momentum behind the Shīʿa was political. Indeed, after spending considerable time explaining the various battles that culminated in the events at the plains of Karbala, Aslan concludes that such events led directly to the distinctive Shīʿī practice of self-flagellation (ibid.: 180). In this, I would submit, he emphasizes the strange or the exotic at the expense of anything resembling theological or historical difference.[6] It is a chapter, moreover, that leads directly into Sufism. If the Shīʿa are defined essentially by their pathos and their political grievances with the Sunnī majority, not to mention their exotic desire to harm themselves ritualistically, Sufism then provides him with an Islam that is "neither law nor theology, neither creed nor ritual … [but] merely the means through which the believer can destroy his ego so as to become one with the creator of the heavens and the earth" (ibid.: 193). The political, in other words, is eclipsed by the spiritual and the experiential.[7] This is reinforced in Mahmoud Ayoub's *Islam: Faith and History* (2004) wherein he further reduces the early Shīʿa to "manifestations of political and economic unrest" (84).

If we take less insider accounts the situation is unfortunately little different. In his *What is Islam?* (1968), W. Montgomery Watt explains the Shīʿa in a chapter titled "The Religious Aspects of Later Political Developments." Once again, there is the tendency to explain the Shīʿa as if they were a *later* and a *political* development that broke away from the normative and mainstream Sunnī position (ibid.: 113–148). Orthodoxy, to repeat, is always imagined as a reflection of the natural order of things, and heterodoxy as somehow a political, unnatural, and subsequent development. The earliest Shīʿīs were, according to him, "a small group of Arabs among the followers of ʿAli; then there were bodies of insurgents at various points until about 687; from then until near the end of the Umayyad period the chief expressions of Shīʿism were in underground movements" (ibid.: 119). The "main body" of Muslims are, once again, too neatly differentiated from these early movements *within* the *umma*. Watt lumps the Shīʿa in with the Khārijites, both of whom he argues were responsible for making Sunnī Muslims aware of features that they might not otherwise have noticed. According to Watt, "Shīʿism, though many of its views were rejected by the main body, made that body aware of its need for a leader who was more than human" (ibid.: 121). In like manner Frederick Mathewson Denny, in his *An Introduction to Islam* (1994), tries to nuance his analysis by writing that although "it is incorrect to call the supporters of ʿAlī by the name Shīʿīs by the time of his death, it should apply only in a social and political sense. The religious doctrines and imamology of Shīʿī Islam developed much later" (81). While I might, under certain conditions, concur with such a statement, it is surely worth noting that Denny here also works on the assumption that the Shīʿa are a later development, whose main doctrines, as he alludes to in this quote, were developed later. He ignores, however, the fact that Sunnī doctrines and practices are also much *later* and, moreover, that these doctrines of Sunnīs and Shīʿa developed contrapuntally to one another. According to Denny's basic narrative:

> The Shīʿīs, strong supporters of ʿAlī, who emerged during the early post-Muhammad years when the Muslim government was centered in Medina, came to claim that Muhammad had designated ʿAlī as his successor well before the Prophet's death. This claim has never been accepted by the majority of Muslims, who eventually evolved into the Sunnīs and consider themselves the mainstream of Islamic faith and practice. The Shīʿat ʿAlī, "party of ʿAlī," developed a peculiar view of Islamic governance centering on the infallible imams, who descended from Muhammad by way of ʿAlī and Fātima.
>
> (Denny 1994: 72–73)

Again, there are problems with such a narrative. While a "Muslim government" existed in Medina, it is assumed that it coincides effortlessly with that of Sunnī Islam. Denny also acknowledges here that such a government was somehow closer to that which "evolved" into the Sunnī tradition. Indeed, I am not so certain that scholars of Islam (or any other religion, for that matter) can or ought to work with a model of evolution and all that it implies (do religions "evolve" or "devolve"?). What became Shīʿī belief and practice is then described as "peculiar," and once again Sunnīsm is held up as both orthodox and normative.

Even Andrew Rippin, in his *Muslims: Their Religious Beliefs and Practices* (2005), writes how "Islam remained, for the most part, unified in its religious manifestations during the classical period" (121). Though he is certainly more sensitive to the notion of the development of the Shīʿa than others examined here, there is once again the assumption that unity (read: the Sunnī tradition) gives way *over time* to minoritarian voices, such as the Shīʿa.

In all of these introductory accounts, which have been composed to introduce students and lay audiences to the tradition, we see to just what an extent the Shīʿa have been marginalized. While some might well argue that such superficial treatment is part and parcel of the textbook market and not the same thing as more specialized and technical studies, I would argue that such textbooks are often written by the same scholars who also write more technical studies. They are thus informed by similar assumptions that reveal real structural problems and that make such oversights inevitable. Even more significantly, at least for the purposes of my argument here, is the notion that the *ahl al-Sunna*, or Sunnī Islam, is simply assumed to be the natural form of Islam and that others "fall off" of it on account of their faulty beliefs and other heresies. Once again, such an assumption does little more than parrot the opinions and beliefs of Sunnī thinkers, those who think that their tradition is normative and those of the Shīʿa, for example, are not.

"Islam" in these studies is thus used as code for Sunnīsm. Shīʿīsm, on the other hand, always needs to be modified by the adjective "Shīʿī." Such approaches mistake one branch of Islam as normative with the result that we potentially overlook a broad and nuanced perspective of the inclusiveness and cosmopolitanism of the Islamic world in earlier times and places. In reproducing such discourses, the non-normative—at least from a Sunnī perspective—becomes the domain of other fields, or better subfields, of study so that the main field no longer needs to worry about them.

While I shall discuss the peculiar case of the Shīʿa in a little more detail below, allow me to focus briefly on two of the other traditions that have played a large role in this study, Judaism and Christianity. While scholars of Jewish studies regularly produce works devoted to the Islamic contexts of medieval Judaism,[8] rarely are scholars of Islam interested in Jewish topics. Jews who lived in the orbit of Islam are simply assumed to be of interest to those who work in Jewish studies, to where they can be farmed out (though see the important study in Krinis 2019). But, it is certainly worth noting in the present context that Jewish studies has its own set of concerns, many of which revolve around—as witnessed in chapter two above—the false premise of showing the uniqueness of the Jewish people who are often extracted artificially from their larger non-Jewish environments. When Jews (or Christians for that matter) are excised from Islam in this manner, the field of Islamic studies—my main concern here—is much the poorer for it.[9] The alternative, that of assuming along with our (Sunnī) sources that groups of retroactively projected normative Jews and Christians existed at the time of Muhammad is also extremely problematic (see, for example chapter 3 above). Rather, as seen with *zindīqs* in the previous chapter, such individuals were literary tropes used by later Muslim scholars to differentiate what they imagined as the early Islamic message from rival religions. They are decidedly not historical reflections, but literary ones. It is incumbent upon us, moreover, to show just how such projections worked and then begin the process of uncovering just what kinds of Jews, Christians and/or others might have existed in this period.

Our interest should be in showing how Jews or Christians (or anyone else for that matter) function *historically* as a part of Arabo-Islamic society and not as somehow existing apart from it. If Jewish studies reifies Jews, the situation in Islamic studies is certainly no better. We do not bother to learn Hebrew or Judeo-Arabic, nor do we bother to learn about the idiosyncrasies of Jewish legal or religious thought and how they ought to be contextualized within Islamic civilization. This deferral, I want to suggest here, comes at a real cost. It means that Jewish studies, among other things, excises Jews from their natural contexts, and unfortunately Islamic studies misses an opportunity to ascertain the complex and intricate reach of Arabo-Islamic ideas and paradigms.

The same could easily be said about late antique Christians. Recent path-breaking work that has tried to situate Islam in the larger context of the late antique period—such as that by the likes of Shoemaker (2012, 2018) or Tannous (2018)—emerges out of the field of late antique studies and not traditional Islamic studies. The question, then, is how do these other traditions fit into the mainframe of contemporary Islamic studies? Where, how, when, and why do Jews and Christians—indeed, does Judaism and Christianity—fit within this field of study? While we may invoke them occasionally in Islamic studies to show, among other things, the multiculturalism and the cosmopolitanism of various times and places, we never pay that much attention to them because we assume that those working in other fields of study will be the ones that deal adequately with them. But they do not always do so (as witnessed, for example, in chapter three).

There are certainly reasons for such oversights and mutual recriminations, not the least of which is the unsavory history of Orientalism, and the many egregious connections it established between scholarship on the one hand, and empire and colonialism on the other. Perhaps no better symbol of this is the formation of the State of Israel in 1948 and the subsequent displacement of indigenous Arab populations.[10] There are, then, also real historical, political, and geographical reasons behind such oversights—and not simply academic ones—when it comes to the study of Jews and Judaism in Islamic studies, just as there are of Arabs and Muslims in Jewish studies. It is an unfortunate state of affairs, to be sure, but our inability to locate Jews and Christians within medieval Islam means that our understanding of Islam will remain incomplete.

Such perspectivalism is also, in large part, the direct result of not being able to deal adequately with non-Sunnī groups in Islamic studies. An emphasis on a Sunnī-centric normativity creates significant blind spots that many seem simply to be unaware of because we, following our sources, have simply conflated Islam with Sunnī Islam. It is incumbent upon us, in other words, to be aware of the various discursive formations and structures of power that help to create such blind spots. Yet, it is the openings and cracks produced by them that ideally provide us with a way to give exclusions and silences an active presence, thereby illumining that which the status quo has rendered marginal and irrelevant. Even when we are aware of such blind spots and oversights, however, it proves difficult to develop appropriate conceptual apparatuses to account for them on account of the structural and epistemological problems that this normativity by definition produces.

Orientalism, Sunnī-centrism, and the Creation of a Western Academic Study

The history of Orientalism and its excesses are certainly well known, and do not need to be rehearsed here.[11] Suffice it to say that since its foundations in the nineteenth century, if not before, the majority of sources available to Western scholars of Islam were by and large those produced by Sunnīs.[12] The dearth of Shīʿī sources created a situation wherein Orientalists, during the formative years of the field, largely bought into Sunnī stereotypes.[13] In his otherwise impressive and path-breaking study of the Qurʾān, to use but one example, Theodor Nöldeke (1836-1930) devoted only four pages out of his three volumes to Shīʿī sources (see Bar-Asher 1999: 27). Whether because of or in spite of such oversight, he had no problem remarking—in a manner that would certainly make any good Sunnī proud—that Shīʿī commentaries on the Qurʾān were "a miserable mixture of lies and nonsense" (*ein elendes Gewebe von Lügen und Dummheiten*) (Nöldeke and Schwally 1909-1938: 180), a locution repeated verbatim by Goldziher in his own study of qurʾānic commentators (1920: 309). Such statements, once again, translate Sunnī theological pronouncements onto an academic register. Though, to his credit, Goldziher did subsequently acknowledge in the same study that an understanding of the Shīʿī commentary tradition would facilitate "a complete knowledge of the religious trends in Islam" (ibid.).

Despite the implicit warnings about partiality and the potentiality for blind spots in Goldziher's caveat, I think it fair to make the assessment that our vision of Islam remains clouded by being viewed through an overwhelmingly Sunnī lens.[14] If in the past this was largely on account of better and easier access to mainly Sunnī manuscripts, in the present it is also the result of wealthy Sunnī benefactors—often from places like Saudi Arabia and the Gulf emirates—who often have very strict or myopic readings of what Islam is or should be. Such wealthy benefactors are responsible for, among other things, the creation of presses that produce and disseminate certain (Sunnī) texts, and who fund university centers or endowed chairs in the West to study them. Without getting into the politics of such centers or chairs, it should suffice to say that minoritarian traditions—including, but not limited to, Twelver Shīʿism—tend to be under-funded, under studied, and their textual productions are often largely ignored.[15] The words of the otherwise apologetical Seyyed Hossein Nasr in his translator's introduction to Tabatabai's *Shiʿite Islam* certainly rings true in the present:

> Until now Shiʿism has received little attention; and when it has been discussed, it has usually been relegated to the secondary and peripheral status of a religio-political "sect," a heterodoxy or even a heresy. Hence its importance in both the past and the present has been belittled far more than a fair and objective study of the matter would justify.
>
> (Nasr 1981: xv)

The detritus of these ideological oversights and concomitant financial malfeasance on the part of university administrators are certainly not irrelevant to Islamic studies. Indeed, I would go so far as to say that such non-academic features actively structure the field. Indeed, such assumptions—whether unintentional or nefarious—make their way into the domain of scholarship, as even the quickest of glances at programs, conferences, and scholarly works reveal. Even the rise of subdisciplines within or cognate to Islamic studies—Shīʿī studies, Jewish studies, late antique studies, Ismāʿīlī studies, and so on—continue, while focusing on their numerous centers, to buy into the normative Sunnī narrative that these other traditions are, by virtue of the fact that they are not Sunnī, marginal to the academic study of Islam. Though issues related to the Shīʿa or Ismāʿīlīs can now be studied using the parameters laid out by Shīʿī studies or Ismāʿīlī studies,[16] they unfortunately remain peripheral to the more dominant narratives of (Sunnī) Islamic studies. The problem is certainly structural and gets to the heart of some of the many problems that beset the study of Islam. "Expertise in [Shīʿism] is seen as a niche within Middle Eastern and Islamic studies," concludes Ron Gleave in a 2009 overview of the field, and "few institutions can afford to hire expertise in both Sunni and Shīʿi Islam. To hire a Shīʿi specialist to teach Sunni Islam is, for some reason, more controversial than hiring a Sunni specialist to teach Shīʿism" (Gleave 2009: 1602). So, while we may now have specialized and very important conferences or collections devoted, say, to particular aspects of Shīʿism or "Jews in the Islamic World," such matters are seen as, to reuse Gleave's term, a "niche" market and of little or no interest to those in the "general" or "mainstream" of the field, which, of course, is always constructed or imagined as Sunnī-normative.

Such an assessment is only exacerbated by the ways in which Islam is produced in the classroom. In our introductory books, as just witnessed, the Sunnī account is always presented as normative, and then followed by a later chapter on Shīʿism as if it is either an afterthought at best or a tacit endorsement of the Sunnī position that imagines Shīʿism as a later political development or as heterodoxy. This is related to the larger problem addressed in this study of mistaking salvation history for history. We cannot believe and maintain that Sunnī texts are somehow normative simply because they tell us that they are.

Non-Shīʿī Traditions: The Case of Judaism and Christianity

If such is the treatment of the Shīʿa and Shīʿī sources, the situation with other religions is equally problematic, but for different reasons. While the desire to reverse a century of Orientalism that wanted to reduce Islam to the sum of its constituent parts is certainly understandable, along with the concomitant need to sever such connections lest some particular feature or doctrine within Islam becomes reducible to some idea or doctrine found or encountered in another religion.[17] The moment we do this, however, we run the risk of assuming that religions emerge whole from hermetically sealed contexts. The result of this oversight is that there is an unfortunate tendency to excise the formative moment of Islam from its larger late antique context, where—as many are now beginning to realize—it firmly belongs. If we ignore such contexts, we simply repeat the refrain from the earliest sources claiming that Arabia was a desert backwater with little or no connection to the outside. Yet, as we know from external sources and from inscriptions (e.g., Hoyland 1997; and see chapter 3 above), the Arabian Peninsula, although largely desert, most certainly was not an isolated oasis. If anything, the Peninsula played an important role in trade routes across its length and breadth; it was certainly on the radar of the region's larger empires which used various tribes as vassals or proxies; and it clearly had connections to other regional monotheisms (Bowersock 2013). We also know that there existed several important towns scattered throughout Arabia. Such towns—for example, Qaryat al-Fāw and Madāʾin Ṣāliḥ—were on important north–south trade routes linking the peninsula to the great economic and cultural centers of Mesopotamia, Syria, and Egypt (e.g., Healey 1993). Pastoralists who subsequently became involved in trade largely settled these towns, and archaeological evidence also links these towns to larger kingdoms in the area (e.g., Nabatea) (e.g., al-Ghabban et al. 2010). There is also evidence that such towns were highly literate, complete with large marketplaces and religious shrines. Yet, for some reason, we like to assume, following our sources, that Arabia was in the middle of nowhere, untouched by previous monotheisms.

When Jews and Christians make appearances in the field of Islamic studies, they—despite what I have just said and given what I have argued in this study—only do so much later and much more discretely, whereupon they can now be the ones influenced by Arabo-Muslim literary and intellectual forms. Their appearance is, as noted, to show the cosmopolitanism of the ʿAbbāsid caliphate and other places such as al-Andalus (Muslim Spain). For the most part, however, other than admitting that such Jews, Christians, and others absorbed numerous intellectual and literary influences from Muslims, these religious others tend to be simply ignored in Islamic studies circles, and this I submit is a real problem for how we understand Islam (and these others) in these centuries. There is, for the most part, little or no interest in Islamic studies, for example, with how Muslim ideas are received among Jewish or Christians thinkers—how, for instance, they built upon or otherwise adapted Muslim ideas to new religious and social contexts. We see no engagement among scholars of Islamic philosophy with the thought of Moses Maimonides (d. 600/1204) or Thomas Aquinas (d. 672/1274), let alone with more "minor" thinkers such as Isaac Israeli (d. ca. 320/932) or Ibn Gabirol (d. 462/1070). Nor do we see any examination of Moses de Leon (d. 704/1305; author of the *Zohar*) among scholars of Islamic mysticism in general, nor of Ibn ʿArabī (d. 637/1240) in particular, despite the fact that they both emerged within a generation of one another in roughly the same geographical locale. Nor do we see any real interest among scholars of Islamic law in Jewish law or Christian law, two forms that developed in the shadow of Islamic jurisprudential traditions.[18]

This means that our understanding of Islamic philosophy, mysticism, and law is partial and, to invoke Goldziher once again, incomplete. If we were to expand our mapping of Islam to include these other contexts, we would have a much different—and, I trust, fuller—understanding.

Conflating Memory and History

A problem endemic to secular Islamic studies (to say nothing of theological treatments within Muslim circles), at least since the time of Orientalism, is the overwhelming tendency to declare a narrative to be historically reliable simply because it contains no improbabilities or merely because some details are accurate.[19] It is important, however, not to confuse memory with history or verisimilitude with authenticity. In this latter case, we not infrequently see a doctrine or belief in the heresiographical literature mischaracterize other traditions and then subsequently use such mischaracterizations as if they were true. If anything, such literature is less about other religions than it is about (Sunnī) Muslims and their construction of what is imagined to be proper Islamic belief.

Instead of operating as though our sources offer stenographic reports of things people really said, or a TV camera recording of things people really did, we have to subject such sources to a more critical hermeneutic that seeks to inform us about the social and other contexts of those who produced them. Rather than take these texts at face value and instead of buying into the assumptions inherent to later texts and interpreters, it is much more profitable to focus on each text as a discrete document produced by a certain ideological reading of events. So, rather than reproduce, for example, the contents of anti-Shīʿī texts, it is necessary to ask ourselves what such texts are doing, and why? And, given the interest of the present chapter, I argue that rather than completely ignore Shīʿī texts, it is much more profitable not only to bring them back into our study of Islam, but to examine the forces that have traditionally marginalized such texts in the first place.

The end result of such approaches will be a much more holistic understanding of Islam in the earliest (and other) periods. This will not only integrate other and minoritarian traditions into Islamic studies, it will simultaneously integrate Islam into other cognate fields of study. A quick examination of secular and normative Islamic studies reveals a replication of the types of normativity seen in the construction of (Sunnī) Islamic orthodoxy. Texts from the latter tradition are neatly differentiated from texts from other religions and then assumed to be representative of the (Sunnī) Muslim take on the world.[20] These texts are often taken at face value with historical settings and intellectual contexts of those who produced them all but ignored. Salvation history, to invoke Wansbrough (1987: 14), is mistaken for history, and the results are both disastrous and univocal at the same time. Rather than assume all the texts produced from the earliest period form an interlocking set produced by those who shared a similar or corresponding vision of what Islam was, is, or should be, it would surely be more worthwhile to pry such texts apart with an eye toward both their specific concerns, in addition to understanding their localized genealogies and contexts.

And rather than imagine them as uncovering the cartography of some hidden or ethereal Islam, I would think that it would be much more profitable to think of them as actively manufacturing mundane Islams both in their own images and, most importantly for my study here, in the inverse or obverse image of all those religious others, whether external or internal, that Muslims thought with and about. Each text, in other words, possesses its own framework, distinctive traits of rhetoric and logic, and must be understood as such instead as part of some larger and inchoate concept such as "(Sunnī) Islam."

Isolating the Problem

Allow me to cite what I consider to be several recent examples of this oversight in the field of Islamic studies where, once again, Islam is simply invoked as code for the Sunnī tradition. As I mentioned in the context of Chapter 1 above, in 2016 the *Journal of the American Academy of Religion* (*JAAR*) ran a roundtable symposium devoted to the theme of "normativity" in Islamic studies. Though it remains unclear to me what exactly the contributors mean by the term "normativity," since it remains undefined or under-defined, it would seem that they use it as a catch-all phrase to engage in a type of liberal Muslim theologizing that is so common in religious studies circles dealing with Islam in North America. The organizer of the project, Juliane Hammer, a scholar otherwise sensitive to nuance and detail, explains her rationale for the collection as follows, "all scholarship is based on normative claims and assumptions" (Hammer 2016: 26).

While I mentioned this in the context of Chapter 1, allow me here to focus on a different aspect, that of "normativity." Hammer unfortunately does not define what she means by the term. The question, then, becomes, at least for me, is: whose normativity? While left uncertain or underdefined, normativity here would seem to be involved in some sort of project of reclamation whose goal is to make the humanities into a "tool for change." Again, I am not sure that this counts as a working definition of "normativity." It becomes clear, however, throughout the several essays that comprise the roundtable that by "normativity" the contributors simply mean "Sunnī" takes on the environment, interfaith dialogue, women, and so on and so forth. There are, then, no Twelver Shīʿī, Ismāʿīlī, Ibāḍī, Aḥmadī or other Muslims voices. Sunnī Islam, not surprisingly, and indeed given what we have seen above, is imagined as normative, orthodox, and the only type of Islam worthy of consideration.

A further example comes by way of another book I examined in Chapter 1: Shahab Ahmed's *What is Islam?* (2016). At the beginning of his first chapter, he makes the following bold statement:

> I am seeking to say that the word "Islam" in a manner that expresses the *historical and human phenomenon* that is Islam in its plenitude and complexity

of meaning. In conceptualizing Islam as a historical and human phenomenon, I am precisely *not* seeking to tell the reader what Islam is as a matter of Divine Commandment, and thus am *not* seeking to prescribe how Islam should be followed as the means to existential salvation. Rather, I seek to tell the reader what Islam has actually been as a matter of human fact in history.

(Ahmed 2016: 5)

Ahmed subsequently tries to circumvent the usual definitions by arguing that, in our desire to define what is Islam and what it is not, what is Islamic and what is its inverse, we often lose sight of actual Muslim lives and the complex and often contradictory ways in which Muslims make sense of their worlds. While his analysis ought, in theory, to make a lot of room for Shīʿism within the much larger rubric of "Islam" or "Muslim," he is surprisingly, or perhaps even worrisomely, reticent. What better way to show the open-endedness or universality of the term "Islam" than to show that it makes room for "non-normative" traditions? There is, however, one startling passage that appears near the end of the book that is certainly worth mentioning. Therein, he writes:

> The most demographically successful group [of minoritarian traditions], the Nizārī Ismāʿīlīs … have not considered it obligatory to perform the *salāt* prayers as established by the example of the Prophet Muhammad, or to fast throughout Ramadan, or to observe other forms in which the majority of Muslims, both Sunni and Shīʿi, enact Divine Truth. But, as Fazlur Rahman pointed out, the alternative truth of the Nizārī Ismāʿīlīs is an extraordinarily authoritarian one …

(Ahmed 2016: 510)

Surprisingly, Ahmed further buys into this Sunnī-centrism. Even in a claim to dislodge a certain normativity, we see its further reinscription. Ahmed's claim that some Muslims, to wit, Nizārī Ismāʿīlīs possess an "alternative truth" and are "extraordinarily authoritarian" would seem to go against some implicit democratic formula that he wants to put at the heart of his analysis. Moreover, his claim that some Shīʿa are antinomian by nature undermines his larger desire to move the study of Islam beyond a traditional nomocentrism. What I find so strange and uncharacteristic about this statement is that it goes against his entire thesis that Islam is many things to many different Muslims, and we have erred in Islamic studies by trying to put it into a particular box or set of boxes. His implications here of law and divine truth would seem to contradict his larger and much more important point.

What do we learn from such examples? At a time when other fields have begun to acknowledge, recognize, and otherwise reinscribe subaltern voices into mainframe narratives, we in Islamic studies should perhaps be a little more vigilant or, at least, cognizant. Moreover, when we simply use Islam as code for Sunnism, we inadvertently mute or silent other Islams or Muslims, and in the process marginalize them as somehow non-normative. But the point I want to make here is that they are not non-normative. On the contrary, and this is why Ahmed's *What is Islam?* should have been of sufficient aid, they provide alternative—*not* non-normative—ways of being Islamic.

Attempts at Reintegration

There have been a number of ways to solve this conundrum, some of them bear more fruit than others. Allow me to move from more recent examples to more traditional mainstays in the literature.

In a recent study of Islamic philosophy that appears in his larger series titled "A History of Philosophy Without Any Gaps," Peter Adamson correctly reasons that in order to appreciate fully the depth and breadth of philosophy in medieval Islam, we need also to take into consideration Jewish and Christian traditions of rationality. "Nowadays," he writes, "scholarship on philosophy written in the Islamic world generally deals with these two [other] faith traditions separately" (Adamson 2016: 3). "A more revealing approach," he continues, "is to look at the whole history of philosophy in the Islamic world in a chronological order" (ibid.: 4).

I certainly agree with Adamson's approach here and much prefer it to the alternative of imaging three discrete religious communities engaging in some sort of ethnic or proto-nationalist project that is somehow different from what thinkers in the other two traditions are doing. The latter model is not only artificial, it produces our current situation wherein scholars in Jewish studies analyze medieval Jewish philosophical texts, scholars in Islamic studies do the same for medieval Islamic philosophical texts, and the same for those engaged in medieval Christian philosophy, but to which we just give the name "philosophy." Rather than see them all as engaged in the project of reconciling Greek philosophy with monotheistic principles, we create anachronistic terms like "medieval Jewish philosophy" or "medieval Islamic philosophy," instead of simply using the term that the philosophers in questions would have employed, to wit, *falsafa*, a term that admits neither ethnic nor religious affiliation.

Nevertheless, despite Adamson's attention to the gaps, there remains a certain degree of reification. He writes, for example, that to "understand the thought of the great early Jewish philosopher Saadia Gaon without knowing something about the early developments in Islamic theology" is incorrect (Adamson 2016: 4). I agree, but would go even further. Why even employ the adjectives "Jewish" or Islamic" in such a locution? Saadia is, after all, not doing "Jewish philosophy" nor is he a "Jewish philosopher"; rather, he is a *mutakallim* engaged in activity of *kalām*, in particular that of the Muʿtazila variety.

Another attempt to overcome such artificial distinctions comes by way of the recently published and important *Oxford Handbook of Islamic Theology* (2016), edited by Sabine Schmidtke. A quick perusal of the Table of Contents reveals an impressive and wide-ranging set of topics. We thankfully begin to hear mention of *some* other voices. Shīʿī *mutakallimūn* receive three separate chapters (out of a total of 41), though I note Jewish *mutakallimūn* receive none. Not unlike Adamson's work, however, despite attempts to redress traditional oversights and blind spots, we still tend to work within a Sunnī-centric narrative. Those traditions that do not subscribe to it are seen as outliers that need to be differentiated from it or as completely separate religions in need of their own fields or subfields. Nor am I convinced that a cognate *Oxford Handbook of Shīʿī Theology* would solve the problem.

If Adamson and Schmidtke at least make room for the subaltern, I am still perplexed by Shahab Ahmed's attempt to universalize Islam through appeals to his "Balkans-to-Bengal Complex." While he wants to destabilize the tradition, he nevertheless still maintains that there is something—we can call it an essence, if we like—that holds the entire enterprise together. There thus would seem to exist some noumenal vision or version of Islam that gives definition to the entire project, but one that cannot be simply reduced to the law or other such factors. This "complex"—whereas others might call it Persianate or Turko-Persian—functions as his "representative case study," which he then uses to examine other areas. Yet, I am not sure just how successful he is in this regard. There is very little reflection, for example, on how this case study illuminates other times and places. His Sunnī-centrism is certainly problematic and would seem to buy into precisely the type of normativity he otherwise seeks to eschew. If his analysis cannot adequately deal with Shīʿism, as witnessed above, then how can he possible account for a non-Islamic tradition like Judaism. In a brief discussion of Maimonides, the great philosopher and codifier of Jewish law, Ahmed argues that we must understand him as an *Islamic* thinker, and in a manner that removes any sort of Jewish element to his thought (Ahmed 2016: 447-449). In theory, I do not have a problem with this.[21] However, and not unlike his discussion of Shiʿism, subaltern voices, if and where they can be made sense of, are reduced to the expression of the majority (read: Sunnī Islam). Shīʿa, Jews, Christians, among others, would seem to only make sense when situated against the backdrop of Sunnī Islam as opposed to that of their own traditions.

If neither of these fit the bill, I find myself constantly returning to Marshall G. S. Hodgson's inclusive category of "Islamicate" (Hodgson 1974: 57-60), of which Ahmed (2016: 113-175) is exceedingly critical. The term, for Ahmed, too neatly differentiates the religious from the cultural. While this is certainly a fair assessment in the context of premodern definitions, it is also appropriate to argue that at risk in Ahmed's critique is the flattening of both concepts into one another. I would instead argue that terms like "Islamicate" have the distinct advantage of making room for minoritarian expressions, showing how they imbibe from Islamic culture, broadly defined, while also maintaining some sort of religio-cultural autonomy. The onus is on us—and I think Hodgson can be read in this manner—to incorporate the Islamicate into our understanding of "Islamdom" (1974: 57-60).

Yet, another model comes by way of Steven Wasserstrom. Following along the path traversed by Shlomo Dov Goitein (1955), he re-posits the term "symbiosis." If Goitein had used the term—as I suggested in Chapter 2—to maintain some eternal and unsubstantiated concept of Jewish difference, Wasserstrom at least interrogates the term in a manner that should be both obvious and helpful to the critical scholar of religion (1995: 224). Though he carefully interrogates the surface or the epidermis on which such symbiosis is imagined to take place, the term—and, more importantly, the concept—nevertheless remains standing at the end of his analysis. I also note that his work is focused solely on Jewish-Muslim interactions.

Again, we are left with a situation in which many of our operative paradigms do not permit us to think—or, at least, think well—with difference, be it religious or otherwise. If our paradigms are unable to afford us the possibility of seeing our collective blind spots, then the operative questions become: How do we know they are there? And, just as importantly how are we to see them?

It strikes me that what none of these models provide is the nuance that the topic needs and deserves. All still seem to work with some sort of normativity—almost always structured as Sunnī—that, in turn, functions as the model to which others, be they internal or external to the tradition, can be compared. Our paradigm for "Islam" thus need to move towards one in which we realize that we cannot know effectively about anything in Islam—the Qurʾān, ḥadīth, kalām, and so on, and so forth—without studying the various, and often competing, conceptions of such topics among other and cognate literatures composed by the likes of Shīʿi, Ibāḍī, Jewish, and Christian thinkers. The category (Sunnī) Islam, to repeat, thus needs to be seen as but one among many contingent development of Muhammad's preaching rather than its necessary historical outcome.

* * *

We access the historical record through our modern epistemic structures, which enable us to see certain things and to overlook others. The modern study of Islam, I have suggested in this chapter, structures the field in such a manner that takes over, rather than questions critically, the worldviews of our sources. Issues of orthodoxy/heterodoxy, normativity/non-normativity, and majoritarian/minoritarian continue to play a significant role in structuring its academic study. The conflation of primary sources seen in previous chapters and secondary ones discussed in the present one is, I submit, not a coincidence, but a natural outgrowth of the latter mistaking the former for historical as opposed to literary and polemical works.

This chapter also emerges from my frustration with certain features of contemporary western Islamic studies. The manner in which the latter frequently and gullibly assumes our sources to be accurate descriptions of what really happened means that we largely buy into these narratives as opposed to interrogating them. When we do this we remove Islam from historical analysis and simply repeat back stories that Muslims told, and continue to tell, themselves to make sense of their social worlds.

Part III

Reboot

Chapter 6

The Study of Islam in the Age of Trump

In October of 1921, Muhammad Ali ibn Khalil al-Najdi, a young Shīʿī, set out on a journey from his village outside the southern Lebanese city of Tyre in search of his love, a Christian girl, whose family had recently sent her to Detroit for fear of upsetting familial honor.[1] The young Muhammad traveled from the Levant to Mexico, erroneously believing it was close to Detroit. Making his way northwards, based on the kindness of strangers and a good business sense that would come to his aid not infrequently throughout his long life, he was able, remarkably, to track down his beloved. She had been working in a restaurant in Dearborn, just outside of Detroit, but the young Muhammad, much to his chagrin, discovered that the girl's family had betrothed her to another, not surprisingly a co-religionist. Not to be deterred, he made his way north to Saskatoon, Saskatchewan, where he would eventually meet a much younger woman, who was trying to escape an unhappy life there with her family.

They wed after a quick courtship and moved much further north to the Canadian Arctic, to Fort Simpson in the Northwest Territories. They lived some 2000 km north of the Canada–US border, on an island at the confluence of the Mackenzie and Liard Rivers, which, given its geography, not surprisingly functioned as a popular trading spot between white traders and the Indigenous Dene First Nation. The Canadian authorities, unfamiliar with the cadences of Arab names, had renamed him, christened him if you will, as "Bud Alley"—assuming that the only ʿAlī could be that of a lane—someone who would go on to become a very successful fur trader in Fort Simpson and beyond. Indeed, his success was based primarily on his kindness in dealing with the Indigenous inhabitants, who preferred to trade with him on account of his fairness than they did with the Hudson's Bay Company, who eventually bought him out of business. At this point Bud Alley, my grandfather, moved to Edmonton. There, as one of the few successful Arab businessmen in that young city, he supplied some of the money to create Canada's first mosque, Masjid al-Rashid, perhaps not surprisingly a Sunni mosque, which officially opened its doors on December 12, 1938.

More family came over, people married—other Muslims and non-Muslims—and had families. Some became farmers in southern Alberta, as early as the 1940s. One, Aliya Saddy, had an affair with the president of Pakistan before marrying him; another, Larry Shaben, was elected to the Alberta provincial legislature in 1975, becoming the first Arab elected in Alberta and among the first Muslims elected to higher political office in North America. One, a grandson, namely me, has an endowed chair in Jewish studies at a major American university.

Why do I mention all this? I assure you that it is not to establish my own "Abrahamic" bona fides, a category of which I have been exceedingly critical over the years (Hughes 2013a; and see the following chapter). On the contrary, my rationale is simple, ridiculously simple. It is to remind us, if in fact we need reminding—and it seems to me, at our current geopolitical moment, we do in fact need reminding—that Muslims are human. They have dreams. They fall in love. They care about their children, their businesses, and their communities. They dare to dream beyond boundaries, nor are they limited by the boundaries imposed upon them. Their agency is independent of the narrative we nowadays construct about them. They cannot, in other words, simply be described using monikers such as "Arab" or "Muslim." Individuals like my grandfather, and he is certainly not sui generis, if he were he would only be of personal and nostalgic interest and not analytic utility, helped to build Canada, and they form an intricate part of Canada's national fabric. But, none of this should come as a surprise to any of us. Indeed, the comment is so obvious that, in 2021, I cannot believe such a point has to be made let alone defended. However, at present in the United States, in Europe, and among a certain dark underbelly in my own country of Canada, "Muslims" functions as a code for all that is incongruous with putative "Western" values. We know the litany of complaints: Muslims stick together; we keep welcoming them, but it is clear that they do not want to be part of "our" system; they take but do not give back; they want to set up their own *sharīʿa* courts that contravene our own secular judicial branch; and the list goes on and on.

Once again, at the risk of belaboring an obvious point, such statements are so ludicrous as to be, if the consequences were not so real, a parody or at least a textbook example of how the West imagines others and, in so doing, replicates a false sense of itself. Indeed, we have seen the exact same arguments supplied to a host of minorities over the years, perhaps none more consistently and cumulatively than that directed toward Jews, which culminated in the middle of the previous century with murderous consequences. Nor do we have to be students of either psychology or of post-colonialism to know that social groups need "others" with which to construct themselves and their imagined values. However, we might do well to pause here for a moment to ask ourselves: just what are "Western" values? Who gets to decide? When were they created and what intellectual, social, and judicial role do they play in our collective consciousness? Social theorists remind us, for example, that identities are never static nor discrete, but always fluid as groups bump up against one another and imagine and reimagine, define and redefine, themselves, in the process of such encounters (e.g., Bourdieu 1984; Bayart 2005; Anderson 2006). To quote from the late Edward W. Said, whose presence will make several appearances throughout this chapter:

> The real question, then, is whether in the end we want to work for civilizations that are separate or whether we should be taking the more integrative, but perhaps more difficult path, which is to try to see them as making one vast whole whose exact contours are impossible for one person to grasp but whose certain existence we can intuit and feel.
>
> (Said 2000: 587)

"Western" values, of course, only begin to take on form and definition once we imagine what their opposites, so-called "non-Western" values, are. The latter can then be neatly put in counterpoint with the former and, quelle surprise, found to be woefully wanting. If Judaism functioned as the opposite of Christian Europe in the premodern world, that pride of place in our modern period is reserved for Islam. This tradition now becomes a cavernous darkness onto which we can project any number of hostile and misinformed attributions. Muslim bodies are now synonymous with insecurity, danger, and risk. The female Muslim body threatens our democratic and aesthetic sensibility; and the male Muslim body threatens to subsume us with its perceived appetite for wanton and irrational violence. We inscribe our own fears and desires not only on Islam, then, but also on the very flesh of Muslims we see both on our screens and in our streets.

The question I wish to address here, however, is what role does the academic study of Islam play in all of these imaginings? Does it help or hinder, correct or exacerbate, these types of negative images? My answer, to be fleshed out in what follows, is that the academic study of Islam—and here I mean the politically correct and largely uncritical version of Islamic studies, of which I have been critical over the years—contributes to the problem because it possesses an intrinsic tendency toward essentialism. In its desire to correct negative stereotypes, this type of Islamic studies, paradoxically to be sure, further reifies Muslims, and, in the process, helps to create the very category "Islam" into which individuals can either be placed or denied entry. In so doing, Islamic studies—in both its American and European contexts—is in the business of constructing good Islam and bad Islam, good Muslims and bad Muslims.[2] Bruce Lincoln, one of the most important theorists writing today, has issued a set of theses that he believes should guide a *critical* academic study of religion (Lincoln 1996). Not unlike Luther's act five hundred years ago, Lincoln has nailed, symbolically if not literally, a set of criticisms on the entrance to our collective guild. I wish to focus, in particular, on the thirteenth and final of his theses, which reads as follows:

> When one permits those whom one studies to define the terms in which they will be understood, suspends one's interest in the temporal and the contingent, or fails to distinguish between "truths," "truth-claims," and "regimes of truth," one has ceased to function as a historian or scholar. In that moment, a variety of roles are available: some perfectly respectable (amanuensis, collector, friend and advocate), and some less appealing (cheerleader, voyeur, retailer of import goods). None, however, should be confused with scholarship.
>
> (Lincoln 1996: 227)

This confusion, it seems to me, is a real problem in the Academy, the North American one in particular, and one that only gets worse when confronted by the types of over-the-top rhetoric that we currently hear from right-wing demagogues. If there is one take-away from Shahab Ahmed's recent, celebrated, and posthumously published *What is Islam?* (2016) it is that he, too, recognized this tendency in contemporary Islamic studies. In our desire to define what is Islam and what it is not, what is Islamic and what is its inverse, he argues that we often lose sight of Muslim lives and the complex and often contradictory ways in which Muslims make sense of their worlds—and in ways that do not neatly fall into Islam and non-Islam.

Can one, Ahmed rhetorically asks, be a "Muslim wine-drinker" (2016: 3)? One hears Salafi preachers, neo-conservative Western political commentators, and many scholars of Islam simultaneously provide an answer to this question in the negative. For a Muslim to drink wine, all of the above would agree, is surely to go against the tenets of Islam. Yet, Ahmed encourages us to suspend what we think we know about Islam, to unlearn that which we have learned, and instead imagine how the act of imbibing wine can be used in a way that defines (some) Muslims. Instead, Islam, as I mentioned in the context of Chapter 1, becomes greater than the set of legal or religious contexts that have traditionally been used to examine what is "Islamic" and what is "non-Islamic." The history of Islam, again returning to the major theme of Chapter 1, has been constructed for various political and ideological purposes as much as anything we might label "intellectual." It is a history, moreover, that has always been predicated on an intricate system of inclusion and exclusion—and what gets to count and what does not is never just based on a natural or an objective set of categories. The present is certainly no different than the past.

Here we must acknowledge that the Western study of Islam has always been a politically fraught field. It has carried out academic activities in the shadow of political expedience. Islamic studies, then, constructs, absorbs, and also resists political discourses. It is the latter that I wish to focus on here. In resisting such discourses, a certain type of Islamic studies opens itself up to an apologetical and often monothetic reading of the tradition. Calls to the contrary of those who purvey this type of apologetic, it is not a natural act, but again one that is heavily invested in the political. Indeed, the current gravitational pull towards identity politics makes the study of Islam, I wish to suggest, no less a detriment to the field than right-wing political discourses. Indeed, they mutually embrace one another and, together, they form a set of discourses that must be resisted.

Islam—as a social, cultural, intellectual, aesthetic, and religious form—is so potentially amorphous that any concept of Islam, again to invoke Ahmed, must denote and connote all possible Islams whether abstract or real, or past and future. This denotation and connotation, however, is lacking, often woefully lacking, in either political or academic discourses. Both work on the assumption that there is one Islam—be it bellicose, on the one hand, or predicated on some amorphous and anachronistic category, such as gender justice or social justice, on the other—that defines the tradition to the exclusion of other forms of belief, practice, or simply being in the world.

I fear that many in Islamic studies, even the most liberal minded, are not unlike conservative political commentators in that both force Muslims to perform their identities in ways with which many may well not be comfortable. Muslims of whatever stripe, denomination or level of observance are forced to renounce terror around the globe or when committed by rogue elements over here. If they do not, then they are somehow imagined to be complicit in such acts. In so doing, the modern West—and here both hostile politicians and well-meaning academics paradoxically converge, and draw inspiration from over a millennium of thinking about Islam—desire to transform such social actors into Muslims. Islam now becomes a discrete and essentialized category that admits of neither subtlety nor nuance. We manufacture this tradition in our Western universities, disseminate it in our writings, and act surprised when our politicians pick away at certain threads and begin to unravel what we thought we had nuanced. Can we be surprised to learn that we have created, inherited, and continue to deploy categories and terms of reference whereby others are forced to define themselves? We do not have to be nuanced anthropologists to acknowledge that where Indigenous populations are frequently content to perceive overlapping identities and live both in and with complexity, we demand strict adherence to the categories that we have invented and then assumed to be natural markers. This, of course, is an intellectual variation on the theme sounded by the Sykes–Picot agreement over a century ago: we carve up regions, without even a passing nod to the specters of ambiguity and indeterminacy, let alone local inhabitants, and adjudicate what and who goes where. Whereas other groups interpret their world, we, in an act of utter hubris, demand that our categories are not only natural, but divinely inspired.

The result is pretty much everywhere the same: nameless, faceless Muslims are denied autonomy and agency except, of course, when they are committing acts of violence against other nameless, faceless Muslims or against people with names and faces, namely, white people in the West. But how does the academic study of religion fit into and contribute to all of this? Or, framed differently, how do we rearrange the faces and supply new names? As I have tried to argue elsewhere: the study of religion is still largely a Protestant endeavor, defining religion as something internal, non-political, spiritual, and non-violent, except of course when "hijacked" or corrupted by external forces (Hughes 2020b). This Protestant orientation becomes the default for many who work in the study of religion and aids in the bifurcation of "authentic" religious forms and those imagined as "inauthentic." This means that scholars of religion in general and of Islam in particular have entered—whether consciously or unconsciously—the political fray of getting to decide or adjudicate who or who is not a good Muslim. But I am not sure this is where we want to or even need to be.

As I hope to show here, however, the more the study of Islam is implicated by and in the current political moment, the more ridiculous and introverted it becomes. Many will invoke, for example, Said's criticism of Orientalism, and continue in the attempt to (1) expose the ideological underpinnings of Western category formation, and to (2) show how such categories have historically deprived Muslim actors of their agency. I have no problem with any of this. In fact, I actively encourage such forms of analysis and have tried to do precisely this in my *Abrahamic Religions* (Hughes 2013a), among other works. We have an obligation to interrogate critically the intellectual genealogies of the fields in which we work, and such interrogation is indeed both a very healthy and very necessary activity. However, it must be systematically applied across the board. We cannot accuse others of being invested in the so-called political all the while ignoring our own investitures in ideological motivations and machinations. In like manner, we cannot say that our own identities or the identities of those we study are complex and complicated, and then simply write off as inconsequential or worse the identities of those of whom we are critical. While many, and I shall bring some egregious examples to bear on my argument shortly, are quick to point out the Orientalist treatment of Islam in Western scholarship, they are often unaware of the problems inherent to reverting to the very Western (read: Protestant) assumption about what gets to count as "good," "real," and "authentic" Islam and what does not. The result is, as in the construction of Orientalism of which they are so critical, the deprivation of agency to Muslim actors. There is a real irony, in other words, when we see the reappearance of Orientalist assumptions emanate from the very same scholarly circles that, at least when it suits them, are willing to point out the political and ideological undertones of the representation of the Other, especially the Muslim Other.

Religious Studies and Politics: An Unhealthy Mix

When we throw into this intellectual-cum-political amalgam the previous leadership in Washington—and the current opposition— we encounter real problems, and not just theoretical and taxonomical ones. It is a political world, one in which (quoting Dylan's song of the same name) "Wisdom is thrown in jail / It rots in a cell / Is misguided as hell / Leaving no one to pick up the trail." I still recall an email I once received from Daniel Pipes, the founder of Campus Watch and the neo-conservative sentinel of appropriate discourses on Islam and Israel. He asked me, long before the thought of (let alone the reality of) a Trump presidency, if I would attend—all expenses paid, plus an honorarium—and go to certain panels at the annual meeting of the Middle Eastern Studies Association (MESA) that he would choose in advance and that I would write about presumably with a slant that would suit him and his organization. "Money doesn't talk," to end this paragraph as I began it, with another quote from Dylan, "it screams."

This one anecdote is revealing for a number of reasons. First, it shows, and I think rather obviously, so there is little reason to belabor the point, just how the study of Islam is encroached upon by various right-wing or, using the *nom du jour*, neo-conservative political actors. This seems to stem from the unfounded fear that the study of Islam produces people who are appreciative of Islam. Second, I find it interesting that because I have been critical of some of the regnant discourses in Islamic studies as far too apologetic and unscholarly (see chapter 1 above), such organizations were somehow aware of this, and they work, moreover, on that age-old adage from Middle Eastern *realpolitik* that the enemy of my enemy must by, definition, be my friend. Third, this action on the part of these right-wing or neo-con social actors, for I do not know what else to call them, must necessarily engender a reaction. Such a reaction, however, and this is my main point in this chapter, is one that recycles, by virtue of the fact that it is a response, the very same problematic terms and categories.

It should also be clear that none of this is necessarily new nor even unprecedented. Another invocation of Said should remind us all that Euro-America has been attempting to think with and regulate Muslim bodies for quite some time. The current obsession with what Muslim women can or cannot, ought or ought not, wear or the xenophobic discourses about refugees and migration is but the latest iteration of this project. What is new now, however, is the outright threat to Muslims in Europe and North America. Muslims are the excuse to bring fascistic-leaning political parties out of the dark recesses in which they have been festering and into the mainstream. Muslims—again nameless, faceless, and displaced because of acts of violence that they are assumed to "perpetrate" on one another—are constructed as a threat to white, Christian Europe. The regulations on Muslims as imagined by Executive Order 13769, titled

"Protecting the Nation from Foreign Terrorist Entry into the United States," but more commonly and simply referred to as the "Muslim ban," makes a mockery of universal human rights, let alone stands in violation of that notoriously problematic and uniquely American of documents, the Constitution.

The Trump administration, of course, did not manufacture all of this, nor did it simply create a discourse from scratch. Instead, it tapped into and responded to a present mood about Islam and about Muslims that is as inaccurate as it is disturbing. The discourse seems to create us, channeling the specter of Foucault for a few seconds, as much as we create it. Islam and Muslims, according to this script, represent a collective threat to "our"—whomsoever "we" are is never entirely clear—values, democracy, well-being, way of life, security, and so on. Muslims are to be feared, pathologized, categorized into "good" and "bad" based on political alliances, and, when and where appropriate, just simply banned. A question we need to ask ourselves is: how does the tendency in Islamic studies to differentiate between "good" and "bad" Muslim bleed over into non-academic discourses? It is easy to see how scholars of Islam respond to those who abnegate Islam for political expediency. But how does it move in the other direction? How do politicians respond to us? Do they just ignore us because we are academics? Here it might be worth mentioning that while the FBI considers Political Scientists and Sociologists to be credible witnesses who can provide expert testimony, it does not grant the same courtesy to scholars of religion (e.g., Weitzman 2013). Is this because scholars of religion—within whose genus we must certainly lump the overwhelming majority of scholars of Islam—insist on terms of reference, invoking Lincoln's thirteenth thesis, that are so apologetic or ecumenical as to be largely unbelievable? Or, is it is some combination of this?

I think articulating this in broad strokes, as I have tried to do here, is the easy part. I now want to go a step further and ask, once again, what role has the academic study of Islam played in all of this? I do not refer simply to the Orientalist tradition, of which it has become fashionable to undermine in certain intellectual circles as of late. Instead I want to put under the microscope the more recent and trendy approach to Islam, the one that is not particularly critical and that desires to offer an antidote to what are perceived to be the excesses of Orientalism. The term that some of my colleagues have used to denote this, and here they invoke the philosopher Kwame Anthony Appiah, is "Cosmopolitanism" (see, e.g., Ernst and Martin 2010).

Cosmopolitanism would, on first blush, appear to be the type of direction in which my argument is ultimately headed. We do, after all, get along better when we realize our interconnections and work, in tandem, to make the world a better place for all of its citizens. But if Orientalism is an academic term, what is "Cosmopolitanism"? The latter certainly does not seem to be an analogue of the former, nor does it function intellectually in the same manner. If Orientalism is about pre-modern texts and, when done properly (and I would be the first to admit the many excesses it has produced over the years), is often critical, what is Cosmopolitanism—modern, post-textual, bricolaged, and what?

If by "cosmopolitanism" we mean, as many do in religious studies, a pluralism of noncritical, nonskeptical, and insider approaches then we are in trouble. Let me give you an example: In a recent work titled *Rethinking Islamic Studies*, and tellingly subtitled *From Orientalism to Cosmopolitanism*, Carl Ernst and Richard Martin invoke Appiah's term. In her chapter, Katherine Pratt Ewing informs us that "cosmopolitanism" is "the foundation of [Appiah's] vision of a harmonious, globalized social order based on pluralism and tolerance" (2010: 53). Okay, fair enough. Who does not prefer tolerance to intolerance or pluralism to monism or exclusivity? But then we might ask, what I imagine is the next or follow-up question: What does this term mean intellectually and what does its invocation mean for scholarship, which is by definition supposed to be critical? Is cosmopolitanism a slogan or a hermeneutic? My argument, rather paradoxically, is that cosmopolitanism, whatsoever it may mean, no less exoticizes Islam and Muslims than Orientalism does precisely because it, too, denies to Muslims autonomy and agency, by forcing them into categories that they may not recognize, and with which they may not agree.

Cosmopolitanism, however, does not seem to have really caught on as either a method or a hermeneutic. It has more recently been replaced by that of "decolonialism" or "decolonial" approaches to the study of Islam, religion, or any other subject in the humanities for that matter. Though I shall discuss this more in the context of Chapter 8 below, it suffices to mention that—though drawing our attention to the important fact that there are other ways of classifying the world around us—such approaches risk being subsumed within the larger issue of identity politics. When this happens, criticism is no longer permitted, except by those within the group in question.

Responses

Every action, as I stated, precipitates a reaction. And it is that reaction that I want to examine in greater detail. Allow me now, in the time that remains, to give a few examples of what I think scholars who are critical of Orientalism have in mind when they say they seek to dislodge Orientalism and replace it with an altogether different set of interpretive lenses.

Although this chapter is titled "in the age of Trump," I confess that I am neither an expert in American politics nor its domestic policies. I do, however, have an abiding interest in the manner whereby such policies influence disciplinary configurations. This is precisely my concern. The sociology of knowledge—and, by extension the sociology of ignorance—instructs us that there exists an intimate relationship between human thought, and lack thereof, and the social contexts within which it arises. There is, then, no world out there waiting to be discovered in an unmediated fashion. On the contrary, knowledge and ignorance are shaped, imagined, manufactured, and disseminated according to established social and cultural frames of references and, of course, political expediency.

This misunderstanding is perhaps the most obvious and the easiest to document. But what I want to do in the time that remains is look at the fallout of this in the academic study of Islam. How does it offer a response to such geopolitical events? The question then becomes, for me, and to reiterate: what is the role of the study of Islam in all of this? For even a rejection of such political categories and discourses—no matter how tacit—ultimately signals their embrace.

In order to nudge the conversation along a little, kindly allow me a confession and let me wax a little autobiographical. My musings in this chapter were precipitated and inspired by a particular event. In the summer of 2017, I interviewed for a chair in Jewish studies at a major state university in the United States. After I presented my so-called job talk on the "Jews" with whom Muhammad might have come into contact, a very early version of which appears as Chapter 3 above, I was informed (not asked, but informed), in the question and answer period, by a potential colleague in Islamic studies that we already know from the *Sira* literature that two of Muhammad's wives were Jewish—so why would I bother to interrogate the matter. When I tried to respond that the *Sira* is problematic chronologically for a number of reasons, another potential colleague—an anthropologist in modern Indonesia and, as I later found out, a convert to Islam—informed me (again informed, not asked) that radio-carbon dating proves that the Qurʾān dates to the period that tradition ascribes to it. I loved the attempt to prove faith by recourse to science, but did not want to point this out in the context of a job interview. So, I tried to point out that radio-carbon dating has a margin of error that could make the Qurʾān later and that such dating tells us only the age of the parchment or vellum and not the script, but it fell on deaf ears because, I would soon learn, nuance was in short supply in that room. But politics, of the identity variety among others, was not. To top it all off, I learned later, another colleague who never once introduced herself to me during my visit, wrote a letter to the search committee and the dean informing them that my talk "insulted her as a Muslim woman," and accused me of having a Zionist and/or neo-conservative agenda.

This really got me thinking. I tried to figure out whence such statements might derive. Are we really so sensitive in the current political moment that a critical and candid posture about what we realistically know, say, about early Islam and the problems associated with its early sources becomes offensive to what are ostensibly other scholars? Is scholarship only skin deep? Does political correctness—and I certainly do not mean this as a conservative critique of the term or concept—become a way to silence voices we do not want to hear or modes of scholarly analysis that might make us uncomfortable?

Allow me to invoke another example that plays off of this, one that speaks volumes to this type of uncritical and politically correct type of approach. In her *The First Muslims* (2007), Asma Afsaruddin argues that the Prophet Muhammad preached "a message of social justice and gender egalitarianism" (18) that was subsequently subverted by white male elites—my term, not hers—in the medieval period. Without getting into the thorny issue of presentism and whether or not "social justice" and "egalitarianism" even existed before the 1970s, we might step back and ask ourselves what might she be trying to accomplish with such a statement. Does she really believe this to be the case? If so, what sources is she using? Presumably the same ones that all of us must use in order to reconstruct the early Islamic period. But these sources pose no problems for her and she feels that all she needs to do is read them as if they provided accurate transcripts of what really happened. But as anyone who works on the topic of Islamic origins knows these sources offer a set of political and chronological problems. They date from a much later period and they are heavily invested in various sectarian propaganda. As opposed to joining, what she calls, "the assertion of the minority rejectionist camp, which has based its contrarian position on its own tendentious reading of the sources and unsubstantiated speculations" (xx), she instead joins ranks with those "careful and responsible scholars" who read the sources with, again, "careful, judicious scrutiny" (xx).

You see the problem. White non-Muslim men run roughshod, according to Afsaruddin, over the sensibilities of a non-white Muslim woman. This returns us to the problem I encountered in my interview at the unnamed American university. The American Academy, which loves charges of white male privilege, swirls in the background like a tornado on the distant horizon. Note what she is doing. One is a careful scholar if one agrees with her and is tendentious if one admits that there might be chronological or other problems with the biographical and other early sources. This, of course, was not unlike what Ernst and Martin were trying to do in their bait-and-switch using a pejoratively and unfairly constructed Orientalism and a more positively framed and equally constructed Cosmopolitanism. Pressed, they would say there is nothing political in their project. But we all know that we live in a political world and no one can venture beyond. What others do is invested in ideology, in other words, but what we do is simply a natural activity.

I lived in Jerusalem at a time when *The Bible Code* just came out. This book, translated into Hebrew as *Hatzofen Hatanachi*, claimed that, encoded in the biblical text, was a series of codes that predicted later events, such as the assassination of the prime minister Yitzhak Rabin. I remember that the Chief Ashkenazic Rabbi at the time issued a statement, which, in typical Israeli directness, basically said, "if you have to lie to people to get them to believe, what's the point?"

Well, I worry that we are heading in a direction where truth is the first casualty. There is a tendency to invoke "normative" and "descriptive" statements that deprive and have the potential to obscure or misrepresent as much as anything constructed by Orientalism. Since when is looking at early Islamic sources and being aware of the problems surrounding them a "tendentious" activity? Or, again, since when has an approach that wants to look seriously into the origins of Islam been labeled as a "contrarian" position? Contrary to what and contrarian to whom? Moreover, why must such an analysis be based on "unsubstantiated speculations"? Unsubstantiated to what or to whom?

Perhaps, rather than label Islamic origins as an activity in which a bunch of angry old white guys engage, it might be profitable to reframe the conversation. Rather than avoid the topic altogether as something that insults the feelings of (some) Muslims, be it academic or non-academic, a responsible approach to Islamic origins provides tremendous insights into a very fluid period of Western history—late antiquity in general and the late antique Arabian Peninsula in particular. Islam, on such a reading, is not the simple sum of other monotheistic sources. On the contrary, its emergence functions as the catalyst for, among other things, the firming up of orthodoxies in other traditions. These are not the discrete traditions of subsequent periods, but represent a moment of fluidity as ideas and those who held them circulated far and wide. How is this tendentious or contrarian? Indeed, if anything, it situates Islam smack dab in the middle of the so-called "West." It neither privileges it nor exoticizes it. Such an approach takes Islamic traditions much more seriously than those who want to focus on, say, the early community's friendliness to gays and lesbians or to its social justice and gender egalitarianism.

The latter topics are less about intellectual or historical integrity and more about theological turf wars between rival Islams in the present that use the quasi-academic jargon of religious studies. In this they are certainly connected to the current political moment. If right-wing politicians say that Islam has no gender equality, what better thing to do than write about how it did in the past and still does in the present. Likewise, if Islamophobes suddenly take up the charge of gay-rights and point to the abhorrent treatment of homosexuals in ISIS controlled territories or in Chechneya, what better than for academics to say that such individuals misunderstand their own beautiful tradition? But, as I hope you might agree with me, such academic presentations come with their own sets of issues.

Conclusions

I began this chapter by invoking my grandfather Muhammad Ali ibn Khalil al-Najdi and his journey to Canada in 1922. I did this for a number of reasons. The first was to make the obvious point that Muslims have been in Canada and North America for a very long time, and this, of course, does not include the Muslim slaves that were forcefully taken to America long before that. Muslims are not just refugees or migrants. They are also builders and quite literally architects of our countries—they our doctors, and our politicians; our layers, and our professors. They are, literally, as Canadian as I am, and I am literally as Arab as they are.

Second, it shows just how potentially ludicrous Islamic studies can become unless we guard it carefully. In many circles, and I used this as my primary example, the study of Islamic origins is *Verboten*. This is in direct response to attempts to undermine Islam on the part of political commentators, many of whom, rather surprisingly, read selectively the Orientalist literature of yesteryear on the emergence of Islam—as any reader on this topic compiled by Ibn Warraq will demonstrate. But as I tried to show, it is no longer intellectually profitable nor sustainable to invoke models that are premised on the assumption that other religions in sixth- or seventh-century Arabia were somehow more stable than our fledgling Islam. A model that, depending upon the metaphor employed, imagines Islam as either the sum of their parts or their simple and illegitimate offspring, no longer holds. Such a model is both ideologically inflected and based on the retroactive projections of later centuries. It privileges Judaism and Christianity as it simultaneously denies Islam and Muslims any agency.

Third, it shows how, returning to Said, we are all intimately connected to one another. Critical scholarship can and must be an important part of Islamic studies. When we ignore certain topics on account of their potential to hurt people's feelings or offend, we are in trouble. What is the alternative? Lies and half-truths peddled by modern-day Sophists?

Fourth, and most importantly, ecumenical and theological ramblings and their concomitant gravitation to certain topics and their avoidance of others are isomorphically tied to the political space we all inhabit. This space constructs Muslims as others, as dangerous, and as foreign. Many, but by no means all, modern scholars of Islam unfortunately respond by going overboard in the opposite direction than the articulations offered by neo-conservative politics. The result, however, is much the same.

Finally, allow me to add that the critical and analytical study of Islam benefits us all. It shows us, both Muslim and non-Muslim, the heights to which historical actors have imagined their tradition. It shows us that Islam is an intricate part of western civilization, whatsoever that may be, and neither its illegitimate child nor its psychological other. Our current political moment—one of fear and distrust, of anger and xenophobia—as worrisome as it may be, cannot hold. The study of Islam has the potential to take an active role in shaping popular opinion of Islam. But this role must eschew simplistic and apologetic formulations, ones predicated simply on responding to ignorant formulations. For such responses, by virtue of the fact that they are responses, internalize that to which they respond. This does not mean that the study of Islam must simply carry on as if nothing were amiss. Instead, it must frame the conversation by, among other things, complicating Islam and Muslim lives.

Chapter 7

Abrahamic Religions: The Second Generation

I remember first hearing the term "Abrahamic religions" and "religions of Abraham" while a graduate student in the late 1990s.[1] Obviously I knew intuitively what they were, but nevertheless the appellation still came as a surprise. The term (or rubric or category) seemed to be used either interchangeably or synonymously with equally murky terms that included the likes of "religions of the West" or "monotheistic religions." While I would like to think that most scholars are well aware of the limited taxonomic validity of such terms and that they do not provide an accurate representation of historical reality, at the time I thought, perhaps naively, that new terms should at least in theory provide more analytical precision than those they were tasked to replace. After all, the use of problematic terms—be they employed in the classroom, popular forms of dissemination, or even in more technical studies—have the potential to contribute to further obfuscation.

Some twenty-five years later, the term has not disappeared. If anything, its use has only increased. There now exist professorships/chairs, book series, conferences, workshops, and academic programs devoted to, at least in theory, the study of Abrahamic religions. It would appear then the term as a system of classification is here to stay. Rather than dismantle or deconstruct the term, as others have done, a more constructive endeavor now might be to expend more intellectual time and energy in better defining what we mean by it and how we can more precisely account for the points of contact between the three religions. To do this, what follows proposes to revisit two foundational questions with the aim of providing much needed nuance to the term. The first is what exactly is an "Abrahamic religion" and, by extension, "Abrahamic religions"? The second, and even more important question, is how ought we to study these religions in an academically rigorous manner?

Others, as mentioned, have already examined the problematic nature of the term, including its lack of precision, its inherent vagueness, and its propensity for ecumenicism.[2] Surely such problems make it not unlike other terms and organizing principles that structure knowledge in the field of religious studies. Terms such as "myth," "ritual," even "religion" have all in recent years been shown to be extremely problematic (see, for example, Segal 1999; Bell 1992; Nongbri 2013). In like manner we could point to very imprecise and monolithic terms used to designate specific religions over diverse geographic areas and temporal periods, such as "Buddhism" or "Islam." None of these terms—despite arguments by some to the contrary—are going away. Rather than argue for their replacement with what would inevitably be more equally problematic terms, I instead want to try to add here some much needed theoretical reflection to the term Abrahamic religions with an eye towards sharpening it as a category of analysis. This necessarily involves thinking about the term in such a manner that it can *include* both the interfaith and the historical, and figuring out the *raison d'être* of each. As things currently stand, the term tends to be confined to the former, and used with caution or sparingly in the latter.

While it is clear that the term is one grounded in the ecumenical and/or the interfaith, such a ground does not have to mean that we cannot transfer more intellectual precision onto it. No one could seriously doubt, for example, that each religion designated as "Abrahamic" has been and indeed continues to be shaped by its contact with the others. Such contact and shaping, however, has less to do with the adjective that purportedly links them and more to do with specifics of real historical interactions. Unfortunately it is this lack of attention to *historical* connections between them—with history functioning as the best antidote to the essentialisms provided by both theologians and comparativists—that has been sorely missing in studies devoted to Abrahamic religions.[3] Indeed, this lack of attention to historicity has been one of the greatest stumbling blocks, I submit, to a proper understanding of the term. This is not to deny however that the term cannot include the interfaith or the theological. But before that can happen, we have to elucidate clearly the parameters of its academic usage.

As we now enter the second generation of the study of Abrahamic religions, we can no longer say that it is a subfield in its infancy or that it is a type of study that is unprecedented.[4] It remains to see if the term can be rehabilitated for the academic study of religion. With this in mind, in what follows I would like to instantiate this process of raising a set of foundational issues surrounding the term "Abrahamic religions," issues that—with the exception of Guy Stroumsa's path-breaking work[5]—do not seem to have been raised sufficiently in the earliest days of its transference from the realm of theology into the domain of the academic study of religion. Since the term seems to have originated primarily in interfaith circles,[6] its rapid appearance within a more secular study risks a certain amount of slippage—and this has happened far too often—that needs to be clarified.

The following study is divided into four parts. In the first part I examine some of the tensions inherent to the term, arguing that several of these tensions result from a lack of clarity when it comes to the various approaches (theological, philosophical, and historical) traditionally used. I detangle such approaches from one another and try to give each one better definition in the process. The second part attempts to define better just what Abrahamic religions are and, in the process, to show that a proper understanding of them demands tremendous linguistic and historical expertise, not slogans. The third part examines the question of how best to study Abrahamic religions. If it is to be an academic field, then there must be some kind of distinct method—or at the very least, some agreed upon first principles—used to study them. Since built into the notion of the term is comparison, it would seem that this method, potentially so problematic, must play some sort of role in this process. If comparison is to be the defining feature of the study of Abrahamic religions, then there is much work to be done to establish their comparative study on firm academic foundations. However, if comparing two things—let alone, two monolithic religions that often do not admit of nuance—is difficult enough, once we add a third, even greater problems will inevitably arise. Finally, the fourth part tries to bring the constituent methods and approaches back together again and chart a potential course for future study.

"Abrahamic Religions": Tensions and Fractures

Implicit in the term Abrahamic religions are a number of tensions that need to be unraveled, one from the other. Until this is done, the term will remain vague, inchoate, and largely unhelpful except for those engaged in the discourses associated with interfaith trialogue. Indeed, it is this latter sense of the term that would, at first blush, certainly seem to be the predominant one. Without rehearsing the entire narrative here, it seems to revolve around the notion that these three discrete religions are imagined to share a bond with the Patriarch Abraham and, by extension, with one another.[7] This shared inheritance then functions as the pretense for the establishment of an ongoing conversation between representatives of the three religions to talk to and engage with one another in a mutually beneficial manner. This sense of the term is perhaps best encapsulated using the words of Leonard Swidler, Professor of Catholic Thought and Interreligious Dialogue at Temple University in Philadelphia, and the founder of the *Journal of Ecumenical Studies*. According to him:

> The three Abrahamic faiths have many more things in common, such as the importance of covenant, of law and faith, and of the community (witness in the three traditions the central role of the terms people, church, and ummah, respectively). But just looking at the list of commonalities already briefly spelled out will provide us with an initial set of fundamental reasons why it is imperative to engage in serious, ongoing dialogue with Muslims.
>
> (Swidler 1990: 123)

Here we see how Swidler—not unlike many others involved in interreligious dialogue—wants to expand the traditional notion of "Judeo-Christian," an equally problematic academic term, which had been coined in the 1950s to try to show the commonality between Judaism and Christianity.[8] The employment of this latter term, not coincidentally, was also the product of non-academic forces—the National Conference of Christians and Jews—whose mandate was to fight anti-Semitism and create a tolerant and inclusive idea of America and articulate a shared set of American values regardless of religious affiliation. "Abrahamic religions," as an interfaith term and category, sought to open this earlier category up to include Muslims into the conversation, something that became increasingly necessary after the events of September 11, 2001, and the ensuing discourses associated with the so-called clash of civilizations. Though, and showing the fluidity of these terms and the political uses to which they can be put, it is worth noting today that when conservative pundits use the term "Judeo-Christian" they do so in a manner that is little more than code for a "Christian" (and mostly evangelical) agenda and which is, by extension, often anti-Muslim or Islamophobic.[9]

If Abrahamic values now supersede Judeo-Christian ones, at least in some quarters, a set of common principles had to be mined beyond just their respective invocations of Abraham. We see an early attempt at this in, for example, the writings of Jürgen Moltmann, the German Reformed theologian and proponent of, among other things, ecumenicism. For him, Abrahamic religions possess a set of essential characteristics the distinguishes them from "non-Abrahamic" religions. According to him:

> Every comparison with the great Asian cosmic religions shows the unique character of the Abrahamic religions: the future is something new; it is not the return of the past. The world is not held in the great equilibrium of the cosmos and its harmony. As God's creation, it is aligned towards the future of his eternal kingdom and hence is temporal.
> (Moltmann 1999: 75)

These three religions are here imagined to possess a set of inherently shared characteristics that make them qualitatively different from other religions, which, in turn, are believed to be in possession of their own unique, yet equally amorphous, essences. Within such a worldview, Abrahamic religions can be compared with and differentiated from, for example, "Eastern religions," the "great Asian cosmic religions," or the "axial religions of Asia and China."[10] Note, though, that since comparison is also one of the main—or at least traditional—methodologies in religious studies, we begin to witness now a certain cross-pollination between ecumenical and religious studies approaches.

We also increasingly begin to witness the connection between the contemporary geopolitical order and the invocation of Abrahamic religions. In the following passage published by the United States Institute of Peace in 2007, for example, we see yet another instance of the way in which the term is used:

> Jews, Muslims, and Christians share and identify as fellow pilgrims on a path—a path all three faiths understand to be profoundly rooted in concepts of truth and peace. Adherents of the Abrahamic faiths believe that right conduct is essential and that sacred texts hold instructions about how to live an ethical, just life that is pleasing to God. Jews, Christians, and Muslims share the belief that God wants them to live a life full of respect for justice, peace, and human relationships. All three believe in the validity of revelation as a sign from God and struggle to maintain unity in spite of splits in their populations (Reform/Orthodox, Shiite/Sunni, Protestant/Catholic).
> (Abu-Nimer, Khoury, and Welty 2007: 19)

What is new here, at least when compared to the previous quotations, is that those who wrote this are scholars and not theologians. While Swidler, Moltmann and others who share their orientation towards Abrahamic religions are clearly theologians and self-identify as such, problems seem to emerge when academics—be they in religious studies, peace studies, Abrahamic religions studies, or the like—invoke it in similar ways and where it is now imagined to function as a historically accurate descriptor. This is where, I submit, the *major* tension inherent to the term resides and, as such, where the greatest energy needs to be expended to clarify. I should be clear that if non-academics want to use the term—without theoretic reflection on it—to encourage interfaith trialogue, they should. If such a trialogue creates meaningful exchanges among Jews, Christians, and Muslims at the grassroots level, in which they can find common ground and shared epistemological space, all the better. This use of the term, though, cannot be simply transferred onto an academic register. The problem however is that—as the quotation from the United States Institute of Peace clearly shows—this is too frequently done, with the result that invocations of "Abrahamic" as an academic category that claims to do analytical work become problematic.

If there is to be an academic sense of the term—and we have to assume that there is if for no other reason than that an academic subfield seems to have grown around the term "Abrahamic religions"—then it needs to be extricated, at least initially, from this interfaith usage. The question then becomes: how might we go about this? For one thing, academic fields have distinct subject matters and distinct methods for undertaking their study. A historical analysis, for example, can neither be a psychological nor a literary one. Likewise for a work of sociology. The problem with religious studies however is that there is not a clearly defined mode of analysis for its subject matter.[11] Indeed, in recent years, the very category "religion" has come under interrogation as little more than a Western construct (e.g., Nongbri 2013; Barton and Boyarin 2016). We might say, then, that an academic treatment of Abrahamic religions runs into precisely the same sorts of issues that its parent field—religious studies—does.

Such a difficulty need not be terminal, though. Just as we are able to recognize the difference between a historical study and a theological or ecumenical one in religious studies, surely we should be able to do the same when it comes to Abrahamic religions. The problem with the latter, however, resides in the fact that historical accounts of Abrahamic religions rarely use the term on account of its ecumenical and often decidedly non-historical usage. I think, for example, of so much of the good work done by scholars who work on the Cairo Genizah, which held over 300,000 manuscript fragments recovered from the storeroom of the Ben Ezra Synagogue in Old Cairo. These manuscripts provide a window onto Jewish history and Jewish–Muslim relations from roughly the ninth to the nineteenth centuries. Written primarily in Hebrew and Arabic, they reveal an intimate portrait of, among other things, Jewish–Muslim business relationships and a shared cultural life among Abrahamic religions.[12] The works supplied in the previous footnote are all historically sophisticated, attentive to requisite linguistic and philological sources, and provide excellent micro-studies of—at least two—Abrahamic religions (i.e., Judaism and Islam). Though I shall leave aside for the moment if a "proper" study of Abrahamic religions has to involve all three, we need to ask: Why do the authors of these micro-studies not invoke the category "Abrahamic religions" in their analyses and, just as importantly, why do those in religious studies tend not to be interested in their studies? Is it because they are too "micro"? Is it because they are too specific or too technical? Is it because they do not make grandiose presumptions about Abrahamic religions? But surely a micro-study ought to provide the perfect ground to think more broadly about intertwined relationships and shared values, be they economic, social, or religious.

The question I want to get at near the end of this study is: how do we transform such technical studies into studies of Abrahamic religions? Before I do, allow me to try to articulate further the problem. In his *The Case for Islamo-Christian Civilization* (2004), the historian Richard W. Bulliet made the case, in the aftermath of 9/11 and Samuel Huntington's problematic concept of the "clash of civilizations," for coining the term "Islamo-Christian" to focus on the shared history and attributes of Islamic and Christian communities, as opposed to their enmity. Using "Judeo-Christian" civilization as his model, Bulliet sought to demonstrate the partially shared—but also mindful of the antagonistic—social, institutional, and political structures that emerged over fourteen centuries of historical interaction. This *historical* basis, he argues with an important caveat, is important "for thinking of the Christian society of Western Europe—not all Christians everywhere—and the Muslim society of the Middle East and North Africa—not all Muslims everywhere—as belonging to a single historical civilization that goes beyond the matter of scriptural tradition" (ibid.: 10). It is the historical relationship, in other words, that Bulliet is most interested in and it is through that relationship, he argues, that we clearly witness historical and structural overlap. He continues:

> A fundamental restructuring of Western thinking about relations with Islam calls for a fresh look at history. The historical development of Western Christendom and Islam parallel each other so closely that the two faith communities can best be thought of as two versions of a common socioreligious system, just as Orthodox Christianity and Western Christendom are considered two versions of the same socioreligious system. For eight centuries, the pathways of development led in the same direction and occasionally virtually overlapped one another.
>
> (Bulliet 2004: 15)

Bulliet's case, as this quotation makes clear, is with the historical record. It is that record, as opposed to a shared scriptural heritage between Christians and Muslims (and Jews), where he sees positive interactions. He thus consciously avoids "Abrahamic religions" because, as he tells us, he is not "looking for a term to signal the common scriptural tradition of these three religions" (9–10). Now, why is this interesting? Rather than focus on Bulliet's book, I wish to focus on how he adapted his case for *The Oxford Handbook of Abrahamic Religions*, wherein he has a chapter titled simply "Islamo-Christian Civilization" (Bulliet 2015: 109). The historian Bulliet is immediately mistrustful—and I think for the reasons I articulated above—of the adjective "Abrahamic," and he instead prefers to use the term that he had earlier coined: "Islamo-Christian." According to him, "as joint inheritors of a Judaic theological and ethical legacy and a Hellenistic philosophical and scientific legacy, Islam and Christianity 'co-evolved' in directions that did not have distinct parallels in Judaism, which remained particularistic rather than universal in nature" (ibid.).

Bulliet thus chooses to focus on the relationship between Islam and Christianity, which he calls a "sub-topic" under the "general rubric" of Abrahamic religions (ibid.). This is important to my argument because it shows that one can do work on two of the three religions without necessarily working on the third or, even more importantly, that one even has to *endorse* the term "Abrahamic religions." Moreover, as I shall argue subsequently, Bulliet's analysis is significant because, even though he does not endorse the category, his analysis certainly bears on the nature of the historical study of Abrahamic religions. We see this, for example, in the following statement:

> Islam and Christianity obviously share certain scriptural elements present in the Old Testament. Does this make it plausible to conceive of a Judaeo-Islamo-Christian civilization? ... The absence of common

scripture-based engagement with Christology, salvation, proselytization, and apocalypse, which arise in Christianity and Islam but only minimally, if at all, in Judaism, provides a narrow base on which to postulate a tripartite civilizational identity. The social reality of Judaism being restricted to a small, kinship defined, population after the destruction of the Second Temple in 70 CE, and of Christianity and Islam becoming enormous, multi-ethnic, world-spanning religious systems in the subsequent centuries, underlines this limitation.

(Bulliet 2015: 113)

That Bulliet's important historical work could be easily repackaged and branded as a study in Abrahamic religions is, it seems to me, potentially a watershed moment in the *academic* study of this young subfield. It shows, for example, that we do not have to eschew critical or historical analysis in the name of essences and the quest to find similarities (at the expense of locating difference). Though similarity is certainly important to Bulliet, he argues that it need not be the subfield's *raison d'être*. And while his goal is in part extra-academic—"the greater the recognition of a sibling relationship between Islam and Christianity, the better the prospects for peaceful coexistence in future years"—his analysis can neither be reduced to nor confined by such an agenda (ibid.: 109).

Significant, and I think this can be found in several (but certainly not all) of the chapters that comprise *The Oxford Handbook of Abrahamic Religions*, is the desire to wrestle with the very category that defines one's object of study. This is, for lack of a better term, a very religious studies move to make.[13] Only by reflecting on the terms we use and employ—being self-conscious of why and how we do so, to invoke Jonathan Z. Smith—are we able to move this subfield forward (Smith 1982: xi). This self-reflexivity, I submit, ought to be a constituent part, perhaps one of the main constituent parts, of a study devoted to Abrahamic religions, regardless of whether it is historical or interfaith.

With this self-reflection, we begin to see the seeds for what an academic study of Abrahamic religions might look like. Yet before I examine the contours of such a study, allow me to examine another tension inherent to the term. "Abrahamic religions" implies, at the very least, three different modes of analysis: the historical; the philosophical; and the theological. Too often these three modes are confused with the result that further confusion ensues. This slippage means that theological treatments can be easily confused with historical ones or even vice versa.

Heuristically, we might define them in the following terms:

- A *historical* study of Abrahamic religions must be one that begins with, emerges from, and remains true to the historical record. It looks at historical interactions—in specific times, regions, and locales—between at least two of the three Abrahamic religions. Rather than deal with generic or essentialized "Jews," "Christians," and "Muslims," it deals with specific and often localized social actors who claims such designations for themselves. They are, by nature and definition, micro-studies, and as I argued above this makes those who engage in them hesitant or unwilling to use an adjective as sweeping and general as "Abrahamic."
- A *philosophical* study of Abrahamic religions is one that necessarily focuses on philosophical texts produced by Jews, Muslims, and Christians. This usually involves showing their common heritage in the Greek philosophical tradition, and how thinkers associated with the Abrahamic traditions adopted that tradition to their own revelatory systems. Such studies tend to be based on influences and anticipations, and can be classified, more broadly, as intellectual history or the history of ideas. Though, as with historical studies, those who engage in such study tend not to see themselves as working in Abrahamic religions at all, but in, say, medieval Aristotelianism or some other philosophical tradition.
- Finally, a *theological* study of Abrahamic religions is the one with which we tend to be most familiar. Every bit as important as the previous two types of study, this one is invested in showing the *commonalities* between the three religions in the service of ecumenicism and peace-building. Like the other two types, this can involve academic monographs (that are clear that they are theological and not historical treatments) or more popular ones to get Muslims, Jews, and Christians talking to one another. Interestingly, if the previous two types can involve two of the three Abrahamic religions, theological study would seem to need to be devoted to all three. I say this because whenever representatives of two of the three religions talk to one another there is the chance that they might either define themselves in light of the third's absence or simply revert to "Jewish-Muslim," "Christian-Jewish," or Muslim-Christian" dialogue.

As I remarked, these are three heuristic types that, by necessity, must have some overlap. But it is important for us to be aware of where these overlaps occur. For example, scriptural reasoning—the practice of people of different faiths coming together with the intention of reading and reflecting on their scriptures—can be both philosophical and theological. Likewise, the study of medieval Jewish, Muslim and Christian philosophical texts can be both historical (e.g., what historical conditions led to the production of such texts) and philosophical. They can, of course, also be theological because the medieval philosophers were primarily interested in understanding God's relationship to the world and, just as importantly, to their respective religious traditions.

With these theoretical issues in mind, allow me to go back to two basic questions—"What is an Abrahamic religion?" and "How does one study Abrahamic religions?"—to shed additional light on the future study of this concept.

What Is an "Abrahamic Religion"?

Others have provided us with the genealogy of the term so there is no need to rehearse here just where, when, why, and how "Abrahamic religions" came into existence (e.g., Hughes 2013a; Stroumsa 2012, 2015b). My interest, to repeat, is not to examine wherefrom and when the term came to be, namely, its past, but how we can proceed with it, to wit, its future. To do this we need to separate, at least initially, the academic sense of the term from the interfaith sense. Too often, as witnessed in the previous section, these two senses cohabit and do so with very mixed and often confused results. Even if we want to re-couple these two senses of the term, and as I shall argue in the final section in many ways we have no alternative, it is still imperative to separate them at least initially with the aim of revealing some of the tensions that contribute to the problems surrounding the term. The main tension stems from the fact that the interfaith and academic senses of the term have different first principles and, by extension, a different set of concerns even if they employ similar methodologies. The interfaith, for example, searches for similarities through the act of comparison between often essentialized Abrahamic religions in the name of ecumenicism (e.g., Abrahamic notions of charity or Abrahamic notions of hospitality). The academic sense of the term—also using the method of comparison—is or ought to be predicated on the articulation of differences with the aim of clarification and ideally analysis (Smith 1982: 19–35; Smith 1990: 36–53; Lincoln 2018: 3–24; Freiburger 2019: 20–44). The difference between the two uses of the term Abrahamic religions would thus seem to turn on the notion of comparison and what the ends of a comparative framework should be.

Though it is perhaps worth pointing out that even if we neatly bifurcate the study of Abrahamic religions into the "interfaith" and the "academic," the line between the two is extremely fuzzy. This fuzziness may well be the result of the fact that many interfaith treatments of the term are carried out not only in obvious theological or ecumenical domains, but often under the guise of academic legitimacy. This is most likely related, as others have duly pointed out, to the theological underpinning of the modern academic study of religion.[14] Is the goal of religious studies understanding or explanation, interfaith work or critical analysis? Again, though, if the field of religious studies or the subfield of Abrahamic religions is to procced, then this fuzziness must be clarified, not necessarily patrolled, with the aim, once again, of sharpening the intellectual tools of which we are already in possession.

If "Abrahamic religions" is to be more than just a slogan, and instead function as an appropriate and academically sophisticated subfield within the academic study of religion, the term—what it is and what it is not, what it can realistically do and what it cannot—needs to be clarified. What, for example, is an "Abrahamic religion," and, even more importantly, what is the best way to study them, both critically and comparatively?

When we think of Abrahamic religions, it would seem that we always have the "big three"—Judaism, Christianity, and Islam—in mind. Unfortunately these big three are rarely subdivided to include all of their basic divisions and "sects." In terms of the latter, we might read, for example, as we did above that all three Abrahamic religions have divisions—Orthodox/Reform in the case of Judaism; Catholic/Protestant in the case of Christianity; and Sunni/Shīʿī in the case of Islam—and that is it. Implicit in such a comparative analogy is the notion that these divisions are somehow analogous. Such an analogy is always presented phenomenologically to show similarity, but almost never historically to show difference. After such divisions are presented, the tendency is to return to the "big three" as if they were monoliths. But academically who can compare three huge and monolithic religions? Scholarship is based on the small-scale not the large-scale, and on the careful study of specific texts (broadly defined) and not gargantuan religions that span millennia and diverse geographic areas. Surely, it is an impossible task. This is why, it seems to me, that those who work in specific periods—returning to the example of the Cairo Geniza—rarely say they work in Abrahamic religions. Though, as I hope to show in the following section, my goal is that, if properly defined, they will begin to do this or at least be encouraged to do so.

In addition to the fact that each of these monoliths is composed of diversity with each in possession of many divisions and sectarian movements, we might ask: how far do we wish to stretch the category? Can or ought we to study Abrahamic religions in isolation from their "pagan" contexts, from ancient Near Eastern religions, from the religions of Greece and Rome, not to mention those of India?[15] If the term is amorphous to begin with, opening it up to these larger contexts risks further inchoateness. Indeed, at that point the term might even become interchangeable with the academic study of religion. But surely no academic treatment of Abrahamic religions—say, the role of the Active Intellect in medieval Jewish and Islamic philosophy—can afford to ignore the role of the Active Intellect in the work of Aristotle and the later Aristotelian commentary tradition. Or, again, do we face the same problem that we do with those studies devoted to the Cairo Geniza, namely, that such studies become too technical to be given the rubric? Are Abrahamic religions only to be invoked, in other words, when they are used in generalist and non-specific studies?

Related to this is the issue of languages. Abrahamic religions, in theory if not always in practice, draw on primary sources in many languages, and very few, if any, have mastered all of them. This is why an important question is: what counts as valid training in Abrahamic religions? Does it involve training in all three religions or, as a recent job description at Cambridge argues, does it involve "the study of at least one of Judaism, Christianity or Islam, and with a focus on the interactions between these traditions...They will be distinguished scholars of at least one of these traditions, with a proven interest in its relations to the other two."[16] These mean different things. Expertise in one religion with an "interest in the relations to the other two" is not the same thing as working on the points of contact—and tensions—between three social groups that identify as Jews, Christians, and Muslims.

Such issues reveal to just what an extent both the category and the study of Abrahamic religions remains under construction. It is a field, in other words, that is still very much in its formative stages and very few—despite the assurances of many—are actually qualified to work in Abrahamic religions. Indeed, I am not even certain that we have established the criteria for what gets to count as expertise in Abrahamic religions. How do we decide, for example, what counts (and what does not) as a valid study in Abrahamic religions? What approaches are valid and invalid?

How Does One Study "Abrahamic Religions"?

Before I examine what an appropriate study of Abrahamic religions might look like, it is—once again—necessary to ask a number of foundational questions, questions that unfortunately are rarely asked.[17] What counts as an academic study of Abrahamic religions? Does one have to study all three or does it suffice to study two of the three, given the need for appropriate linguistic skills? This is a basic question. While I will argue shortly that academic treatments of Abrahamic religions need to deal with only two, an ecumenical treatment *must* by definition take into consideration all three religions. If it does not, it automatically ceases to be "Abrahamic" and defaults to one of dialogue (as opposed to trialogue) between two of the three. It would seem, then, that an ecumenical study of Abrahamic religions has a different set of criteria from academic treatments of the same topic.

Leaving aside the interfaith or ecumenical for the time being, we return to the question already raised at several points in this study: Do technical studies count as treatments of Abrahamic religions (e.g., Cohen 2005; Ackerman-Lieberman 2013)? Currently it would seem that they do not. It is unclear just who is to blame for this. Is it the fault of those who engage in such study not wanting to be associated with an amorphous and inchoate term? Or, is it the case that those who have been responsible for trying to define the field of Abrahamic religions maintain that studies have to be generalist, of broad appeal (e.g., Ma'oz 2009), or—most worrying from an academic perspective—necessarily deal only with interfaith or ecumenical issues?

Religious studies, the parent field of the study of Abrahamic religions, tends to be generalist, largely interested in matters of theory and method (broadly defined to include the critical and the ecumenical), and increasingly does both at the expense of language work. The result is that it tends to eschew technical studies of texts in the manner that, say, Islamic studies does. This tension between the particular and the universal itself creates a sense of confusion. At what point is a study too technical, of interest to only a few other specialists, or when does it become too general and unrecognizable to fellow specialists outside of religious studies?

Allow me to provide an example. In 1947, the late Harry Austryn Wolfson (1887–1974) published his important *Philo: Foundations of Religious Philosophy in Judaism, Christianity, and Islam* (1947). The work first provides an examination of Philo of Alexandria's (d. ca. 50 CE) philosophic principles, before going on to show how these principles became the common foundation of the subsequent medieval Jewish, Christian, and Islamic philosophical traditions, before being attacked by Spinoza in the seventeenth century. At the end of the first volume, for example, Wolfson remarks:

> In Philo's conception of human freedom we have an adumbration of all the elements of the problem as it presented itself to the minds of religious philosophers, whether Christian, Moslem, or Jewish, throughout the ages. Like Philo, they all as a rule start out with the assumption that there are laws of nature but that these laws were established in the world by God and that God has reserved for himself the freedom to upset these laws on certain occasions and for good reason in the form of miracles.
> (Wolfson 1947, vol. 1: 458)

Wolfson did not call his work a work of Abrahamic religions, primarily because I am certain that he would not have even known of the term. Indeed, the 1940s, the date of *Philo's* publication, was coincidentally around the same time that the term was coming into vogue. Yet, given the fact that Wolfson presents a linguistically competent and historically accurate account of one specific aspect of these *three* religions, it must surely count as a study of Abrahamic religions?

I mention Wolfson's work in this context because it raises a number of interesting questions. The first is, are we able to label a study as one of "Abrahamic religions" retroactively? If we answer this in the affirmative, and I can think of no good reason to see why we should not, then we could surely label a host of other studies going back to at least the mid-nineteenth century as studies in Abrahamic religions. But, to raise another question: Could we label works such as Abraham Geiger's (1810–1874) *Was hat Mohammed aus dem Judenthume aufgenommen?* (Geiger 1970 [1833]) as a work of Abrahamic religions? This work, which seeks to show the Jewish and rabbinic roots of the Qurʾān certainly engages two of the three religions. Some might object and say that Geiger's work could not be considered Abrahamic on account of the fact that his operating assumption is that Muhammad actively took or stole Jewish ideas in order to appeal to his audience. Though it is worth noting that he was certainly more sensitive to the genius of Islam than his Christian contemporaries and certainly more grounded than the excesses of those Orientalists surveyed in Said's *Orientalism* (see Heschel 1998; Koltun-Fromm 2006). This raises an additional question: does a work of Abrahamic religions have to work with a general spirit of magnanimity between the religions? Could a study that focused on, for example, disputations between Jews and their former coreligionists, now Christians, over the veracity of the Talmud—in Barcelona in 1263 or Tortosa in 1412–1414—that often led to violence and persecution be classified as a work of Abrahamic religions (e.g., Lasker 1977; Maccoby 1982)? If we are willing to include Geiger's work or those devoted to the less sanguine elements of the relationship between the three religions, then a host of other works in Abrahamic religions open up before us. For example: Heinrich Speyer's "Von den biblischen Erzählungen im Koran" (1923–1924), Josef Horovitz's *Koranische Untersuchungen* (1926), Shlomo Dov Goitein's *Jews and Arabs* (1955). From such works we could presumably include even more technical ones, such as Shlomo Pines's "Shi'ite Terms and Conceptions in Judah Halevi's Kuzari" (1980) or his "Notes on Islam and on Arabic Christianity and Judaeo-Christianity" (1985).

The reason I want to open the category up in this manner is, I hope, obvious. If scholars have been working on Abrahamic religions—without necessarily calling their work by that name—then we have a precedent and a genealogy for its modern study. All of the works mentioned in the previous paragraph are historical, small-scale, and linguistically competent. They all involve, moreover, a theoretical concern for the intersection of at least two of the three religions. If we are willing to grant this to works that existed before the term "Abrahamic religions" came into existence, then it would seem that we could also open up the term a little further to include more recent works that deal with these religions but for some reason or set of reasons are not regarded as works or studies in Abrahamic religions. Into this category we might include important—and often technical—works such as Patricia Crone's *Roman, Provincial, and Islamic Law* (2009), Elliot R. Wolfson's *Language, Eros, Being* (2004), or Emran El-Badawi's *The Qur'ān and the Aramaic Gospel Traditions* (2014), to name but a few. Opening up the study of Abrahamic religions to include such historical works and more modern ones allows us to further sharpen the category, while simultaneously encouraging those who engage in more technical studies to contribute to a larger conversation with a presumably larger readership than that found in their own technical fields and subfields.

This brings me to one of my main points, namely, what counts as a valid *academic* study of Abrahamic religions. It seems quite clear what a valid *theological* or *ecumenical* study is. The latter includes a study of all three religions in a spirit or ecumenicism (as opposed to, say, that of supersessionism) to show commonalities—and to a lesser extent differences—between the three Abrahamic religions. That would seem to be the easy rubric to define. Now in the space that remains in this section, allow me to try to define more specifically what ought to count as an academic work of Abrahamic religions.

First, an academic study of Abrahamic religions has to involve at least two of the three religions and has to be done at the "micro" level (broadly defined as historical, sociological, anthropological, dealing with material culture, etc.). For the sake of scholarly norms, it is simply impossible to work on or with grandiose concepts such as "Judaism," "Christianity," or "Islam." For example, a study on charity in the Abrahamic religions is too vague and would, most likely, be a candidate for an interfaith study. However, a study in, say, charitable institutions as they emerge from documents associated with the Cairo Geniza would surely be an appropriate academic study. To use another example, "Abrahamic mysticism" would also seem to be far too broad to be scholarly, but a study of, say, textual strategies to convey illuminative experiences in Ibn Arabi's (d. 1240) *Bezels of Wisdom* (*fuṣūṣ al-ḥikam*) and the *Zohar*, the major work of thirteenth-century Jewish mysticism, is certainly much more narrow and focused, and would provide the data for an in-depth study.[18]

Second, a valid academic study of Abrahamic religions has to show linguistic and historical competence in the period and geographic region concerned. One cannot work, for example, in medieval Muslim-Jewish relations in al-Andalus without a knowledge of Hebrew and Arabic. Such a knowledge ideally prevents imaginative flights of fancy about ecumenicism that betray the historical record.

Third, such a study has to reflect on how the data examined help us to better define the term Abrahamic religions. Within this context, one of the quintessential moves in religious studies is to reflect on the category "religion"—not at the expense of our data (though this can frequently happen) but in light of the data. A study in Abrahamic religions therefore ought to be able to make second-level order reflections on how one's particular study helps us to sharpen, expand, or otherwise finesse the category.

Fourth, and relatedly, since I have argued that a study in Abrahamic religions need only involve two of the three religions on account of linguistic expertise, historical training, and so on, it would seem that a study needs to at least invoke the third religion in one's theoretical reflections. Such reflections could, for example, take the form of invoking the third religion in one's introduction or conclusion with the acknowledgment that one's study will be a technical examination of topic "x," say, in some aspect of Christianity and Islam, but nevertheless this study also helps us to better understand how that topic can function in either the third or in all three.

I am calling, then, for studies in Abrahamic religions—in this, their second generation of study—to be specific so that one can speak to other specialists in one's chosen subfields, but also with some sort of reflection—be it theoretical, practical, or methodological—on the larger ramifications of what one is studying for the more general field. A good academic study of Abrahamic religions, it seems to me, must include all of these features. Linguistic skill, sensitivity to the historical record, and theoretical sophistication. Without these we will see more of the same overlap between the academic and the interfaith.

Abrahamic Religions: Moving Forward

Having separated the interfaith from the academic senses of the term, it now remains to try to put them back together. Whereas some, most notably myself, have argued that the term has little or no heuristic value as an academic term (Hughes 2013a: 1–14), I would argue that this criticism is confined to what I have called the "first generation" of the study of Abrahamic religions. Now, as the term—and its concomitant study—moves out of its infancy, it is time revisit their study, if for no other reason that it would appear that the term is here to stay.

Here it might be worth looking at other traditions within the academic study of religion. In term of Christianity, for example, it is quite obvious that there are theological treatments of that tradition—or, perhaps better, certain aspects of the tradition—and that there are more critical and academic ones.[19] Of course, there also exist studies that straddle the two types, namely, that present themselves as academic treatments, but have theological intentions. And, for the most part, we are able to recognize these types of approaches to Christianity. The same situation exists in each of the other two religions dubbed "Abrahamic." And, again, scholars in those fields are able to recognize the differences between such approaches. No one, for example would conflate studies with a title like *Memories of Muhammad: Why the Prophet Matters* (Safi 2009) with, say, one titled *The Death of a Prophet: The End of Muhammad's Life and the Beginnings of Islam* (Shoemaker 2012).

It should be clear that my comments here are confined to the study of Abrahamic religions. I will leave it to others to comment on the larger field of religious studies, which some feel is perhaps a little too comfortable with such fuzzy borders between the ecumenical and the theological. Moreover, and just for the sake of reiteration, I am not trying to say that either (1) the academic is superior to the theological or (2) that theological treatments cannot be academic. On the contrary, they simply—and, again, for the most part—represent what should be two different types of treatment that can, in theory, learn from and be informed by one another.

Rather, my point here is much simpler. If those of us trained in specific religions are able to recognize, often with relative ease, the difference between a theological and an academic treatment, why should we not be able to do the same thing when it comes to Abrahamic religions? The problem, however, is that much of the first generation of the study of Abrahamic religions was largely confined to the ecumenical. If we open it up, in the manner that I have suggested in the previous section, then we will increasingly get more historical and critical studies. In which case, we should be able to recognize the difference between a critical and historical treatment of Abrahamic religions on the one hand, and one that is interested in ecumenical concerns on the other.

Abrahamic religions, in other words, must be seen as an inclusive category, under which one can do any number of things and using a variety of approaches and methodologies. But I would add to this and argue that, most importantly, it is up to us—those of us who ostensibly work in Abrahamic religions—to be relentlessly self-conscious about our use of the category, clear on why we are invoking it, and what we imagine to be doing by its invocation. If we want to engage in historical studies, we have to make it clear that this is what we are doing; if we want to deploy the term ecumenically, then again we need to be clear that this informs our approach and will, most likely, structure our conclusions. It is when there is a confusion of method and goals that we witness a confusion of results.

Conclusions

If the first generation of the study of Abrahamic religions saw a great deal of confusion between the interfaith and academic senses of the term, the second generation will ideally witness a corrective—one that is based on the clarification of the two approaches and a recalibration of their coexistence. If we are to engage in this recalibration, it is necessary to realize what each of these two accounts can realistically do (and not do). Academic studies of Abrahamic religions reveal that Jews, Muslims, and Christians have always bumped up against one another, and thought about themselves by thinking about the other two. But such encounters and thinking were always specific to distinct places and time periods wherein such interactions occurred. We can certainly extrapolate from such interactions to make interfaith points, but we cannot engage in eisegesis and/or run roughshod over the historical and textual record. In like manner, interfaith accounts of Abrahamic religions remind scholars that the historical subjects we work with were once members of living and vibrant communities that sought to make sense of themselves in dialogue with their religious neighbors.

Chapter 8

The Study of Religion as a National and Nationalist Project

The academic study of religion,[1] for all intents and purposes, began in Germany in the nineteenth century.[2] There have, however been recent attempts to locate it elsewhere, both temporally and geographically. Daniel Boyarin, for example, has tried to put it in the late antique period and argues that it arose on account of the need to differentiate early Jews from early Christians when they were, for all intents and purposes, taxonomically very similar to one another (e.g., Boyarin 2004). Steven M. Wasserstrom (1988) instead locates it in the heresiographical literature associated with medieval Islam, and connects it to the desire to figure out how to establish the minority status of other religious traditions, something that would determine, among other things, rates of taxation. And Guy G. Stroumsa (2010) puts it later, in early modern Europe, where he triangulates its rise between (1) the emergence of empires that led to ethnological curiosity, (2) the Reformation, which permanently altered Christianity's landscape by creating new religious forms, and (3) the invention of philology, a discipline that transformed Western intellectual thought.

Regardless of where we locate its origins, the ostensible goal of the academic study of religion was, as indeed it still is, to understand the religions of the globe from an ostensibly scientific (or neutral or objective) perspective. There are, of course, a number of problems with this—many of which have been articulated in previous chapters. Defining religion, for example, tends to be done using the fiat of those in and with power (early Christians, medieval Muslims, and early modern Europeans in the case of Boyarin, Wasserstrom, and Stroumsa, respectively). Imagining religion not infrequently means examining the beliefs of others and finding them wanting because they do not measure up to those who imagine their own beliefs and traditions to be God-given. Thinking about and taxonomizing religions is often akin to fitting alterity and the beliefs of others into the categories—deemed to be both natural and self-evident—of a dominant group, which imagines its own local context as somehow universal in scope. This is as true for Christian and Muslim heresiologists as it is for those engaged in the contemporary academic study of religion. Theorizing about religion, most significantly, is almost never done in a disinterested manner, but often instead for other purposes—often, to clarify oneself by clarifying the beliefs and deeds, but more often than not the misbeliefs and misdeeds, of others.

Why, we might ask, should things be any different today? Can we talk about the religions of others without committing the same taxonomic violence as heresiographers and theorists of centuries past (see Chapter 5 above)? Does switching the discourse from religions to faiths or spiritualities signal a change in intent and does it help to transform the ideological desires of earlier times to ones that we today imagine to be more inclusive and interfaith? Does transforming the conversation to the level of species, as our cousins in Cognitive Science of Religions (CSR) want us to do help us overcome our field's collective baggage (e.g., White 2017)? Can we have a natural history of religion (see Ambasciano 2018)? I have my doubts given the fact that CSR runs roughshod over the historical and cultural records of humans, and instead tries to distill something called "religion" in the brain or the DNA.

The traditional way to give definition to the academic study of religion is very easy, but simultaneously very unsatisfying. It is premised simply upon a negative, and I am sure many have frequently heard the refrain: "We do *not* do theology" or "we are *not* theologians." We instead engage in something much more academically rigorous, something that we subsequently call "the academic study of religion." This, of course, all sounds very good in theory, but since we never actually define what makes a study of religions "academic" other than the fact that we teach it at secular universities as opposed to seminaries, it lacks weight and would seem to be devoid of meaning. Recall Eliade's famous statement that the academic study of religion is defined by its ability to understand the morphology of the sacred (e.g., Eliade 1958). While we may well think that such a *raison d'être* guided a previous generation's understanding of our field and that we now know better, it still persists. While many today might feel uncomfortable about charting its morphology, the field remains very contented to talk about the sacred as if it named an aspect of reality that was somehow supra-human and thus special. But how does one study the supra-human and the special?

I remember being an undergraduate student at the University of Alberta in Edmonton, Canada, and recall that every course I took in the Department of Religious Studies there began with a faculty member repeating ad nauseum the first week of term that what we were about to engage in was the *academic* study of religion and not theology. After the first week the phrase would be quickly retired and replaced with often detailed descriptions of the religious beliefs and practices of others, often in ways that would make those of the particular religion in the class nod their heads in assent. The last week of the class would then witness the phrase reappear, whereupon we would be told again that we did not do theology over the course of the semester, but religious studies. I found this very odd. And I am sure that many in the field could recount similar stories. It would be tantamount, I realize in hindsight, to a historian saying to her class that they were going to study history, but not salvation history, and then go on to spend the rest of the semester studying the latter, and then subsequently ending the course emphasizing the former once again.

When it came to the study of Islam, what would go on to become my own area of specialization, this was often done in such a manner that would make any *salafi* (Muslim "fundamentalist") immensely happy. "Real" and "authentic," read Sunnī, Islam was presented as normative, and then there would be a healthy dose describing what Sufis do, the briefest description of the Shīʿa, and then just as minor a description of the visitation to the shrines of saints that would be described as "popular" or "unofficial" Islam. This continues to be our model for teaching Islam at the introductory level and, as I described in Chapter 5 above, is extremely problematic. I always find it curious—comical if the stakes were not so high—that, in order to justify and legitimate our academic selves, those of us in religious studies have ostensibly distanced ourselves from more confessional or theological approaches, even though we actually engage in precisely such activities. A critical approach to the study of religion means massive structural changes, and not simply removing a thin veneer, that many seem unwilling or unable to undertake. It categorically does not involve repeating the mantra "We are scholars, not theologians" until we believe this to be true.

In order to firm up this line, it has become fashionable—and, I would add, important—in the present day to debate the merits and utility of the very term "religion" (e.g., Nongbri 2013; Barton and Boyarin 2016).

If theologians and many in religious studies (see Chapter 1 above) are in the business of procuring "good" religion, their more critical colleagues are now engaged in analyzing the very discourses that bring religion into focus as a category of analysis.[3] This usually entails a quasi-"meta" and a quasi-historical analysis to show how "religion" is nothing more than a Western construct that is heavily invested in European intellectual and imperial hegemony. Indeed, the very term "religion," as people like Brent Nongbri (2013: 3) have argued, may not be as universal as many in the field have traditionally held or assumed. This is not to imply that peoples in different times and different places were not "religious," whatever that term might mean, but rather that the act of distinguishing between "religion" and "non-religion" is a distinctly modern development, with a very specific genealogy, that cannot be neatly retrofitted onto the past, let alone other cultures. We thus have to be cautious of assuming that people have always carved up the world—for example, into a realm of the sacred and another of the profane—in the same manner that we do today. Using antiquity, as an example, Nongbri writes:

> the real problem is that the particular concept of religion is absent in the ancient world. The very idea of "being religious" requires a companion notion of what it would mean to be "not religious," and this dichotomy was not part of the ancient world. To be sure, ancient people had words to describe proper reverence of the gods, but these terms were not what modern people would describe as strictly "religious." They formed part of a vocabulary of social relations more generally.
>
> (Nongbri 2013: 4)

Rather than help us understand other cultures, it is now argued, Western discourses created by the field of religious studies actually succeed in misreading and distorting other cultures, shaping them to fit problematic Western terms and categories of analysis.[4] These discourses have created "religions" for others—Hindu-ism, Buddh-ism, Shinto-ism, Juda-ism—not to mention, as Tomoko Masuzawa (2005) has shown, an entire discourse called "world religions" into which we can all too conveniently lump them. Because of this, as many who have made guest appearances in the pages above have well argued, the axioms and first principles of religious studies need to be systematically rethought, if not actually dismantled.

Recent years have witnessed terms such as "myth," "ritual," "Abrahamic religions" become extremely problematic.[5] In like manner we could point to very imprecise and monolithic terms used to designate specific religions over diverse geographic areas and temporal periods. These can include the likes of "Buddhism" or "Islam" (e.g., Josephson 2012). None of these terms—despite arguments by some to the contrary—are going away, especially not anytime soon.[6] Arguments for replacing them, while occasionally of interest, never possess much staying power. Think, for example, of Daniel Dubuisson's argument to replace "religion" with "cosmographic formation." While certainly an interesting suggestion, it went nowhere precisely because we are in the habit of speaking of "religions." So rather than argue for their replacement with what would inevitably be more and probably equally problematic terms, we need to add much-needed theoretical reflection on our existent ones with an eye towards sharpening them as categories of analysis. Though, this is not infrequently met with consternation at best and hostility at worst from our more traditionally minded colleagues, it is an endeavor that we must constantly engage in.

If we switch from our genealogical past to our postmodern or bricolaged present, is it possible to overcome our collective angst and arrive, as many now seem to want us to, at a set of critical *and* decolonial approaches to religion? What might that look like? In good academic fashion, it might be nice to tease out some of the tensions inherent to the so-called decolonial study of religion. The first, and most basic, issue that arises comes in the form of a question: Can a decolonial approach to the study of religion be critical?

Now, from what I can tell, a "decolonial" approach is an attempt to undo the logic of colonialism, especially its concomitant notions of hegemony, which is often associated with the Enlightenment project wherein, of course, we must also situate the roots of the modern university.[7] The goal of decolonial approaches, it seems to me, is to replace the logic that structures western civilization, including its systems of knowledge production, with a set of critical Indigenous methodologies (e.g., Smith 2012: 1–19). Or, if not actually replace them, then at least to call our attention to the fact that there are other ways of classifying the world around us. Without wanting to undermine the desire for such a replacement, I will say that there is an inevitable tension between critical and Indigenous methodologies, one that needs to be worked out, especially as far as the academic study of religion is concerned. What, in particular, defines "critical"? And, perhaps just as importantly, who is allowed to critique using such methodologies? In like manner, who is silenced in the process? There is an implicit danger that a decolonial approach to the study of religion might become—this, of course, is not to say that it has to—little more than a description using a set of Indigenous categories. This may well be just the other side of the coin where "other" local traditions are understood in terms of western (and thus themselves local) categories that are assumed to be universal in both nature and scope.

Within this context, there is a danger that a decolonial approach to religion might mean little more than taking an insider or non-critical approach to the beliefs of others, something one could argue is little different from the status quo in the field already. A decolonial approach, in other words, need not necessarily be a critical one. A decolonial approach to the study of Islam might well be one where the study of that tradition simply reverts to Indigenous terms and categories, and in such a manner that it become largely untranslatable using the categories of the modern Academy. Recall the situation in which Neusner found himself (Chapter 2 above), wherein Jewish texts were studied in Jewish seminaries in the same way they had been for centuries, and with little regard for the historical record. A decolonial approach also might mean that only those who are part of the tradition—and, in the case of Islamic studies, this would include converts to the tradition—can have a voice. Non-Muslims, in other words, would then simply have to refrain from entering the conversation, and function as cheerleaders to their Muslim colleagues. There is also the risk that the boundary between the academic study of Islam and Islamic perspectives on a particular topic might blur so that one does not know where the one begins and the other ends. There is a danger, in other words, that a decolonial approach to the study of religion might default to a set of largely noncritical, nonskeptical, and insider approaches. There are, of course, those who might argue that this is little different from the manner in which the academic study of religion is currently carried out in the North American Academy.

Religion and the Modern Nation State

Now we can undermine the imperialist, Protestant, Orientalist, and other problematic aspects of the category "religion" until we are blue in the face. But there is nothing we can do on account of the fact that the category "religion" is intimately caught up with the modern nation state (see, e.g., Sullivan 2018; Sullivan, Yelle, and Taussig-Rubbo 2011). It is that state—with is overlapping legal, political, and social infrastructures—that is the ultimate arbiter of what gets to count as a religion and what does not, and who is religious and who is not. It might well come as a surprise, but it is the courts, and not scholars of religion, that ultimately define what is and is not a religion or a religious act/belief. It would seem, then, that the study of religion is heavily invested in various nationalist or other regional contexts.[8]

While I certainly agree that "religion" is a modern term, that it is assumed to be universal, and has been used problematically to identify and/or taxonomize various actions or people in the recent or distant past, my goal here in the remainder of this chapter is to come at this rethinking from a somewhat different angle. While I certainly want to reinforce the above position, I want to suggest that this could not have been otherwise because there can be no Archimedean point from which to adequately describe or analyze religion on account of the study of religion's investment in the modern nation-state. In other words, the study of religion—and, for the moment, I am not even going to differentiate between theology and religious studies—in every Western country, is ultimately dependent upon, reflected in, and complexly intertwined with decidedly non-academic contexts. Religion is thus imagined, constructed, and situated in specific national frames of reference.[9] All of these factors, in turn, structure the study of religion.

What follows, then, provides a test case to illumine some of the intellectual and extra-intellectual contexts—the material conditions, if you will—that went into the production of a national discourse about the place, role, and function of religion as both a category and a set of discourses.[10] I work on the assumption that no discipline or field of study that has as its subject matter "religion" can escape being influenced by a complex set of demographic, social, political, legal, and other debates about the public and political understanding of religion. Such debates, I suggest, help structure the way religion is imagined nationally and subsequently reflected in how it is studied institutionally. Rather than speak about the study of religion as a generic field, then, it might be more profitable to think of various national (and nationalist) fields. This is not to say that transnational concerns do not exist; but it is to claim that every country has an often idiosyncratic set of anxieties that structure—legally, socially, politically, and so on—issues about, for example, what gets to count as a religion, how religion is discussed in the public sphere, and ultimately what the appropriate institutional setting or settings are wherein religion should be taught, and, of course, to whom it should be taught.

To test this hypothesis, I will focus on a couple of examples from Canada. I do this not only because I am a Canadian and a product of its system but also because the Canadian context is frequently ignored or bypassed when it comes to the study of religion in general and of North America in particular. When one thinks about the academic study of religion in North America, it is always the American context that is privileged. Given its history, and reinforcing my point, the overwhelming focus of this topic has been on the legal rulings that made the secular study of religion possible in the United States. More often than not this has involved an examination of the *School District of Abington Township, PA v. Schempp* Supreme Court case of 1963 (see, e.g., Imhoff 2016). This ruling forbade public school readings of the Bible as a violation of the Establishment Clause of the American Constitution, but just as significantly it also ruled in favor of teaching about religion as part of a general humanistic education. This ruling led directly to the founding of the American Academy of Religion (AAR) in the same year and the subsequent creation of departments of religion or religious studies in state universities throughout the country. That ruling, for all intents and purposes, made the secular study of religion possible in the United States.

Indeed, the impetus for this chapter is to provide a direct response to the American desire to make their narratives universal. I recall a conversation I had with Canadian graduate students at the American Academy of Religion (AAR) about nine years ago. We talked about the history of religious studies in Canada, and several in that group mentioned the Schempp Supreme Court ruling in the United States that helped create the non-denominational study of religion in American state universities. I still remember how they tried to tell me that the Canadian model was also influenced by the US Supreme Court decision since, after all, departments of religious studies began to flourish in Canada at around the same time. While I did not object to the chronological convergence, the underlying cause did not seem right to me. So, I have spent much of the following decade trying to provide an accurate and informed response to this group (the results of this may be found in Hughes 2020b).

It would be a mistake to assume that the American story was standard, let alone normal. Instead, I would suggest that the American story is precisely that, a story that developed out of a set of idiosyncratic concerns unique to that country. We could similarly argue that how the study of religion came to be—indeed, how it continues to be configured in places such as Britain, France, Italy, Germany, Belgium, Switzerland, Austria,

Greece, and so on—is the direct product of those countries' own distinct and often idiosyncratic legal, theological, denominational, judicial, and social frameworks, all of which have been, and continue to be, forced to deal in some way, shape, or form with religion broadly conceived.

In this context, the story of the study of religion in Canada is, in many ways, the story of Canada itself. Its unfolding reveals its development from religious exclusion to secularism, from Christocentrism to multiculturalism, and from theology carried out in seminaries to the study of religion carried out in secular universities. Within a much larger context (as I try to set out in Hughes 2020b), it is intimately connected to the story of geographic expansion and growing national confidence in the face of British and subsequent American influence. Finally, it is the story of institutional tensions, legal battles, and constitutional patriation over the course of the twentieth century. The story of the study of religion in any country is, after all, the story of how that country imagines itself, of its ability to deal (or not) with difference, religious or otherwise, and, in the final analysis, of how it situates itself in the world and in the community of nations. Canada is certainly not unique in this respect, but merely, as the present study shows, exemplary.

Now in order to test this hypothesis I want to focus on two examples. The first is the United Church of Canada, and the second is the transition from the *Canadian Journal of Theology* to *Studies in Religion/sciences religieuses* in the early 1970s. My goal in doing this is to show that the study of religion does not fall from the sky, but emerges slowly and gradually from a set of nationalist narratives and institutional spaces that situate religion—and more importantly for my narrative, the place of the study of religion—within a set of larger national contexts. I do not think that here is either the time or the place to go into lots of details with these examples. I mention them briefly not to provide a study of a forgotten aspect in Canadian history, but only to show that the study of religion comes from somewhere. And this somewhere is, more often than not, tied to a host of political and legal factors that ultimately determine how the modern nation state thinks about religion and, in the process, itself.

United Church of Canada

The first example I want to look at is the formation of the United Church of Canada in the first decades of the twentieth century. In 1924, three large mainline Protestant denominations—Presbyterian, Methodist, and Congregationalist—joined forces to found what would become known as the United Church of Canada with the goal of establishing a unified national Church for the young country (Grant 1967; McIntire 2012). Though it could never of course fulfil that role, especially since the Anglican and Baptist churches refused to join, I mention it here because the creation of the United Church, unbeknownst at the time, actually succeeded in destabilizing the denominationalism that had plagued Eastern Canada for much of its history, even predating Dominion in 1867. This, in turn, would play a crucial role in the creation of the academic study of religion in Canada because such destabilization cleared the necessary intellectual space for a less sectarian and potentially more ecumenical approach to the study about religion.

Within this context it might be worth noting that Canada, unlike the United States, was never seen as a religious haven or refuge for Christians escaping persecution in the Old World (Grant 1967: 7). Canada has no myth of origins: people went there to make money in, for example, the fur trade. Isolation, large-scale immigration (with more than a million immigrants arriving from Britain and Europe between 1815 and 1850) (Buckner 1993), and the need for theological creativity thus triangulated to produce a situation that was well-disposed toward new forms of or experiments with traditional Christian denominations that had not been entertained in the Old World. The United Church of Canada was inaugurated on June 10, 1925, in a ceremony held, perhaps fittingly enough, in the Mutual Street Arena, the main hockey arena in Toronto prior to the opening of Maple Leaf Gardens in 1931 (Stebner 2012: 40).

In order to train clergy, there was a need for seminaries. Here we should not forget that if one of the main reasons, historically, to study the religions of others was to understand better one's own beliefs, one of the main reasons to study one's own involved the training of clergy. In the new seminaries associated with the United Church, unlike those of its predecessors or rivals, the teachings of modern biblical criticism were taught. Training for the ministry, as outlined in its Basis of Union, was predicated on the attainment of a BA that included Greek; this was to be followed by three years in the study of theology, as "strongly recommended by the Church" (United Church of Canada 1925: II.3(I)). Theological study, as the document goes on to recount in its listing of "suggested subjects," could be fulfilled by courses such as the following:

Old Testament Language and Literature, including Textual Criticism. Exegesis, Biblical Theology Introduction, Old Testament History and Old Testament Canon; New Testament Language and Literature, including Textual Criticism, Exegesis, Biblical Theology, Introduction, New Testament History and New Testament Canon; English Bible; Church History, including Symbolics; Systematic Theology; Apologetics, including Philosophy of Religion, History of Religion, and Comparative Religion; Christian Ethics and Sociology; Christian Missions; Practical Training, including preparation and delivery of sermons.

(United Church of Canada 1925: II.3(I))

We see from this list that the newly formed United Church of Canada was not averse to the teachings of modern biblical criticism and so-called comparative religion. Indeed, the church was highly ecumenical from the start, and its policies, perhaps not surprisingly, were, at least relatively speaking, inclusive and liberal. It tended, in other words, to feel less threatened than the more traditional denominations by higher criticism.

This was an important precursor to the study of religion (Moir 1982). On account of its liberalism and ecumenicism, higher criticism seems to have posed less of a threat to the United Church than traditional mainline denominations. The dismantling of traditional denominations when combined with the rise and eventual broad-based dissemination of higher biblical criticism associated with secular institutions such as the University of Toronto, and with the United Church's willingness to have potential clergy trained in this criticism, created a situation in which Canadians could begin to think more critically about religion, including things like biblical inerrancy (ibid.).

I do not want to go into too much detail here, but I will close this first example by saying that the formation of the United Church of Canada, from the vantage point of hindsight, played an important role in the ways Canadians thought about religion. If a previous generation was mistrustful of higher criticism, especially when it was coupled with Darwinism, a new generation was not and this was because a new church in Canada led the way in thinking about religion in a relatively new manner. This was an important and necessary first step in the formation of the non-theological study of religion in the Canadian context.

Canadian Journal of Theology to *Studies in Religion/Sciences religieuses*

A second example that made this possible concerns the venues of dissemination for discussing religion in the Canadian context. There have been three main journals over the years devoted to the subject, the *Canadian Journal of Religious Thought* (1924–1932), which, despite the inclusive title is exclusively Christian and theological, though often of the same ecumenical spirit that powered the formation of the United Church of Canada in the same years. The second was the *Canadian Journal of Theology* (1955–1970), hereafter *CJT*, and *Studies in Religion/Sciences religieuses* (1971–present), hereafter *SR*. I want to focus in particular on the transition from *CJT* to *SR*, especially as framed within the larger national context about immigration and multiculturalism. My argument, once again, is that the study of religion as an academic process and discourse is intimately connected to much larger national conversations that structure and shape it.

The focus of *CJT* was solely Christian, and a perusal of the contents quickly bears this out. In an editorial from the third issue of the first volume, the journal's aim is set out:

> to discuss those issues of Christian faith and practice which bear directly on the life of the Church and on the thinking and action of the Christian believer, and to do this against the background of the past history and the present circumstances of the Christian communions of Canada. It is, in other words, essentially a journal of theology, devoted to the expression of Christian truth and to the clarification of the way of life which that truth involves.
>
> (CJT Editors 1955a: 139)

The new journal was published by the University of Toronto Press with an initial subscription of 750 (CJT Editors 1955b: 67), which had jumped to 1,300 by volume 3 (CJT Editors 1957: 68). Although more amenable to higher criticism, the journal still saw its primary mandate as being to advocate for Christian theological positions. "One of the most disturbing development of our time is the abandonment, by the individual, of moral responsibility," the editors write in a 1956 editorial, and "our situation has arisen because we have largely lost our theological concern for life" (CJT Editors 1956: 125).

Though change was certainly in the air as several articles between that editorial and the mid-1960s begin to acknowledge the need for a non-sectarian study of religion. It is, however, unclear what the authors meant by that term given the fact that the journal's mandate remained devoted to Christianity and to theological method. An editorial from 1958 encouraged more pastors, ministers, and priests to contribute so that the journal might become more relevant to preaching activities (CJT Editors 1958: 163–164). A glaring instance of the journal's Christocentrism is the curious case of Ismail al-Faruqi, a scholar of Islam at McGill. In 1961 he wrote an article titled "On the Significance of Niebuhr's Ideas of Society," which is significant for at least two reasons. First, though a scholar of Islam, al-Faruqi could only appear in the pages of the journal if he wrote on a topic relevant to Christian theology. This in itself might not be surprising given the journal's mandate. The second reason, though, is jarring. Since al-Faruqi was not a Christian, the article had to be introduced by the editor, who writes that "it is not usual to preface a contribution to this journal with an introductory paragraph, but the article which follows has certain unusual features which perhaps justify an exception in this instance" (CJT Editors 1961: 99).

Following this, the editor moves to assure his readers that although al-Faruqi is not a Christian, he is at the very least a devout religious person:

> Dr. Faruqi is a devout Muslim whose faith has impressed all his colleagues by its qualities of conviction and sincerity ... His present assignment is a critique of the Christian ethic from the Muslim point of view ... Not everyone will accept his estimate of Jesus and his teaching ... Nevertheless it is important that we in the West should discover how we appear to eastern eyes.
>
> (CJT Editors 1961: 99)

Despite the patronizing tone, however, clearly the winds of change were in the air, if not necessarily in the pages of the journal. We see this, for example, in changing immigration patterns, the constitutional definition of Canada as an officially bilingual and multicultural country, the stirrings of counterculture, and related diminution of attendance at mainline churches. On July 19, 1963, for example, Prime Minister Lester B. Pearson struck a Royal Commission on Bilingualism and Biculturalism in order "to recommend what steps should be taken to develop the Canadian Confederation on the basis of an equal partnership between the two founding races, taking into account the contribution made by the other ethnic groups to the cultural enrichment of Canada and the measures that should be taken to safeguard that contribution."[11]

The commission recommended, among other things, that bilingual districts be created in regions of Canada where members of the minority community, be they French or English, made up 10 per cent or more of the local population; that children be able to attend schools in the language of their parents' choice in regions where there was sufficient demand; that Ottawa become a bilingual city; and that English and French be declared the official languages of Canada.

In 1969, Pearson's successor, Pierre Elliot Trudeau passed the Official Languages Act/Loi sur les langues officielles that made Canada officially bilingual. Two years later, in a speech to the House of Commons on October 8, 1971, Trudeau announced the new policy of multiculturalism:

> It was the view of the royal commission, shared by the government and, I am sure, by all Canadians, that there cannot be one cultural policy for the Canadians of British and French origins, another for the original peoples and yet a third for all others. For although there are two official languages, there is no official culture, nor does any ethnic group take precedence over any other. No citizen or group of citizens is other than Canadian, and all should be treated fairly.[12]

He then proposed that the cultural freedom of all individuals be preserved and that the cultural contributions of diverse ethnic groups to Canadian society be recognized:

> The policy I am announcing today accepts the contention of the other cultural communities that they, too, are essential elements in Canada and deserve government assistance in order to contribute to regional and national life in ways that derive from their heritage yet are distinctly Canadian.[13]

Relatedly, the Immigration Act of 1976 further contributed to this more inclusive pattern of immigration. For example, it was the first immigration act to include refugees—as defined by the UN's Convention Relating to the Status of Refugees—as a distinct class. It also sought to "[e]nsure that any person who seeks admission to Canada on either a permanent or temporary basis is subject to standards of admission that do not discriminate on grounds of race, national or ethnic origin, colour, religion or sex."[14]

The question then arises: How could a national journal devoted to religion that was solely anglophone and exclusively engaged in Christian theological apologetics possibly continue to justify its existence in the face of such rapid changes in Canadian society?

Well, it became increasingly difficult, if not impossible. The *CJT*'s final editorial, announcing the journal's termination, makes this explicit. Therein, the Rev. Eugene R. Fairweather, the journal's last editor, writes: "Early in 1971 the University of Toronto Press will issue the first number of a new quarterly journal devoted to a wide range of religious studies, including those scholarly disciplines which have been regularly represented in the pages of this Journal" (Fairweather 1970: 127). He calls the new journal "a fresh and promising venture in religious publishing" (ibid.). He also notes:

> In 1970 a Canadian university which fails to provide for religious studies, Christian and non-Christian, invites the criticism that its curriculum is anachronistic and inadequate. In 1970 the Canadian theological faculty or seminary which tries to work in isolation from the wider community of theological and religious scholarship is on the way to becoming the underprivileged exception to a recognized rule. We may reasonably hope that the coming decade will see an unprecedented flowering of religious and theological studies in the great academic centers of this country.
>
> (Fairweather 1970: 128)

As Canadian society became increasingly diverse and as the federal government began to encourage such diversity, journals like the *CJT* were now ineligible for federal funds. Just as Canadian society was diversifying, so, too was the study of religion. Departments of religious studies, funded solely by taxpayer dollars, began to appear in select Canadian universities, scholarly organizations were beginning to develop, and *CJT*, as Fairweather duly noted, was increasingly anachronistic. These new departments, moreover, increasingly sought out new methodologies as they set out to switch their purview to all religions and not just Christianity and its theological elaboration. The study of religion now shifted from the context of the religious seminary to the secular university. In the place of *CJT* a new journal, *SR*, now appeared. The latter journal, as articulated in its inaugural editorial, would be bilingual (and it definitely succeeded in this respect) and engage with other religious traditions. I quote from that editorial:

> The editors of *Studies in Religion / Sciences religieuses* have accepted the task of creating a Canadian journal to cover the whole field of the academic study of religion. As the successor to the Canadian Journal of Theology, SR will continue to serve scholars in the various theological disciplines who formally looked to CJT as an organ for the publication of their work. But the special interest of these scholars will now take their place in a

wider context of the academic study of religion and religions by a variety of methodologies.

(Nicholls 1971: 1)

The study of religion, then, became part of Canada's multicultural self-definition. The federal government's policy of Multiculturalism made the study of religion possible, and *not* vice versa. Coincidentally, at around the same time the US also began to develop departments of religious studies in public universities thanks to the Supreme Court ruling mentioned earlier. But Canada, not unlike the UK, never had such separation between church and state. If the reason for the change of institutional context in the United States was legal, in Canada it was demographic and the direct result of a more liberal immigration policy and the rise of multiculturalism as official federal policy. This is not to imply that the academic study of religion looked (or continues to look) different in Canada than it does in the United States or even in other European countries. On the contrary, and much more modestly, it is only to suggest that the larger legal, demographic, and social conditions that facilitated such study are considerably different in various countries. This is why, it seems to me, we have to pay attention to precisely these sorts of national and legal anxieties about religion.

Conclusions

Allow me now to move towards something of a conclusion. I have presented these two examples not because I necessarily think that they are interesting in and of themselves. On the contrary, I have done so because, it seems to me, they are exemplary of a much larger issue that I have tried to get at here. That issue is how the modern nation state thinks about religion. I trust you will agree with me when I say that there is no one-size-fits-all way to go about this. The Canadian situation is much different from the American one, which in turn is much different from the UK, the French, and the German contexts to name only a few Western countries with fairly lengthy histories of academic religious studies.

Though there is a field of religious studies that crosses international borders, how that field came to be in each of the countries wherein the field exists is by no means uniform. How are departments funded? How are they structured? Where are they situated, and so on and so forth. It is incumbent upon us to investigate the ways in which these processes took shape—and indeed continue to take shape—in specific nationalist contexts. Indeed, I would go so far as to say that such discourses are just as important, if not more so, than those that want to argue that religion is a woefully inaccurate term to use. Before we can rethink different terms for "religion" or argue about its inaccuracies—which it most certainly possesses—we need to be cognizant of the fact that religion and its taxonomy, is an important part of the modern nation state.

The study of religion, be it confessional or non-confessional, accordingly is heavily invested in the modern nation-state. That investment points to a number of decidedly non-academic contexts—demographic, social, political, legal—that define how we talk about, or want to talk about, religion in the public sphere. Those contexts subsequently help structure the way religion is envisioned nationally and how it is studied institutionally.

Religion, then, is imagined, constructed, and situated within specific national frames of reference. The present chapter has made the case that we need to take seriously the various localized contexts in which modern nation-states came into existence simultaneously with the production of various discourses on religion. The anxieties generated as a result of this coexistence constantly reappear in the way religion is taught—where, by whom, to whom, and about what. This is not to imply that there are not transnational concerns that help define the study of religion in a global context. But it is to state that every liberal, Western democracy has its own specific and unique concerns and anxieties over religion that determine where and how it ought to be located and that structure religion's place within legal and political systems in addition to institutions of higher learning.

Afterword

Most academic fields have fairly clear and, for the most part circumscribed, objects of study. Art history, for example, studies art. Political science examines political systems. Mathematics examines numbers. And so on. The subject matter of religious studies, by contrast, is a little more complicated. One would think it studies "religion." But then we quickly get bogged down in definitions of just what "religion" is (see Hughes and McCutcheon 2021). Is it an interior state or emotion? Is it a political will to power? Or, is it something grounded in social or psychological forces? While people working in the Cognitive Science of Religion (CSR) have recently come on the scene seeking to understand religion's root causes in the laboratory, the results are often technical and frequently too narrow in their focus, especially for anyone interested in matters historical or textual. Moreover, CSR give us very little to no sense of how religion either functions or operates in society.

Others have argued that religious eperiences are too difficult to get at and ascertain with any degree of precision, and that more time and energy should be devoted to analyzing the external effects of such emotions and states. We thus see courses and books devoted to topics as diverse as "religion and politics," "religion and art," religion and theory," and/or "religion and society." Often left unqueried, however, is the first term, not to mention the conjunction that connects it to the set of second words. Recent years have witnessed a tendency on the part of some to include "lived religion" or "material religion" as a way to signal that we should focus not just on elites, but also on more popular forms. Again, though, the emphasis is on the "lived" or the "material" and less the "religion," which continues to remain problematically out of focus.

Despite all these internal and external approaches, including a concomitant set of theoretical interventions that argue that religion is nothing but a Western construct, religious studies as a field of study remains largely rudderless. Theological interests have once again—if in fact they ever left—coopted the field. To this there has been added a large dose of political correctness brought on by identity politics. The result is that interfaith dialogue and a desire for justice has largely replaced critical analysis. Or, perhaps more accurately, these features have not replaced critical scholarship—something that has been, after all, woefully lacking in the academic study of religion—so much as they have replaced an equally problematic quest for the sacred including a phenomenological method used to undertake the task. While there is certainly nothing wrong with religious groups talking to one another and a socially just society is what we all should work for, I remain unconvinced that both topics should be singled out as paramount research agenda for the field. A focus on these issues, as I hope should be clear by now, is predicated on a number of assumptions about the nature of religion, not to mention the numerous fissures and blind spots that travel in their wake.

Instead of such approaches, the essays in this volume have tried to call attention precisely to some of these assumptions, fissures, and blind spots. Though my points of departure were the study of Islam and the study of Judaism, the issues raised above should be of interest to all in the field of religious studies and, I would hope, those in cognate fields and disciplines who examine features of "religion." Collectively, the above chapters have argued that data is constructed, not natural, and that it is necessary to reflect on whence, wherefrom, why, and how we do what we do. What terms, for example, bring data into existence? What narratives structure our data, whether through inclusion or—just as importantly, if not more so—exclusion? Our terms and narratives, much like fields and disciplines that are constructed out of them, come from somewhere and they have been used to argue for all sorts of things, often time at cross purposes with one another. Fields of study, after all, are full of dominant narratives that have created a consensus and a status quo. Rather that follow consensus, however, it is important to try to undermine the hegemony and dominance it creates. This ought not be done solely for the sake of deconstruction or disciplinary nihilism, but to show how in order to move forward we need to revisit—constantly—how we got to where we are in the first place.

This study, like all of my work, emerges from the critical wing of religious studies. However, because the field tends to be a generalist one, increasingly interested in matters of interfaith relations and justice issues, it often does so at the expense of language work, historical analysis, and criticism. Religious studies, thus, tends to eschew technical studies of texts in the manner that, say, more traditional subfields such as Islamic or Jewish studies have done. This tension creates a sense of confusion that weaves throughout the chapters above. At what point is a study too technical, of interest to only a few other specialists, or when does it become too general and unrecognizable to fellow specialists outside of religious studies? Within this context, the greatest task for those of us who work in religious studies is to translate between the highly technical specifics of our chosen subfields, in this case Islamic and Jewish studies, and the often too general framework provided by our disciplinary home.

Reflection upon my own position as "somewhere between" Islam and Judaism, and occupying intellectual space "somewhere between" Islamic studies and Jewish studies, ultimately returns me to the importance of dislocation. In the final analysis, it would seem to be more intellectually profitable to occupy such uncertain terrain because, from it, one is able—from the vantage point of one subfield—to point out some of the structural issues and systemic problems of the other, and of course vice versa. This middle ground, however, need not be defined either by loneliness or alienation so much as by a desire to reach a different point of repose. A place in which those in each subfield unfortunately seem to be unaware. When we are blinded by our own discourses and when we lack attunement to critical thinking then, at that instance, we are no longer between, but truly lost.

Notes

Introduction

1. For a good critique of this "world religions" paradigm, see the essays collected in Cotter and Robertson 2016.

Chapter 1

1. This chapter began as a lecture that was to be delivered at the Institute for Ismaili Studies on March 24, 2020, that was unfortunately cancelled on account of the COVID-19 pandemic. Some of these comments, especially those in the opening section, were recycled in Hughes 2021a.
2. The classic account, of course, being Said 1978. To this we could also add the much bolder account of Hallaq 2018.
3. As a Canadian I prefer to use the Canadian term LGBTQ2S (lesbian, gay, bisexual, transgender, queer, and two spirited) as opposed to the more customary LGBTQ.
4. To quote from that year's call for papers: "This year's annual meeting theme is Revolutionary Love. Neither word captures the complexity of the theme, but I use the word 'love' in the broadest possible sense, including love as a social and political force, a structural reality, a collective endeavor, a shared social practice, a language, a relationship, a moment, a gesture, an identity, a quest. The membership of the AAR includes scholars who study religious traditions and historical moments of enormous variety. It's hard to imagine any area of study, however, that does not reflect on the topic of 'love'—again, defined as broadly and creatively as possible—in one form or another. I use the term 'revolutionary' next to 'love' to turn our attention to love that seeks to transform the world, which includes love that both tears down and builds up. To provoke our thinking, let me offer the prophetic words of James Baldwin, 'I use the word love here not merely in the personal sense but as a state of being, or a state of grace—not in the infantile American sense of being made happy but in the tough and universal sense of quest and daring and growth.'"

5. Here I will list my usual conversation partners, both literal and literary: Arnal and McCutcheon 2013; Cotter and Robertson 2016; Dubuisson 2003, 2006 [1993]; Fitzgerald 2000; Lincoln 2000; Martin 2014; Masuzawa 2005; McCutcheon 1997, 2003, 2014; Owen 2011; Sheedy 2018; J. Z. Smith 1990, 2004; Touna 2017.
6. Most important in this regard is Lincoln 2006.
7. Just as one does not need to be Jewish to study Judaism or, to use the words of Gershom Scholem—the pioneering scholar of Kabbalah or Jewish mysticism, when asked if he was a kabbalist—"one does not need to be a square to study geometry."
8. Unfortunately, Schubel's essay (2014a), "Thoughts on Dissecting an Octopus," which was housed at the *Religion Bulletin Blog* is no longer available. A synopsis of it, however, may be found at https://bulletin.equinoxpub.com/2014/12/rethinking-contested-ground-the-study-of-islam-inand-the-study-of-religion.
9. Schubel (2014b) had also written an online review essay of Hughes 2012c in the Society for Contemporary Thought and the Islamicate World (SCTIW). Unfortunately, the link is no longer active.
10. Though some have tried to put the origins of the "objective" study of religion earlier. Most notable are Barton and Boyarin (2016), who put it in late antiquity. Wasserstrom (1988) located it in the literature associated with the medieval Islamic heresiographcial traditions. Stroumsa (2010) puts it later in early modern Europe and the Age of Empires.
11. See, for example, the names cited in note 5 above.
12. Parts of the following three paragraphs rework Hughes 2017a.
13. This section reworks Hughes 2021a.
14. For a recent treatment of some of the salient issues, see Sheedy 2018.
15. Interestingly, Norton's learned discussion lumps Jews in with Europeans (e.g., 16–18). While I certainly understand why, it alas overlooks the plight of Jews—and the contortions they had to put themselves in—so as to be "accepted" by mainstream (read: Christian) European cultures.
16. I am grateful to Francesco Chiabotti and Marco Schöller for their help in formulating this paragraph. Any mistakes are mine alone.
17. One such Center may be found at Frankfurt/Gießen. Their webpage, including an English description of its structure, may be found at www.goethe-university-frankfurt.de/50747235/Center_for_Islamic_Studies.
18. On the tensions between these approaches—scholarly, structural, and financial—see the essays in Schöller and Khorchide 2012.

Chapter 2

1. Parts of this chapter originated as a lecture "It's Dark Outside: Destabilizing 'Judaism' in Late Antique Judeo-Islam," delivered at a workshop titled "Looking Outward: Reframing Jewish Studies" held at Emory University in Atlanta.
2. See, for example, the comments in Wiese 2005. I have tried to tell this larger story in Hughes 2013c: 39–56.
3. This is why someone like Hermann Cohen (1842–1918) could proclaim that Jews had to be stateless because, unlike other peoples, their gift of monotheism was spiritual, not territorial. "Monotheism, however, did not come to a final close in the Bible," he would write, "thus Israel, as a nation is nothing other than the mere symbol for the desired unity of humankind. The Greek people could not present such a symbol; for it did not know the concept of humankind. The idea of one humankind could only arise under the one God. The one God, however, arose in the one people. Therefore this one people had to endure" (Cohen 1995 [1919]: 252–253).
4. This is not the place to chart this history. I try to do so in Hughes 2013c: 57–76. See also the important study in Ritterband and Wechsler 1994.
5. For a study of the study of religion in Canada, which offers a somewhat different paradigm, see Hughes 2020b.
6. And subsequently recycled by the likes of Lewis 1984: xi, 191; Sarah Stroumsa 2011: 3–6.
7. Parts of this section rework Hughes 2016b.
8. This note comes from the Neusner archives that may be found at the American Jewish Archives in Cincinnati, which I consulted regularly in writing his authorized biography (Hughes 2016a).
9. Retrieved from https://networks.h-net.org/node/28655/discussions/2616718/job-irving-m-and-marilyn-c-shuman-visiting-assistant-professor.
10. After my experience I complained to the Association for Jewish Studies, the main organization devoted to Jewish studies in the US. They said and did nothing. I also lodged a complaint with the *Chronicle of Higher Education*, which did pick up the story (Adams 2017).

Chapter 3

1. Versions of this chapter were originally given as the David Patterson Lecture at the Oxford Center for Hebrew and Jewish Studies and then again at the Centre for Jewish Studies at the University of Manchester in November of 2019, and then at the University of Chester in January of 2020. Parts of this chapter also rework Hughes 2020a, but with a much different theoretical focus.

2. Indeed, we still largely divide Jewish Studies along their lines—history, philosophy, kabbalah and hasidut, parshanut, and so on—and perhaps as we try to rethink the internal gaze, we need to rethink such neat and tidy divisions.
3. Mazuz (2014), for example, can opine (without a shred of evidence) that: "Our findings demonstrate that the Medinan Jews were Talmudic-Rabbinic Jews in almost every respect. Their sages believed in using homiletic Interpretation (*derash*) of the Scriptures, as did the sages of the Talmud. On many halakhic issues, their observations were identical to those of the Talmudic sages. In addition, they held Rabbinic beliefs, sayings, and motifs derived from Midrashic literature" (99). I shall discuss this in greater detail below.
4. On the trope of "midwife," see Hughes 2017b: 36–61.
5. Witness, for example, the omission in the otherwise excellent work by Schäfer 1995.
6. The metaphor and language here is indebted to Bulliet 1994.
7. Parts of this section draw on examples I have used in Hughes 2017b: 50–51.
8. Pre-Islamic Arabia, for example, was composed of quite distinctive peoples. See Hoyland 2001: 11. On the notion of "Arabs" as a much later construct to unify the fledgling empire, see Webb 2016.
9. A family tomb erected in 42CE that refers to a Jew comes from Hegra (roughly 50 km to the northwest of Yathrib). See Healey 1993: no. 4.
10. Most of the pre-Islamic Arab sources are found in inscriptions and papyri. See, e.g., Healey 1993; al-Ghabban et al. 2010. On the non-Muslim sources, see Hoyland 1997.
11. On these traditions, see Gil 1984: 208. Newby (1988: 47) seems to accept them; cf., Goitein 1955: 48–49.
12. Bowersock 2013. Though see also *Pseudo-Dionysus of Tel-Mahre, Chronicle II*, ed. J.B. Chabot 1996 [1933]: 54–56. See also Hatke 2013.
13. Indeed, as Nebes (2010) suggests, it is "quite understandable to find the Ḥimyar joining the other form of monotheism a short time later, if only as an ideological countermeasure against their traditional Aksumite rivals and in order to stem the growing influence of the Byzantine Empire in the region" (39–40).
14. *Raḥmānān*, for example, is also used in the largely Christian Syriac to refer to God. See Levy 1876–1889: 417b.
15. For a facsimile, see Naveh 1999–2000: 619–635.
16. Here I differ from Newby (2013: 39) who argues that these "Arabian Jews were rabbinic in that they were organized into congregations headed by rabbis, and they were in touch, at least limitedly, with the Babylonian academies." But then he acknowledges, and in this sense I do agree with him, that "it is clear that practices and beliefs of the Arabian Jews were different from the Judaism idealized in the Babylonian Talmud." But rather than leave it at that, I

am here interested in examining the contours and contents of South Arabian "Judaism."
17. Robin 2004: 891. A facsimile of the inscription may be found in Naveh 2003: 117–120.
18. See, for example, the sixth-century Christian *Book of the Himyarites* (Moburg 1924).

Chapter 4

1. By the phrase "framers of Islam," I refer to, among others, qurʾānic redactors, ḥadīth collectors, early legists, *mutakallimūn*, and popular preachers. On the social, political, and historical setting of these types of individuals who sought to understand their past, the historical record, and how they differed from other genres of contemporaneous Arabic literature, see Robinson 2002: 3–17.
2. Perhaps most recently and forcefully put in Fowden 2014: 1–17.
3. For relevant context, see Harries and Wood 1993; Matthews 2000; Millar 2006.
4. I realize that recent years have witnessed a great deal of criticism of the category "religion," and whether or not it is anachronistic to apply it to other times and places beyond the modern Euro-American West. Most recently, see McCutcheon 1997; Fitzgerald 2000; Nongbri 2013; Barton and Boyarin 2016. While I sympathize with the sentiment, I remain convinced that, as per the *Theodosian Code*, there nevertheless remains some sort of idea—metaphysical, ethical, cultural, whatever we want to call it—that people hold that makes them perceive themselves as different from other social groups. Whether we want to call this "religion," especially as the term came to be defined in Protestant circles wherefrom the modern academic study of religion emerged, or something else is not my main concern here.
5. See, for example, McClure 1979; Cameron 2003; Flower 2013.
6. Karamustafa (2010: 95–97), for example, has argued that one of the Qurʾān's main concerns is with *ummāt* (sg. *umma*, to wit, "religious communities") than it is with other descriptors, such as *shuʿūb* ("race/ethnicity"). See also Denny 2005: 372–373.
7. See the recent and important work of Tannous 2018: 225–232; Sahner 2018: 1–7.
8. For the complexities of this rapid spread, see Hoyland 2014. For an account of some of the various Christian responses to it, see Penn 2015b. More generally, see Penn 2015a: 102–140. See also Griffiths 2010: 23–44.
9. A particularly good example of an interpretive grid that situates this process is Powers 2009: 3–31.

10. The first date in each of these configurations refers to the year in the traditional Muslim calendar (*anno hegirae*), whereas the second refers to the Gregorian calendar.
11. Crone and Hinds 1986: 4–23. Indeed, Hinds (1960–2005) subsequently argues that it was the *miḥna*, or inquisition of al-Maʾmūn (d. 218/833) that succeeded in putting an end to this conception of the caliphate.
12. E.g., Ibn al-Nadīm 1872 (vol. 2): 327–338. English translation: Ibn al-Nadīm 1970 (vol. 2): 773–806 (vol. 2).
13. Perhaps the most famous Jew in all of Islamic literature, ʿAbd Allāh Ibn Sabaʾ, is believed to have been a Jew from Yemen who converted to Islam after the death of Muhammad. More than anyone else, he is credited with subverting the pristine unity of the early Muslim community. Were it not for him and his deceitful actions, it is imagined that the originary community would have remained unified and immune from subsequent sectarianism. Relevant literature is Friedländer 1909–1910. Most recently, see Anthony 2012. Though not important to my argument here, it is perhaps worth pointing out that his Jewish bona fides have been questioned by some. Most notable is Hodgson 1955, 1960–2005.
14. Lieu 1985: 82–83. Though as Stroumsa and Stroumsa (1988) argue, this "tolerance" may well have been only indirect as a result of the Umayyad preoccupation with other matters (39).
15. On Wāṣil b. ʿAtāʾ, more generally, see S. Stroumsa 1990.
16. This is certainly not the place to discuss the formation of the legal schools, only to note that they were, like so much in this period, under construction. For relevant background, see Melchert 1997: 1–31; Calder 1993: 223–243; Schacht 1950: 11–20; Lowry 2007: 23–59; Hallaq 2001: 1–10.
17. Hodgson 1974: 386–392. See further the discussion in Melchert 2002. The term "*ḥadīth* folk" has the distinct advantage of avoiding the idea that they were somehow older or more authoritative than their adversaries, especially the rationalist theologians (*mutakallimūn*).
18. On the general fear of their infiltration, see al-Murtaḍā 1373/1954: 127.
19. On Abd al-Karīm b. Abī al-ʿAwjāʾ, see al-Bīrūnī 1879: 67–68; al-Baghdādī 1910 [1328]: 167–168. More generally see Chokr 1993: 131–140. See further Stroumsa and Stroumsa 1988: 55–57.
20. E.g., "Say, 'If mankind and the jinn gathered in order to produce the like of this Qurʾān, they could not produce the like of it, even if they were to each other assistants'" (Q 17/88; c.f., 52/30–34).
21. Indeed, it is a charge that would continue to be levelled against critics. Maribel Fierro (2012), for example, has shown how the Andalusī thinker Ibn Ḥazm (994–1064) charged an unknown Jew, believed to be Ismāʿīl Ibn Naghrīla, with being a *zindīq* for trying to imitate the Qurʾān.

22. See van Ess 1991–1997, vol. 2: 29, 34–36. See further, van Ess 1981: 156. See also Cassarino 2000: 101–114.
23. Our sources do not give a clear indication of the reason for the persecution, but, as de Blois notes, it may surely be no coincidence that it occurred shortly after the conversion of the Uyghur rulers to Manichaeism in 762. This meant that Manichaeism suddenly became the state religion of an important neighboring kingdom to the ʿAbbāsid Empire and was evidently perceived as a threat to the security of the caliphate. See de Blois 1960–2005: 512.
24. Ibn al-Nadīm relates a story that subsequent to the period under discussion here, Manichaeans freely migrated back and forth between Transoxania and Iraq, and that, during the reign of al-Muktadir (r. 295–320/908–932), the Manichaeans in Samarqand were actually protected from the Muslim overlords through an intervention of "the king of China." See Ibn al-Nadīm 1872 (vol. 2): 337 (English: 1970 (vol. 2): 802–803). The story, according to de Blois, "bristles with anachronisms and has little historic value" (1960–2005: 512).
25. On the denial of any connection, see Zaman 1997: 136–138. He argues that whereas al-Mahdī's *miḥna* was an attempt to weed out heresy, al-Maʾmūn's, on the contrary, was directed "at those who defined themselves in opposition to 'heretics,' 'innovators'" (136).
26. On al-Maʾmūn's *miḥna* more generally, see Nawas 1994; Kennedy 1986: 163–170; Watt 1973: 178–285; Sourdel 1962; Lapidus 1975; Crone and Hinds 1986: 93–96; Turner 2013: 118–150.
27. Though, as Nawas duly notes, "The promulgation of the doctrine and the order for enforcing its acceptance were not simultaneous; the first preceded the second by six years. They therefore cannot be treated, although it is often done, as a single event, because the circumstances that prompted al-Maʾmūn to set the *miḥna* in motion may well have been different from those that led him to declare that the Qurʾan was created" (Nawas 1994: 615).
28. See al-Maʾmūn's letter quoted in al-Ṭabarī 1879–1901: 1112. English translation: Bosworth 1985: 199–200.

Chapter 5

1. This chapter originated as a lecture titled "'The Shīʿa are the Jews of Our Umma': Rethinking Alterity in Medieval Islam" that was delivered at the Institute of Arab and Islamic Studies, University of Exeter, on February 12, 2019.
2. I have spent considerable time elucidating some of the excesses of Islamic studies in the past. I see no reason to replicate them here. I refer the interested reader to Hughes 2006, 2012c, 2015.

3. Obviously, I am not thinking here about important subfields—such as Shiʿī studies or Ismāʿīlī studies, or even Jewish studies. Instead, my analysis is based on the generic field of Islamic studies, a field that should ideally account for these others, but rarely does.
4. On "Islamic religious studies," see Hughes 2012c: 3–5, 118–132. See more recently Daneshgar 2020: 15–27.
5. The situation finds a parallel in Jewish studies where Judaism, at least in the premodern period, is code for Rabbinic Judaism. Other forms, most notably that of Karaites, is—following rabbinic precedent—then marginalized or ignored. I would only add however that this parallel is at least in part faulty because Karaite Judaism is, from the perspective of today, not nearly as prominent as the Shīʿa are in the context of Islam.
6. For a much more realistic account of ritual and other differences, see Haider 2011: 1–8. See further Hughes 2013b: 115–131.
7. The chapter on Sufism is titled "Stain Your Prayer Rug with Wine."
8. To take but a few recent examples, see Goldberg 2012; Ackerman-Lieberman 2013; Russ-Fishbane 2015.
9. This is certainly exacerbated by the identity politics of the modern humanities, wherein one is supposed to write or examine only about one's own ethnic and/or religious group or the group to which one has converted, and not talk about the ethnic/religious identities of others.
10. This can then lead to a set of field-wide exchanges that are helpful for neither. The rise of Israel studies, for example, gave rise to that of Palestine studies. In like manner, some Israeli scholars seek to undermine the apologetics of Islamic studies and its inability to predict events such as September 11, 2001—as if the goal of fields of study is solely for political expediency. One of the most egregious examples of this is Kraemer 2001.
11. Though, of course, the classic treatment remains Said's *Orientalism* (1978). There were, however, important precursors to his work. In this regard, see, e.g., Owen 1973; Asad 1973; Laroui 1976. More recently, see Rodinson 1987; Turner 1994; Marchand 2009.
12. According to Kohlberg: "The Shia which the Western world first came to know from distinct experience was that of the Fatimids and, somewhat later, the Assassins. It was the Fatimids, not the Twelver Shiis, whom the Crusaders confronted as immediate enemies; and though they may well have come across Twelver Shiis in Syria and Palestine, these were neither organized in an independent state like the Fatimids, nor possessed the mystical aura of the Assassins. They were therefore much less attractive to Crusader writers" (1987: 31).
13. One of the few exceptions being Goldziher 1920. Though, it is worth pointing out that even Goldziher had to undertake his analysis with a dearth of Shīʿi sources.

14. Only in recent years have works of Shīʿī thinkers grown in prominence thanks to the path-breaking scholarship of the likes of Wilfred Madelung, Etan Kohlberg, Mahmoud Ayoub, Hossein Modarressi, Hasan Ansari, Sabine Schmidtke, Mohammad Ali Amir-Moezzi, and Sajjad Rizvi. In 2017, the scholarship of such individuals paved the way for the creation of *Shii Studies Review*, published by Brill and edited by Ansari and Schmidtke. Despite their efforts, however, the field, as this chapter shows in considerable detail, still remains under the undue influence of Sunnism.
15. Such a phenomenon, of course, is not unique to the study of (Sunnī) Islam. As I demonstrated in Chapter 2 above, it is not uncommon, for example, to find donors with pro-Zionist agendas funding chairs in Israel studies or Jewish studies.
16. See, for example, Daftary and Meri 2003; Ali-de-Unzaga 2007; Kohlberg and Ehteshami 2019.
17. The secondary literature is chock full of such studies. See, for example, Geiger 1970 [1833]. Katsh 1954; Goitein 1955. For a discussion of these and related works, see Hughes 2017b: 17–35.
18. Certainly exceptions abound. One, for example, is Neusner, Sonn, and Brockopp 2000; though I should add that the authors are more interested in phenomenological similarities than in historical ones.
19. One of the most egregious examples of this in recent years is Afsaruddin 2007, to which must be coupled the comments in Robinson 2009.
20. Such an approach unfortunately and inevitably leads to the overwhelming tendency in religious studies to focus on interfaith dialogue. While having such religions talk to one another is certainly important, such an activity ignores the real *historical* and *textual* connections between these religions and is, I would argue, more appropriate for a church/mosque/synagogue setting than the secular academy.
21. Though to see just what is at stake in the political and politicized world of Jewish studies, see Ivry's scathing rebuke of Oliver Leaman's attempt to argue the same position in Ivry 1993.

Chapter 6

1. This chapter originated as a lecture given at Aga Khan University in London in November 2017 and then in December of the same year at Albert-Ludwigs-Universität Freiburg.
2. On the relevance of the European context, see my comments in Chapter 1 above.

Chapter 7

1. This chapter originated in a lecture given to the Faculty of Theology at St. John's College at the University of Cambridge in March of 2020.
2. For critiques of the term, see Levenson 2012: 1–17; Hughes 2013a: 15–33; Brague 2015.
3. Important exceptions are the books in the series "Oxford Studies in the Abrahamic Religions" published by Oxford University Press and edited by Guy G. Stroumsa.
4. The remarks found in the inaugural lectures of the two chairs devoted to the study of Abrahamic religions in England—at Oxford (inaugurated in 2009) and Cambridge (inaugurated in 2013) respectively—are telling. For the former, see G. Stroumsa 2011, and for the latter, see Fowden 2015.Though, it is perhaps worth mentioning in the present context, that the precursor to much in the study of Abrahamic religions would seem to be Peters 2003.
5. I think in particular of his *The Making of the Abrahamic Religions in Late Antiquity* (Stroumsa 2015a). In an important methodological statement, for example, he writes: "Suffice it here to say that, in any domain, research demands an intellectual effort to identify common denominators of various phenomena (for instance, multiple religious sects and groups). Such common denominators allow us to retrace central trends underlying the complexity of observable reality. One cannot fulfill this task without creating categories, the primary justification of which is their heuristic usefulness. Gnosticism and Jewish-Christianity are examples of such categories, which cannot be abandoned, although they must be used with care, without forgetting what they are not: a truthful representation of historical reality" (140).
6. I have located this transference at the point when scholars of Islam in the early and mid-twentieth century—most notably those associated with the "school" of Louis Massignon (1883–1962)—began to employ it as a way "to imagine and designate a commonality or a wistful paternity among three monotheisms at a time when they were increasingly at odds with one another" (Hughes 2013a: 58). This notion was subsequently picked up by the Second Vatican Council in the 1960s, with Pope Paul VI being a confidant of Massignon (ibid.: 65–66).
7. Though as Remi Brague well notes, the three religions "[s]imply because the names are the same does not mean that their personages are. Their personal traits are embedded and revealed in the particular narratives of the different writings. And what is recounted in the holy books of the three with respect to these figures is not uniform, far from it" (2015: 94).
8. See Silk 1984: 65–85. For criticism of the term, see Cohen 1970.
9. On the uses to which the term can be put, see Gaston 2019: 1–19.

10. See, for example, Werner 1993. In some of these treatments, Abrahamic religions are on the receiving end and can be, when compared to "Eastern faiths," described as intolerant and bellicose. On the latter, see Carter and Smith 2004: 286.
11. I point here to works such as McCutcheon 1997; Wiebe 1999; Fitzgerald 2000; Dubuisson 2003.
12. I think of works such as Rustow 2008; Goldberg 2012; Franklin 2013; Secunda 2014; Ackerman-Lieberman 2013.
13. Though, of course, I should be clear that by "religious studies," I refer to the more critical wing of religious studies, which is sometimes used interchangeably with the term "theory and method" or, now, "critical religion."
14. Perhaps best articulated in Bruce Lincoln's "Theses on Method." In his thirteenth thesis, for example, he writes: "When one permits those whom one studies to define the terms in which they will be understood, suspends one's interest in the temporal and the contingent, or fails to distinguish between 'truths,' 'truth-claims,' and 'regimes of truth,' one has ceased to function as a historian or scholar. In that moment, a variety of roles are available: some perfectly respectable (amanuensis, collector, friend, and advocate), and some less appealing (cheerleader, voyeur, retailer of import goods). None, however, should be confused with scholarship" (1996: 227).
15. A particularly good attempt to do this, and a work that in many ways functions as a model for the type of analysis I am encouraging here, is Stroumsa 2015a: 1–22.
16. Retrieved from www.hr.admin.cam.ac.uk/files/qaboos.pdf.
17. Again, one of the few to ask such questions is Guy Stroumsa, with the relevant literature cited in the notes above.
18. One could point in this context to the excellent study found in Sells 1994. Though, interestingly and perhaps tellingly, he nowhere invokes the term "Abrahamic religions" in this study.
19. This exists throughout the tradition from biblical studies to history. An example of an undeniably theological or evangelical treatment of the New Testament might include the likes of Hamilton 2004. Then I could point to more critical and academic studies of the New Testament, such as Arnal 2005; Rollens 2014; Eyl 2019. Or, for those that are more theological, but published with academic presses, see Hill 2012; Rowe 2016. But, again, most scholars working in the field are able to differentiate these three approaches from one another. In this regard, see Young forthcoming.

Chapter 8

1. This chapter was first presented as a lecture to the "Critical Religion" seminar at Mansfield College, Oxford, in March 2020. It derives from and reworks Hughes 2020b.
2. For historical precedents, see Waardenburg 2017; Sharpe 1986; Capps 2000.
3. This is perhaps best put in the language of the late Jonathan Z. Smith (1938–2017), who provocatively stated—perhaps the most often cited locution in the field—that "there is no data for religion. Religion is solely the creation of the scholar's study" (1982: xi; his italics).
4. See further McCutcheon 1997: 127–157; Fitzgerald 2000: 3–32; Dubuisson 2003: 99–114.
5. See, for example, Segal 1999; Bell 1992; Nongbri 2013; Hughes 2013a.
6. Arguments for replacing terms, while controversial, never possess much staying power. I think, for example, of Daniel Dubuisson's argument to replace "religion" with "cosmographic formation" (2003: 189–194).
7. One of the best accounts of this approach may be found in Nye 2019.
8. Parts of this section builds on the arguments I developed in Hughes 2020b.
9. I say "Western country" because the academic study of religion is, by and large, a Western initiative.
10. For an attempt to divide this along regional lines, see the essays collected in Alles 2010; although it is worth noting that neither Canada nor North America is mentioned therein.
11. Report of the Royal Commission on Bilingualism and Biculturalism, Appendix 1: The Terms of Reference (1963), 173. The report may be found at http://epe.lac-bac.gc.ca/100/200/301/pco-bcp/commissions-ef/dunton1967-1970-ef/dunton1967-70-vol1-eng/dunton1967-70-vol-part2-eng.pdf.
12. Rt. Hon. P. E. Trudeau (prime minister), "Announcement of Implementation of Policy of Multiculturalism within Bilingual Framework," October 8, 1971. Retrieved from www.pier21.ca/research/immigration-history/canadian-multiculturalism-policy-1971.
13. Ibid.
14. Ibid.

References

Abu-Nimer, Mohammed, Amal Khoury, and Emily Welty. 2007. *Unity in Diversity: Interfaith Dialogue in the Middle East.* Washington, DC: United States Institute of Peace.

Ackerman-Lieberman, Phillip I. 2013. *The Business of Identity: Jews, Muslims, and Economic Life in Medieval Egypt.* Palo Alto, CA: Stanford University Press.

Adams, Liam. 2017. "Anxieties Over a Donor's Role in a Faculty Search Boil Over at Case Western." *Chronicle of Higher Education.* October 12. Retrieved from www.chronicle.com/article/anxieties-over-a-donors-role-in-a-faculty-search-boil-over-at-case-western.

Adamson, Peter. 2016. *Philosophy in the Islamic World: A History of Philosophy Without Any Gaps.* Oxford: Oxford University Press.

Afsaruddin, Asma. 2007. *The First Muslims: History and Memory.* Oxford: Oneworld.

Ahmed, Shahab. 2016. *What is Islam?: The Importance of Being Islamic.* Princeton, NJ: Princeton University Press.

Ahroni, Reuben. 1986. *Yemenite Jewry: Origins, Culture and Literature.* Bloomington, IN: Indiana University Press.

Ali-de-Unzaga, Omar, ed. 2007. *Fortresses of the Intellect: Ismaili and Other Islamic Studies in Honour of Farhad Daftary.* London: I. B. Tauris.

Alles, Gregory D., ed. 2010. *Religious Studies: A Global View.* New York: Routledge.

Ambasciano, Leonardo. 2018. *An Unnatural History of Religions: Academia, Post-truth and the Quest for Scientific Knowledge.* London: Bloomsbury.

Anderson, Benedict. 2006. *Imagined Communities: Reflections on the Origins and Spread of Nationalism.* Rev. ed. London: Verso.

Amir-Moezzi, Mohammad Ali. 1994. *The Divine Guide in Early Shiʿism: The Sources of Esotericism in Islam.* Trans. David Streight. Albany, NY: State University of New York Press.

Anthony, Sean W. 2012. *The Caliph and the Heretic: Ibn Sabaʾ and the Origins of Shiʿism.* Leiden: Brill.

Arjomand, Said Amir. 1994. "ʿAbd Allah Ibn al-Muqaffaʿ and the ʿAbbasid Revolution." *Iranian Studies* 27.1–4: 9–36. https://doi.org/10.1080/00210869408701818

Arnal, William E. 2005. *The Symbolic Jesus: Historical Scholarship, Judaism and the Construction of Contemporary Identity*. London: Equinox.

Arnal, William E., and Russell T. McCutcheon. 2013. *The Sacred is the Profane: The Political Nature of "Religion."* Oxford: Oxford University Press.

Asad, Talal, ed. 1973. *Anthropology and the Cultural Encounter*. Amherst, NY: Humanity Books.

Aslan, Reza. 2005. *No god but God: The Origins, Evolution, and Future of Islam*. New York: Random House.

Ayoub, Mahmoud M. 2004. *Islam: Faith and History*. Oxford: Oneworld.

al-Baghdādī. 1910 [1328]. *Al-Farq bayn al-Firaq*. Ed. Muhammad Badr. Cairo: Maṭbaʿat al-Maʿārif.

Badawi, ʿAbd al-Raḥman. 1993. *Min tāʾrīkh fi al-ilḥād fi al-islām*. Cairo: Sīnā lil-Nashr.

Bar-Asher, Meir M. 1999. *Scripture and Exegesis in Early Imāmī Shiism*. Leiden: Brill.

Barton, Carlin A., and Daniel Boyarin. 2016. *Imagine No Religion: How Modern Abstractions Hide Ancient Realities*. New York: Fordham University Press.

Bausi, A., and A. Gori. 2006. *Tradizioni orientali del Martirio di Areta*. Florence: University of Florence.

Bayart, Jean-François. 2005. *The Illusion of Cultural Identity*. Trans. Steven Rendall, Janet Roitman, Cynthia Schoch, and Jonathan Derrick. Chicago, IL: University of Chicago Press.

Beeston, A.F.L. 1984. "Himyarite Monotheism." In Abdelgadir M. Abdalla, Sami al-Sakkar, Richard T. Morter, Abd al-Rahman al-Ansary, and Gami'at al-Malik Sa'ūd, *Studies in the History of Arabia*, vol. 2, 149–154. Riyadh: King Saud University Press.

Bell, Catherine. 1992. *Ritual Theory, Ritual Practice*. Oxford: Oxford University Press.

al-Bīrūnī. 1879. *Al-Āthār al-bāqiyya min al-qurūn al-khāliya* [*The Chronology of Ancient Nations*]. Trans. Edward Sachau. London: Minerva GMBH.

Bosworth, C. E., trans. 1985. *The Reunification of the ʿAbbasid Caliphate: The Caliphate of al-Maʾmun, A.D. 813-833/A.H. 198-218*. Vol. 32 of *The History of al-Ṭabarī*. Albany, NY: State University of New York Press.

Bourdieu, Pierre. 1984. *Distinction: A Social Critique of the Judgment of Taste*. Trans. Richard Nice. Cambridge, MA: Harvard University Press.

Bowersock, Glen W. 2013. *The Throne of Adulis: Red Sea Wars on the Eve of Islam*. Oxford: Oxford University Press.

Boyarin, Daniel. 2004. *Border Lines: The Partition of Judaeo-Christianity*. Philadelphia, PA: University of Pennsylvania Press.

Brague, Remi. 2015. "The Concept of the Abrahamic Religions: Problems and Pitfalls." In Adam J. Silverstein and Guy G. Stroumsa, eds., *The Oxford Handbook of Abrahamic Religions*, 88–107. Oxford: Oxford University Press.

Buckner, Philip. 1993. "Whatever Happened to the British Empire?" *Journal of the Canadian Historical Association* 4.1: 3–32.

Bulliet, Richard. 1994. *Islam: The View From the Edge*. New York: Columbia University Press.
Bulliet, Richard. 2004. *The Case for Islamo-Christian Civilization*. New York: Columbia University Press.
Bulliet, Richard. 2015. "Islamo-Christian Civilization." In Adam J. Silverstein and Guy G. Stroumsa, eds., *The Oxford Handbook of Abrahamic Religions*, 109–120. Oxford: Oxford University Press.
Calder, Norman. 1993. *Studies in Early Muslim Jurisprudence*. Oxford: Oxford University Press.
Cameron, Averil. 2003. "How to Read Heresiology." *Journal of Medieval and Early Modern Studies* 33: 471–492. https://doi.org/10.1215/10829636-33-3-471
Capps, Walter H. 2000. *Religious Studies: The Making of a Discipline*. Minneapolis, MN: Fortress Press.
Carter, Judy, and Gordon S. Smith. 2004. "Religious Peacebuilding: From Potential to Action." In Harold G. Coward and Gordon Smith, eds., *Religion and Peacebuilding*, 279–301. Albany, NY: State University of New York Press.
Cassarino, Mirella. 2000. *L'aspetto morale e religioso nell'opera di Ibn al-Muqaffaʿ*. Soveria Mannelli, Italy: Rubbettino Editore.
Chabot, J. B., ed. 1996 [1933]. *Pseudo-Dionysus of Tel-Mahre, Chronicle II*. Trans. Witold Witakowski. Liverpool: Liverpool University Press.
Chokr, Melhem. 1993. *Zandaqa et zindiqs en Islam au second siècle de l'hegire*. Damascus: Institut Français de Damas.
CJT Editors. 1955a. "Theological Scholarship." *Canadian Journal of Theology* 1.3: 139–140.
CJT Editors. 1955b. "Editorial." *Canadian Journal of Theology*: 67–68.
CJT Editors. 1956. "A Theological Need." *Canadian Journal of Theology* 2.3: 125–128.
CJT Editors. 1957. "Editorial." *Canadian Journal of Theology* 3.2: 68–69.
CJT Editors. 1958. "Editorial." *Canadian Journal of Theology* 4.3: 163–164.
CJT Editors. 1961. "Preface to On the Significance of Niebuhr's Ideas of Society." *Canadian Journal of Theology* 7.2: 99.
Cohen, Arthur A. 1970. *The Myth of the Judeo-Christian Tradition*. New York: Harper and Row.
Cohen, Hermann. 1995 [1919]. *Religion of Reason Out of the Sources of Judaism*. Trans. Simon Kaplan. Atlanta, GA: Scholars Press.
Cohen, Mark R. 2005. *Poverty and Charity in the Jewish Community of Medieval Egypt*. Princeton, NJ: Princeton University Press.
Cohen, Shaye J.D. 2006. *From the Maccabees to the Mishnah*, 2nd ed. Louisville, KY: Westminster John Knox Press.
Cotter, Christopher R., and David G. Robertson, eds. 2016. *After World Religions: Reconstructing Religious Studies*. New York: Routledge.
Crone, Patricia. 2009. *Roman, Provincial, and Islamic Law: The Origins of the Islamic Patronate*. Cambridge: Cambridge University Press.

Crone, Patricia. 2016. "Ungodly Cosmologies." In Hanna Siurua and Patricia Crone, eds., *Islam, the Ancient Near East, and Varieties of Godlessness*, vol. 3 of *Collected Studies in Three Volumes*, 118–150. Leiden: Brill.

Crone, Patricia, and Martin Hinds. 1986. *God's Caliph: Religious Authority in the First Centuries of Islam.* Cambridge: Cambridge University Press.

Daftary, Farhad, and Josef W. Meri, eds. 2003. *Culture and Memory in Medieval Islam: Essays in Honour of Wilferd Madelung.* London: I. B. Tauris.

Daneshgar, Majid. 2020. *Studying the Qur'an in the Muslim Academy.* Oxford: Oxford University Press.

Daneshgar, Majid, and Aaron W. Hughes. 2020. "Introduction." In Majid Daneshgar and Aaron W. Hughes, eds, *Deconstructing Islamic Studies*, 1–8. Cambridge, MA: Harvard University Press.

de Blois, François. 1960–2005. "Zindīḳ." *EI2* 11: 510–513.

Denny, Frederick Mathewson. 1994. *An Introduction to Islam*, 3rd ed. Upper Saddle River, NJ: Pearson.

Denny, Frederick Mathewson. 2005. "Community and Society in the Qurʾān." In Jane MacAuliffe, ed., *Encyclopaedia of the Qurʾān*, vol. 1, 367–386. Leiden: Brill.

Donner, Fred M. 2010. *Muhammad and the Believers: At the Origins of Islam.* Cambridge, MA: Harvard University Press.

Dubuisson, Daniel. 2003. *The Western Construction of Religion: Myths, Knowledge, and Ideology.* Trans. William Sayers. Baltimore, MD: Johns Hopkins University Press.

Dubuisson, Daniel. 2006 [1993]. *Twentieth Century Mythologies.* 2nd ed. Trans. Martha Cunningham. London: Equinox.

El-Badawi, Emran. 2014. *The Qurʾān and the Aramaic Gospel Traditions.* New York: Routledge.

Eliade, Mircea. 1958. *Patterns in Comparative Religion.* Trans. Rosemary Sheedy. New York: Sheed and Ward.

Ernst, Carl, and Richard C. Martin, eds. 2010. *Rethinking Islamic Studies: From Orientalism to Cosmopolitanism.* Chapel Hill, NC: University of North Carolina Press.

Ewing, Katherine Pratt. 2010. "The Misrecognition of a Modern Islamist Organization: Germany Faces 'Fundamentalism.'" In Carl Ernst and Richard C. Martin, eds., *Rethinking Islamic Studies: From Orientalism to Cosmopolitanism*, 52–71. Chapel Hill, NC: University of North Carolina Press.

Eyl, Jennifer. 2019. *Signs, Wonders, and Gifts: Divination in the Letters of Paul.* Oxford: Oxford University Press.

Fairweather, Rev. Eugene R. 1970. "Editorial: Canadian Journal of Theology, 1955–1970." *Canadian Journal of Theology* 16.3–4: 127–128.

al-Faruqi, Ismail. 1961 "On the Significance of Niebuhr's Ideas of Society." *Canadian Journal of Theology* 7.2: 99–107.

Fernando, Mayanthi L. 2014. *The Republic Unsettled: Muslim French and the Contradictions of Secularism*. Durham, NC: Duke University Press.

Fierro, Maribel. 2012. "Ibn Ḥazm and the Jewish *Zindīq*." In Camilla Adang, Maribel Fierro, and Sabine Schmidtke, eds., *Ibn Ḥazm of Cordoba: The Life and Works of a Controversial Thinker*, 497–509. Leiden: Brill.

Fitzgerald, Timothy. 2000. *The Ideology of Religious Studies*. New York: Oxford University Press.

Flower, Richard. 2013. "'The Insanity of Heretics Must be Restrained': Heresiology in the *Theodosian Code*." In Christopher Kelly, ed., *Theodosius II: Rethinking the Roman Empire in Late Antiquity*, 172–194. Cambridge: Cambridge University Press.

Fowden, Garth. 2014. *Before and After Muhammad: The First Millennium Refocused*. Princeton, NJ: Princeton University Press.

Fowden, Garth. 2015. *Abraham or Aristotle? First Millennium Empires and Exegetical Traditions*. Cambridge: Cambridge University Press.

Franklin, Arnold E. 2013. *This Noble House: Jewish Descendants of King David in the Medieval East*. Philadelphia, PA: University of Pennsylvania Press.

Freiburger Oliver. 2019. *Considering Comparison: A Method for Religious Studies*. Oxford: Oxford University Press.

Friedländer, Israel. 1909–1910. "ʿAbd Allāh ibn Sabā, der Begründer der Šīʿa, und sein jüdischer Ursprung," *Zeitschrift für Assyriologie A* 23: 296–327, 24: 1–46. https://doi.org/10.1515/zava.1910.24.1.1

Fück, Johann, 1935. "Spuren des Zindīqtums in der islamischen Tradition." In W. Heffening and W. Kirfel, eds., *Studien zur Geschichte und Kultur des nahen und fernen Ostens: Paul Kahle zum 60 Geburtstag*, 95–100. Leiden: Brill.

Gabrieli, Francesco. 1961. "La «Zandaqa» au Ier siècle abbaside." In *L'Élaboration de l'islam: colloque de Strasbourg (12–13 juin 1959)*, 23–38. Paris: Presses Universitaires de France.

Gajda, Iwona. 2009. *Le royaume de Ḥimyar à l'époque monothéiste*. Paris: Académie des Inscriptions et Belles-Lettres.

Gaston, K. Healan. 2019. *Imagining Judeo-Christian America: Religion, Secularism, and the Redefinition of Democracy*. Chicago, IL: University of Chicago Press.

Geiger, Abraham. 1970 [1833]. *Judaism and Islam*. Trans. F. M. Young. Madras: MDCSPK Press.

al-Ghabban, A. et al, eds. 2010. *Routes d'Arabie: Archeologie et Histoire du Royaume d'Arabie Saoudite*. Paris: Somogy.

Gil, Moshe. 1984. "The Origins of the Jews of Yathrib." *Jerusalem Studies in Arabic and Islam* 4: 203–223.

Gillot, Claude. 2009. "Christians and Christianity in Islamic Exegesis." In David Thomas and Barbara Roggema, eds., *Christian-Muslim Relations. A Bibliographical History. Volume 1 (600–900)*, 31–56. Leiden: Brill.

Gleave, Robert. 2009. "Recent Research into the History of Early Shīʿism." *History Compass* 7.6: 1593–1605.

Goitein, Shlomo Dov. 1955. *Jews and Arabs: Their Contact Through the Ages*. 3rd rev. ed. New York: Schocken.

Goldberg, Jessica. 2012. *Trade and Institutions in the Medieval Mediterranean: The Geniza Merchants and their Business World*. Cambridge: Cambridge University Press.

Goldziher, Ignác. 1920. *Die Richtungen der islamischens Koransauslegung*. Leiden: Brill.

Graetz, Heinrich. 1955. *History of the Jews*. Vol. 3. Philadelphia, PA: Jewish Publication Society of America.

Grant, John W. 1967. *The Canadian Experience of Church Union*. Richmond: John Knox Press.

Grewal, Zareena. 2016. "Destabilizing Orthodoxy, De-territorializing the Anthropology of Islam." *Journal of the American Academy of Religion* 84.1: 44–59. https://doi.org/10.1093/jaarel/lfv095

Griffiths, Sidney. 2010. *The Church in the Shadow of the Mosque: Christians and Muslims in the World of Islam*. Princeton, NJ: Princeton University Press.

Gross, Rachel B. 2021. *Beyond the Synagogue: Jewish Nostalgia as Religious Practice*. New York: New York University Press.

Gruen, Erich S. 2011. *Rethinking the Other in Late Antiquity*. Princeton, NJ: Princeton University Press.

Haider, Najam. 2011. *The Origins of the Shiʿa: Identity, Ritual, and Sacred Space in Eighth-Century Kūfa*. Cambridge: Cambridge University Press.

Haider, Najam. 2014. *Shīʿī Islam: An Introduction*. Cambridge: Cambridge University Press.

Hallaq, Wael B. 2001. *Authority, Continuity, and Change in Islamic Law*. Cambridge: Cambridge University Press.

Hallaq, Wael B. 2018. *Restating Orientalism: A Critique of Modern Knowledge*. New York: Columbia University Press.

Halm, Heinz. 1988. *Die Schia*. Darmstadt: Wissenschaftliche Buchgesellschaft.

Hamilton, James M. 2004. *God's Indwelling Presence: The Holy Spirit in the Old & New Testaments*. n.l.: B & H Publishing.

Hammer, Juliane. 2016. "Introduction: Roundtable on Normativity in Islamic Studies." *Journal of the American Academy of Religion* 84.1: 25–27.

Harries, Jill and Ian Wood, eds. 1993. *The Theodosian Code: Studies in the Imperial Law of Late Antiquity*. Ithaca, NY: Cornell University Press.

Hatke, George. 2013. *Aksum and Nubia: Warfare, Commerce, and Political Fictions in Ancient Northeast Africa*. New York: New York University Press.

Healey, John. 1993. *The Nabataean Tomb Inscriptions of Mad'in Salih*. Oxford: JSS.

Heschel, Susannah. 1998. *Abraham Geiger and the Jewish Jesus*. Princeton, NJ: Princeton University Press, 1998.

Hill, C. E. 2012. *Who Chose the Gospels?:Probing the Great Gospel Conspiracy*. Oxford: Oxford University Press.
Hinds, Martin. 1960–2005. "Miḥna." *EI2* 7: 2–6.
Hodgson, Marshall G.S. 1955. "How Did the Early Shīʿa Become Sectarian?" *Journal of the American Oriental Society* 75: 1–12.
Hodgson, Marshall G.S. 1960–2005. "ʿAbd Allāh ibn Sabaʾ" *EI2* 1: 51.
Hodgson, Marshall G.S. 1974. *The Venture of Islam: Conscience and History in a World Civilization*. Vol. 1. Chicago, IL: University of Chicago Press.
Horovitz, Josef. 1926. *Koranische Untersuchungen*. Berlin: W. de Gruyter.
Hoyland, Robert G. 1997. *Seeing Islam as Others Saw It: A Survey and Evaluation of Christian, Jewish, and Zoroastrian Writings on Early Islam*. Princeton, NJ: Darwin Press.
Hoyland, Robert G. 2001. *Arabia and the Arabs: From the Bronze Age to the Coming of Islam*. New York: Routledge.
Hoyland, Robert G. 2014. *In God's Path: The Arab Conquests and the Creation of an Islamic Empire*. Oxford: Oxford University Press.
Hughes, Aaron W. 2006. *Situating Islam: The Past and Future of an Academic Discipline*. London: Equinox.
Hughes, Aaron W. 2012a. "The Study of Islam Before and After September 11: A Provocation." *Method & Theory in the Study of Religion* 24.4–5: 314–336. https://doi.org/10.1163/15700682-12341234
Hughes, Aaron W. 2012b. *Theorizing Islam: Disciplinary Deconstruction and Reconstruction*. Sheffield: Equinox.
Hughes, Aaron W. 2013a. *Abrahamic Religions: On the Uses and Abuses of History*. Oxford: Oxford University Press.
Hughes, Aaron W. 2013b. *Muslim Identities: An Introduction to Islam*. New York: Columbia University Press.
Hughes, Aaron W. 2013c. *The Study of Judaism: Authenticity, Identity, Scholarship*. Albany, NY: State University of New York Press.
Hughes, Aaron W. 2014a. "Jewish Studies is Too Jewish." *Chronicle of Higher Education*. Retrieved from www.chronicle.com/article/jewish-studies-is-too-jewish.
Hughes, Aaron W. 2014b. "When Bad Scholarship is Just Bad Scholarship: A Response to Omid Safi." *Bulletin for the Study of Religion*. Retrieved from https://bulletin.equinoxpub.com/2014/02/when-bad-scholarship-is-just-bad-scholarship-a-response-to-omid-safi.
Hughes, Aaron W. 2015. *Islam and the Tyranny of Authenticity: An Inquiry into Disciplinary Apologetics and Self-Deception*. Sheffield: Equinox.
Hughes, Aaron W. 2016a. *Jacob Neusner: An American Jewish Iconoclast*. New York: New York University Press.
Hughes, Aaron W. 2016b. "Jewish Studies and Local Communities." *JewSchool*. Retrieved from https://jewschool.com/2016/05/76638/jewish-studies-and-local-communities.

Hughes, Aaron W. 2017a. "Review of Shahab Ahmed's *What is Islam?*" *Reading Religion.* Retrieved from https://readingreligion.org/books/what-islam.

Hughes, Aaron W. 2017b. *Shared Identities: Medieval and Modern Imaginings of Judeo-Islam.* Oxford: Oxford University Press.

Hughes, Aaron W. 2020a. "Arabian Judaism at the Advent of Islam: A Forgotten Chapter in the History of Judaism." In Gwynn Kessler and Naomi Koltun-Fromm, eds., *A Companion to Jews and Judaism in the Late Antique World, 3rd Century BCE–7th Century CE,* 291–304. Oxford: Wiley-Blackwell.

Hughes, Aaron W. 2020b. *From Seminary to University: An Institutional History of the Study of Religion in Canada.* Toronto: University of Toronto Press.

Hughes, Aaron W. 2020c. "Good Muslim, Bad Muslim: Neo-Orientalism and the Study of Religion." In Leslie Dorrough Smith, Steffen Führding, and Adrian Hermann, eds., *Hijacked: A Critical Treatment of the Public Rhetoric of Good and Bad Religion,* 12–22. Sheffield: Equinox.

Hughes, Aaron W. 2021a. "Introduction." *Method and Theory in the Study of Religion* 33.2: 107–113.

Hughes, Aaron W. 2021b. "South Arabian 'Judaism,' Himyarite Rahmanism, and the Origins of Islam." In Carlos Segovia, ed., *Remapping Emergent Islam,* 15–43. Amsterdam: Amsterdam University Press.

Hughes, Aaron W., and Russell T. McCutcheon, eds. *What Is Religion?: Debating the Academic Study of Religion.* Oxford: Oxford University Press, 2021.

Hurvitz, Nimrod. 2002. *The Formation of Hanbalism: Piety into Power.* New York: Routledge.

Ibn Hishām, ʿAbd al-Malik. 1858–1860 [English translation: 1955]. *Kitāb sīrat rasūl Allāh.* Ed. Ferdinand Wüstenfeld. Göttingen. English translation: *The Life of Muhammad: A Translation of Ibn Ishaq's Sirat Rasul Allah.* Trans. A. Guillaume. Oxford: Oxford University Press.

Ibn al-Nadīm. 1872. *Kitāb al-Fihrist.* Ed. Gustav Flügel. 2 vols. Leipzig: Verlag von F. C. Vogel.

Ibn al-Nadīm. 1970. *The Fihrist.* English translation by Bayard Dodge. 2 vols. New York: Columbia University Press, 1970.

Ibn Taymiyya, Taqī al-Dīn Aḥmad ibn ʿAbd al-Ḥalīm. 2009. *Kitāb al-īmān.* Trans. Salman Hassan al-Ani and Shadia Ahmad Tel. Kuala Lampur: Islamic Book Trust.

Ibrahim, Mahmood. 1994. "Religious Inquisition as Social Policy: The Persecution of the 'Zanadiqa' in the Early Abbasid Caliphate." *Arab Studies Quarterly* 16.2: 53–72.

Imhoff, Sarah. 2016. "The Creation Story, or How We Learned to Stop Worrying and Love Schempp." *Journal of the American Academy of Religion* 84.2: 466–497. https://doi.org/10.1093/jaarel/lfv060

Ivry, Alfred L. 1993. "Review of *Moses Maimonides* by Oliver Leaman." *AJS Review* 21.2: 306–308. https://doi.org/10.1017/s0364009400005055

Johansen, Birgitte Scheperlen and Riem Spielhaus. 2019. "Quantitative Knowledge Production on Muslims in Europe as a Practice of 'Secular Suspicion.'" In Monique Scheer, Nadia Fadil, and Birgitte Scheperlen Johansen, eds., *Secular Bodies, Affects and Emotions: European Configurations*, 171–185. London: Bloomsbury.

Josephson, J. 2006. "The Hellenistic Heritage of the zanādiqa." In L. Edzard and J. Retsö, eds., *Current Issues in the Analysis of Semitic Grammar and Lexicon II: Oslo-Göteborg Cooperation 4th-5th November 2005*, 175–194. Wiesbaden: Harrassowitz Verlag.

Josephson, Jason Ananda. 2012. *The Invention of Religion in Japan*. Chicago, IL: University of Chicago Press.

Juasson, Antonin, and Rafaël Savignac. 1909–1922. *Mission archéologique en Arabie*. Paris: E. Leroux.

Karamustafa, Ahmet. 2010. "Community." In Jamal J. Elias, ed., *Key Themes for the Study of Islam*, 93–103. Oxford: Oneworld.

Katsh, Abraham I. 1954. *Judaism in Islam: Biblical and Talmudic Backgrounds of the Koran and Its Commentaries*. New York: Sepher-Hermon Press.

Kelsey, John. 2012. "Islam and the Study of Ethics." *Method and Theory in the Study of Religion* 24.4–5: 357–370.

Kennedy, Hugh. 1981. *The Early Abbasid Caliphate: A Political History*. London: Croom Helm.

Kennedy, Hugh, trans. 1985. *Al-Manṣūr and al-Mahdi*. Vol. 29 of The *History of al-Ṭabarī*. Albany, NY: State University of New York Press.

Kennedy, Hugh. 1986. *The Prophet and the Age of the Caliphates*. London: Longman.

Kohlberg, Etan. 1987. "Western Studies of Shiʿa Islam." In Martin Kramer, ed., *Shiʿism, Resistance and Revolution*, 31–44. Boulder, CO: Westview.

Kohlberg, Etan, and Amin Ehteshami, eds. 2019. *In Praise of the Few: Studies in Shīʿite Thought and History*. Leiden: Brill.

Koltun-Fromm, Ken. 2006. *Abraham Geiger's Liberal Judaism: Personal Meaning and Religious Authority*. Bloomington, IN: Indiana University Press.

Kramer, Martin, ed. 1999. *The Jewish Discovery of Islam: Studies in Honor of Bernard Lewis*. Tel Aviv: Moshe Dayan Center for Middle Eastern and African Studies.

Kramer, Martin. 2001. *Ivory Towers in Sand: The Failure of Middle East Studies in America*. Washington, DC: The Washington Institute for Near East Policy.

Krinis, Ehud. 2019. "Directions in Jewish-Shīʿī Studies." *Shii Studies Review* 3: 183–210. https://doi.org/10.1163/24682470-12340042

Kristó-Nagy, István. 2013. *La pensée d'Ibn al-Muqaffaʿ: Un «agent double» dans le monde persan et arabe*. Versailles: Éditions de Paris.

Lapidus, Ira. 1975. "The Separation of State and Religion in the Development of Early Islamic Society." *International Journal of Middle East Studies* 6: 363–385. https://doi.org/10.1017/s0020743800025344

Lapidus, Ira. 1988. *A History of Islamic Societies.* Cambridge: Cambridge University Press.

Laroui, Abdallah. 1976. *The Crisis of the Arab Intellectual: Traditionalism and Historicism.* Trans. Diarmid Cammell. Berkeley, CA: University of California Press.

Lasker, Daniel J. 1977. *Jewish Philosophical Polemics Against Christianity in the Middle Ages.* Liverpool: Liverpool University Press.

Laskier, Michael M., and Yaacov Lev, eds. 2011a. *The Convergence of Judaism and Islam: Religious, Scientific, and Cultural Dimensions.* Gainesville, FL: University of Florida Press.

Laskier, Michael M., and Yaacov Lev, eds. 2011b. *The Divergence of Judaism and Islam: Interdependence, Modernity, and Political Turmoil.* Gainesville, FL: University of Florida Press 2011.

Lauzière, Henri. 2016. *The Making of Salafism: Islamic Reform in the Twentieth Century.* New York: Columbia University Press.

Lentin, Ronit. 2018. *Traces of Racial Exception: Racializing Israeli Settler Colonialism.* London: Bloomsbury.

Levenson, Jon. 2012. *Inheriting Abraham: The Legacy of the Patriarch in Judaism, Christianity, and Islam*, Princeton NJ: Princeton University Press.

Levy, Jakob. 1876–1889. *Chaldäisches Wörterbuch über die Targumim und einen grossen Teil des rabbinischen Schriftthums.* Vol. 2. Leipzig: Verlag von Baumgärtner's Buchhandlung.

Lewis, Bernard. 1984. *The Jews of Islam.* Princeton, NJ: Princeton University Press.

Lieu, Samuel N. C. 1985. *Manichaeism in the Later Roman Empire and Medieval China: A Historical Survey.* Manchester: Manchester University Press.

Lincoln, Bruce. 1996. "Theses on Method." *Method and Theory in the Study of Religion* 8: 225–227.

Lincoln, Bruce. 2000. *Theorizing Myth: Narrative, Ideology, and Scholarship.* Chicago, IL: University of Chicago Press.

Lincoln, Bruce. 2006. *Holy Terrors: Thinking About Religion After September 11.* 2nd ed. Chicago, IL: University of Chicago Press.

Lincoln, Bruce. 2018. *Apples and Oranges: Explorations In, On, and With Comparison.* Chicago, IL: University of Chicago Press.

Lowry, Joseph E. 2007. *Early Islamic Legal Theory: The "Risala" of Muhammad Ibn Idris al-Shafiʿ.* Leiden: Brill.

Maccoby, Hyam. 1982. *Judaism on Trial: Jewish-Christian Disputations in the Middle Ages.* Rutherford: Fairleigh Dickenson University Press.

Ma'oz, Moshe. 2009. *The Meeting of Civilizations: Muslim, Christian, and Jewish.* Eastbourne: Sussex Academic Press.

Marchand, Suzanne L. 2009. *German Orientalism in the Age of Empire: Religion, Race, and Scholarship.* Cambridge: Cambridge University Press.

Martin, Craig. 2014. *Capitalizing Religion: Ideology and the Opiate of the Bourgeoisie.* London: Bloomsbury.

Martin, Richard. 2012. "The Uses and Abuses of Criticism in the Study of Islam: A Response to Aaron Hughes." *Method and Theory in the Study of Religion* 24.4-5: 371-388. https://doi.org/10.1163/15700682-12341238

Masuzawa, Tomoko. 2005. *The Invention of World Religions: Or, How European Universalism was Preserved in the Language of Pluralism*. Chicago, IL: University of Chicago Press.

Matthews, John F. 2000. *Laying Down the Law: A Study of the Theodosian Code*. New Haven, CT: Yale University Press.

Mazuz, Haggai. 2014. *The Religious and Spiritual Life of the Jews of Medina*. Leiden: Brill.

McClure, Judith. 1979. "Handbooks Against Heresy in the West from the Late Fourth to the Late Sixth Centuries." *Journal of Theological Studies* 30: 186-197. https://doi.org/10.1093/jts/xxx.1.186

McCutcheon, Russell T. 1997. *Manufacturing Religion: The Discourse on Sui Generis Religion and the Politics of Nostalgia*. Oxford: Oxford University Press.

McCutcheon, Russell T. 2003. *The Discipline of Religion: Structure, Meaning, Rhetoric*. New York: Routledge.

McCutcheon, Russell T. 2014. *Entanglements: Marking Place in the Field of Religion*. Sheffield: Equinox.

McCutcheon, Russell T. 2018. "Afterword: The Meaning and End of Scholarship on Religion." In Matt Sheedy, ed., *Identity, Politics, and the Study of Islam: Current Dilemmas in the Study of Religions*, 202-223. Sheffield: Equinox.

McIntire, C. T. 2012. "Unity among Many: The Formation of the United Church of Canada, 1899-1930." In Don Schweitzer, ed., *The United Church of Canada: A History*, 3-38. Waterloo: Wilfrid Laurier University Press.

Meddeb, Abdelwahab and Benjamin Stora, eds. 2013. *A History of Jewish-Muslim Relations: From the Origins to the Present Day*. Princeton, NJ and Paris: Princeton University Press and Albin Michel.

Melchert, Christopher. 1997. *The Formation of the Sunni Schools of Law, 9th-10th Centuries CE*. Leiden: Brill.

Melchert, Christopher. 2002. "The Piety of the Hadith Folk," *International Journal of Middle East Studies* 34.3: 425-439.

Melchert, Christopher. 2003. "The Early History of Islamic Law." In Herbert Berg, ed., *Method and Theory in the Study of Islamic Origins*, 293-324. Leiden: Brill.

Millar, Fergus. 2006. *A Greek Roman Empire: Power and Belief Under Theodosius II (408-450)*. Berkeley, CA: University of California Press.

Moburg, Axel, ed. and trans. 1924. *Book of the Himyarites: Fragments of a Hitherto Unknown Syriac Work*. Lund: G. W. K. Gleerup.

Moir, John S. 1982. *A History of Biblical Studies in Canada: A Sense of Proportion*. Chico, CA: Scholars' Press.

Moltmann, Jürgen. 1999. *God for a Secular Society: The Public Relevance of Theology*, trans. Margaret Kohl. Minneapolis, MN: Fortress Press.

Morgenson, Eric B. 2019. "Review of *Traces of Racial Exception: Racializing Israeli Settler Colonialism* by Ronit Lentin." *H-Judaic*. Retrieved from https://networks.h-net.org/node/28655/reviews/4797269/morgenson-lentin-traces-racial-exception-racializing-israeli-settler.

al-Murtaḍā, al-Sharīf. 1373/1954. *Ghurar al-fawāʾid wa-durar al-qalāʾid* Ed. Muḥammad Abu al-Faḍl Ibrāhīm. Vol. 1 Cairo: Dār Iḥyāʾ al-Kutub al-ʿArabiyya.

Nakissa, Aria. 2021. "Cognitive Science of Religion and the Study of Islam: Rethinking Islamic Theology, Law, Education, and Mysticism Using the Works of al-Ghazālī." *Method and Theory in the Study of Religion* 32.3: 205–232.

Nasr, Seyyed Hossein. 1981. "Translator's Preface," to Sayyid Muḥammad Ḥusayn Ṭabāṭabāʾī, *Shiʿite Islam*, xv–xxxviii. Kuala Lumpur: Islamic Book Trust.

Naveh, Joseph. 1999–2000. "Seven New Epitaphs from Zoar" (Hebrew). *Tarbiz* LXIX: 619–635.

Naveh, Joseph. 2003. "A Bilingual Burial Inscription from Saba" (Hebrew). *Leshonenu* LXV.2: 117–120.

Nawas, John A. 1994. "A Reexamination of Three Current Explanations for al-Maʾmun's Introduction of the Miḥna." *International Journal of Middle East Studies* 26.4: 615–629. https://doi.org/10.1017/s0020743800061134

Nebes, Norbert. 2010. "The Martyrs of Najrān and the End of Ḥimyar: On the Political History of South Arabia in the Early Sixth Century." In Angelika Neuwirth, Nicolai Sinai, and Michael Marx, eds., *The Qurʾān in Context: Historical and Literary Investigations into the Qurʾānic Milieu*, 27–59. Leiden: Brill.

Neusner, Jacob, Tamara Sonn, and Jonathan E. Brockopp. 2000. *Judaism and Islam in Practice: A Sourcebook*. New York: Routledge.

Newby, Gordon D. 1988. *A History of the Jews of Arabia: From Ancient Times to Their Eclipse Under Islam*. Columbia, SC: University of South Carolina Press.

Newby, Gordon D. 2013. "The Jews of Arabia at the Birth of Islam." In Abdelwahab Meddeb and Benjamin Stora, eds., *A History of Jewish-Muslim Relations: From Their Origins to the Present Day*, 39–51. Princeton, NJ and Paris: Princeton University Press and Albin Michel.

Nicholls, William. 1971. "Editorial: A New Journal and Its Predecessor." *Studies in Religion / Sciences religieuses* 1.1: 1–3.

Nöldeke, Th., and F. Schwally. 1909–1938. *Geschichte des Qorans*. Vol. 2. Leipzig: Dieterich'sche Verlagsbuchhandlung.

Nongbri, Brent. 2013. *Before Religion: A History of a Modern Concept*. New Haven, CT: Yale University Press.

Norton, Anne. 2020. *On the Muslim Question*. Princeton, NJ: Princeton University Press.

Nyberg, H. S. 1929. "Zum Kampf zwischen Islam und Manichäismus." *Orientalistische Literaturzeitung* 32: 427–448.
Nye, Malory. 2019. Decolonizing the Study of Religion. *Open Library of Humanities* 5.1. Retrieved from https://olh.openlibhums.org/articles/10.16995/olh.421.
Owen, Roger. 1973. "Studying Islamic History" *Journal of Interdisciplinary History* 4.2: 287–298.
Owen, Suzanne. 2011. *The Appropriation of Native American Spirituality*. London: Continuum.
Penn, Michael Phillip. 2015a. *Envisioning Islam: Syriac Christians in the Early Muslim World*. Philadelphia, PA: University of Pennsylvania Press.
Penn, Michael Phillip. 2015b. *When Christians First Met Muslims: A Sourcebook of the Earliest Syriac Writings on Islam*. Berkeley, CA: University of California Press.
Peters, Francis E. 2003. *The Monotheists: Jews, Christians, and Muslims in Conflict and Competition*. 2 vols. Princeton, NJ: Princeton University Press.
Pines, Shlomo. 1980. "Shiʿite Terms and Conceptions in Judah Halevi's Kuzari." *Jerusalem Studies in Arabic and Islam* 2: 165–251.
Pines, Shlomo. 1985. "Notes on Islam and on Arabic Christianity and Judaeo-Christianity." *Jerusalem Studies in Arabic and Islam* 4: 135–152.
Powers, David S. 2009. *Muhammad Is Not the Father of Any of Your Men: The Making of the Last Prophet*. Philadelphia, PA: University of Pennsylvania Press.
Rabin, Shari. 2017. *Jews on the Frontier: Religion and Mobility in Nineteenth-Century America*. New York: New York University Press.
Ramadan, Tariq, 2017. *Islam: The Essentials*. London: Penguin.
Rippin, Andrew. 2005. *Muslims: Their Religious Beliefs and Practices*, 3rd ed. New York: Routledge.
Rippin, Andrew. 2012. "Provocation and Its Responses." *Method and Theory in the Study of Religion* 24.4–5: 408–417. https://doi.org/10.1163/15700682-12341247
Ritterbrand, Paul, and Harold S. Wechsler. 1994. *Jewish Learning in American Universities: The First Century*. Bloomington, IN: Indiana University Press.
Robin, Christian J. 2004. "Ḥimyar et Israël." *Comptes-Rendus de l'Académie des Inscriptions et Belles-Lettres*: 831–908. Retrieved from www.persee.fr/doc/crai_0065-0536_2004_num_148_2_22750.
Robinson, Chase F. 2002. *Islamic Historiography*. Cambridge: Cambridge University Press.
Robinson, Chase F. 2009. "The Ideological Uses of Early Islam." *Past and Present* 203 (May): 205–228. https://doi.org/10.1093/pastj/gtp021
Rodinson, Maxime. 1987. *Europe and the Mystique of Islam*. London: I. B. Tauris.
Roggema, Barbara. 2009. *The Legend of Sergius Baḥīrā: Eastern Christian Apologetics and Apocalyptic in Response to Islam*. Leiden: Brill.
Rollens, Sarah E. 2014. *Framing Social Criticism in the Jesus Movement: The Ideological Project in the Sayings Gospel Q*. Tübingen: Mohr Siebeck.

Roubekas, Nickolas P. 2016. "Review of Aaron W. Hughes, *Theorizing Islam: Disciplinary Deconstruction and Reconstruction.*" *Contemporary Islam* 10.1: 119–121. https://doi.org/10.1007/s11562-015-0330-6

Rowe, C. Kavin. 2016. *One True Life: The Stoics and Early Christians as Rival Traditions.* New Haven, CT: Yale University Press.

Russ-Fishbane, Elisha. 2015. *Judaism, Sufism, and the Pietists of Medieval Egypt: A Study of Abraham Maimonides and His Circle.* Oxford: Oxford University Press.

Rustow, Marina. 2008. *Heresy and the Politics of Community: The Jews of the Fatimid Caliphate.* Ithaca, NY: Cornell University Press.

Safi, Omid. 2009. *Memories of Muhammad: Why the Prophet Matters.* New York: HarperCollins.

Safi, Omid. 2014. "Reflections on the State of Islamic Studies." *Jadaliyyah.* Retrieved from www.jadaliyya.com/Details/30175.

Sahner, Christian C. 2018. *Christian Martyrs under Islam: Religious Violence and the Making of the Muslim World.* Princeton, NJ: Princeton University Press.

Said, Edward W. 1978. *Orientalism.* New York: Vintage Books.

Said, Edward W. 2000. *Reflections on Exile and Other Essays.* Cambridge, MA: Harvard University Press.

Sarna, Jonathan. 2019. "A Note from Jonathan Sarna, Chair, H-Judaic." *H-Judaic.* Retrieved from https://networks.h-net.org/node/28655/discussions/4815412/note-jonathan-sarna-chair-h-judaic

Schacht, Joseph. 1950. *The Origins of Muhammadan Jurisprudence.* Oxford: Clarendon.

Schäfer, Peter. 1995. *The History of the Jews in Antiquity.* Trans. David Chowcat. Amsterdam: Harwood Academic Publishers.

Schmidtke, Sabine, ed. 2016. *Oxford Handbook of Islamic Theology.* Oxford: Oxford University Press.

Schöller, Marco, and Mouhanad Khorchide, eds. 2012. *Das Verhältnis zwischen Islamwissenschaft und Islamischer Theologie.* Münster: Agenda Münster Verlaf.

Schorsch, Ismar. 1994. "Scholarship in the Service of Reform." In his *From Text to Context: The Turn to History in Modern Judaism,* 303–333. Hanover, NH: University Press of New England.

Schubel, Vernon James. 2014a. "Thoughts on Dissecting an Octopus." *Religion Bulletin Blog.* Synopsis may be found at https://bulletin.equinoxpub.com/2014/12/rethinking-contested-ground-the-study-of-islam-inand-the-study-of-religion.

Schubel, Vernon James. 2014b. "New Nostalgia for Old Orientalism: A Review Essay of Aaron Hughes' *Theorizing Islam,*" SCTIW Reviews. Retrieved from http://sctiw.org/sctiwreviewarchives/wp-content/uploads/2014/08/006-Theorizing-Islam-Vernon-Schubel.pdf (link no longer active).

Secunda, Shai. 2014. *The Iranian Talmud: Reading the Bavli in Its Sasanian Context.* Philadelphia, PA: University of Pennsylvania Press.

Segal, Robert A. 1999. *Theorizing Myth.* Boston, MA: University of Massachusetts Press.

Sells, Michael. 1994. *Mystical Languages of Unsaying.* Chicago, IL: University of Chicago Press.

Sharpe. Eric J. *1986. Comparative Religion: A History.* 2nd ed. London: Duckworth.

Sheedy, Matt. 2018. *Identity, Politics, and the Study of Islam: Current Dilemmas in the Study of Religions.* Sheffield: Equinox.

Shoemaker, Stephen J. 2012. *The Death of a Prophet: The End of Muhammad's Life and the Beginnings of Islam.* Philadelphia, PA: University of Pennsylvania Press.

Shoemaker, Stephen J. 2018. *The Apocalypse of Empire: Imperial Eschatology in Late Antiquity and Early Islam.* Philadelphia, PA: University of Pennsylvania Press.

Silk, Mark. 1984. "Notes on the Judeo-Christian Tradition in America." *American Quarterly* 36.1: 65–85. https://doi.org/10.2307/2712839

Smith, Linda Tuhiwai. 2012. *Decolonizing Methodologies: Research and Indigenous Peoples.* 2nd ed. London: Zed Books.

Smith, Jonathan Z. 1982. *Imagining Religion.* Chicago, IL: University of Chicago Press.

Smith, Jonathan Z. 1990. *Drudgery Divine: On the Comparison of Early Christianities and the Religions of Late Antiquity.* Chicago, IL: University of Chicago Press.

Smith, Jonathan Z. 2004. *Relating Religion: Essays in the Study of Religion.* Chicago, IL: University of Chicago Press.

Sourdel, Dominique. 1962. "La politique religieuse du calife ʿabbaside al-Maʾmun" *Revue des études islamiques* 30: 27–48.

Speyer, Heinrich. 1923-1924. "Von den biblischen Erzählungen im Koran." *Korrespondenzblatt*: 7–26.

Spielhaus, Riem. 2018. "Der Umgang mit innerreligiöser Vielfalt im Islamischen Religionsunterricht in Deutschland und seinen Schulbüchern." In Zrinka Štimac and Riem Spielhaus, eds., *Schulbuch und religiöse Vielfalt. Interdisziplinäre Perspektiven*, 93–116. Göttingen: V&R unipress.

Stebner, Eleanor J. 2012. "The 1930s." In Don Schweitzer, ed., *The United Church of Canada: A History*, 39–56. Waterloo: Wilfrid Laurier University Press.

Stewart, Devin. 2018. "A Modest Proposal for Islamic Studies." In Matt Sheedy, ed., *Identity, Politics, and the Study of Islam: Current Dilemmas in the Study of Religions*, 157–200. Sheffield: Equinox.

Stroumsa, Guy G. 2010. *A New Science: The Discovery of Religion in the Age of Reason.* Cambridge, MA: Harvard University Press.

Stroumsa, Guy G. 2011. "From Abraham's Religion to the Abrahamic Religions" *Historia Religionum* 3: 11–22.

Stroumsa, Guy G. 2012. "The History of Religions as a Subversive Discipline: Comparing Judaism, Christianity and Islam." In Volkhard Krech and Marion Steinicke, eds., *Dynamics in the History of Religions Between Asia and Europe: Encounters, Notions, and Comparative Perspectives*, 149–158. Leiden: Brill.

Stroumsa, Guy G. 2015a. *The Making of the Abrahamic Religions in Late Antiquity.* Oxford: Oxford University Press.

Stroumsa, Guy G. 2015b. "Three Rings or Three Imposters? The Comparative Approach to the Abrahamic Religions and Its Origins." In Adam J. Silverstein and Guy G. Stroumsa, eds., *The Oxford Handbook of Abrahamic Religions,* 56–70. Oxford: Oxford University Press.

Stroumsa, Sarah. 1990. "The Origins of the Muʿtazila Reconsidered." *Jerusalem Studies in Arabic and Islam* 13: 265–293.

Stroumsa, Sarah. 1999. *Freethinkers of Medieval Islam: Ibn al-Rawāndī, Abū Bakr al-Rāzī, and their Impact on Islamic Thought.* Leiden: Brill.

Stroumsa, Sarah. 2011. *Maimonides in His World: Portrait of a Mediterranean Thinker.* Princeton, NJ: Princeton University Press.

Stroumsa, Sarah, and Gedaliahu G. Stroumsa. 1988. "Aspects of Anti-Manichaean Polemics in Late Antiquity and under Early Islam," *Harvard Theological Review* 81.1: 37–58. https://doi.org/10.1017/s0017816000009949

Sullivan, Winni. 2018. *The Impossibility of Religious Freedom.* New ed. Princeton, NJ: Princeton University Press.

Sullivan, Winni, Robert A. Yelle, and Mateo Taussig-Rubbo, eds. 2011. *After Secular Law.* Stanford, CA: Stanford University Press.

Swidler, Leonard. 1990. *After the Absolute.* Minneapolis, MN: Fortress Press.

al-Ṭabarī, Abū Jaʿfar Muhammad ibn Jarīr. 1879–1901. *Taʾrīkh al-rusul wa-l-mulūk.* Ed. M. J. de Goeje. 3 vols. Leiden: Brill.

Tannous, Jack. 2018. *The Making of the Medieval Middle East: Religion, Society, and Simple Believers.* Princeton, NJ: Princeton University Press.

al-Tirmidhī, Abū ʿĪsā Muḥammad b. ʿĪsā b. Sawra. 1978 [1398]. *Al-Jāmiʿ al-ṣaḥīḥ, wa-huwa Sunan al-Tirmidhī.* Ed. Aḥmad Muḥammad Shākir. 5 vols. Cairo: Sharikat Maktabat wa-Maṭbaʿat Muṣṭafā al-Bābī al-Ḥalabī wa-Awlādihi.

Touna, Vaia. 2017. *Fabrications of the Greek Past: Religion, Tradition, and the Making of Modern Identities.* Leiden: Brill.

Turner, Bryan S. 1994. *Orientalism, Postmodernism and Globalism.* New York: Routledge.

Turner, John P. 2013. *Inquisition in Early Islam: The Competition for Political and Religious Authority in the Abbasid Empire.* London: I. B. Tauris.

United Church of Canada. 1925. "The Basis of Union." Retrieved from https://commons.united-church.ca/Documents/Legal/Laws%20and%20Regulations/The%20United%20Church%20of%20Canada%20Act.pdf.

Vajda, Georges. 1937–1939. "Les zindîqs en pays d'Islam au debut de la période abbaside," *Rivista degli studi orientali* 17: 173–229.

van Ess, Josef. 1968. "Skepticism in Islamic Religious Thought." *Al-Abhath* 21: 1–14.

van Ess, Josef. 1981. "Some Fragments of the Muʿaradat al-Qurʾan attributed to Ibn al-Muqaffaʿ." In Wadad al-Qadi, ed., *Studia Arabica & Islamica: Festschrift for Ihsan ʿAbbas,* 151–163. Beirut: American University of Beirut.

van Ess, Josef. 1991–1997. *Theologie und Gesellschaft im 2. und 3. Jahrhundert Hidschra: Eine Geschichte des religiösen Denkens im frühen Islam*. 6 vols. Berlin: de Gruyter, Berlin.

Waardenburg, Jacques. 2017. *Classical Approaches to the Study of Religion: Aims, Methods, and Theories of Research*. 2nd ed. Berlin: De Gruyter.

Wansbrough, John. 1987. *Res Ipsa Loquitur: History and Mimesis*. Jerusalem: Israel Academy of Sciences and Humanities.

Wasserstrom, Steven M. 1988. "Islamicate History of Religions." *History of Religions* 27.4: 405–411.

Wasserstrom, Steven M. 1995. *Between Muslim and Jew: The Problem of Symbiosis Under Early Islam*. Princeton, NJ: Princeton University Press 1995.

Watt, W. Montgomery. 1968. *What is Islam?* London: Longmans.

Watt, W. Montgomery. 1973. *The Formative Period of Islamic Thought*. Edinburgh: Edinburgh University Press.

Webb, Peter. 2016. *Imagining the Arabs: Arab Identity and the Rise of Islam*. Edinburgh: Edinburgh University Press.

Weitzman, Steven P. 2013. "Religious Studies and the FBI: Adventures in Academic Interventionism." *Journal of the American Academy of Religion* 81.4: 959–995.

Werner, Roland. 1993. *Transcultural Healing: The Whole Human: Healing Systems Under the Influence of Abrahamic Religions, Eastern Religions and Beliefs, Paganism, New Religions, and Mixed Religious Forms*. Kuala Lumpur: University of Malaya Press.

White, Claire. 2017. "What the Cognitive Science of Religion Is (and Is Not)." In Aaron W. Hughes, ed., *Theory in a Time of Excess: Beyond Reflection and Explanation in Religious Studies Scholarship*, 95–114. Sheffield: Equinox.

Wiebe, Donald. 1999. *The Politics of Religious Studies: The Continuing Conflict with Theology in the Academy*. New York: Palgrave Macmillan.

Wiese, Christian. 2005. *Challenging Colonial Discourse: Jewish Studies and Protestant Theology in Wilhelmine Germany*. Trans. Barbara Harshav and Christian Wiese. Leiden: Brill.

Wisse, Ruth. 2007. *Jews and Power*. New York: Schocken.

Wolfson, Elliot R. 2004. *Language, Eros, Being: Kabbalistic Hermeneutics and Poetic Imagination*. New York: Fordham University Press.

Wolfson, Harry Austryn. 1947. *Philo: Foundations of Religious Philosophy in Judaism, Christianity, and Islam*. 2 vols. Cambridge, MA: Harvard University Press.

Young, Stephen L. forthcoming. "'Let's Take the Text Seriously': The Protectionist Doxa of Mainstream New Testament Studies." *Method and Theory in the Study of Religion*.

Zaman, Muhammad Qasim. 1997. *Religion and Politics Under the Early ʿAbbāsids: The Emergence of the Proto-Sunnī Elite*. Leiden: Brill.

Index

ʿAbbāsid caliphate 80, 82, 83–7, 101
Abrahamic religions 7, 112, 117,
    127–46, 150
  defining 127, 136, 137–40
  expertise in 140
  interfaith nature of 128, 129, 132,
    137–8
  and languages 139–40
  problems with 127, 128
  rehabilitating 129, 132, 138, 143–5
  second generation of 128–9, 144–5
Adamson, Peter 105–6
Afsaruddin, Asma 122–3
ahl al-kitāb 73, 75, 77
Ahmed, Shahab 18, 24–5, 103–5, 106,
    107, 114–15
American Academy of Religion (AAR)
    14, 23, 29, 32, 154
  conceptualization of religion 14–5
  and "radical love" 14
  see also religious studies; September
    11, 2001 (9/11)
al-Andalus 3, 101, 143
anti-Semitism 34–5, 37, 90, 130
Apocalypse of Sergius Baḥīrā 12, 13
Appiah, Kwame Anthony 119–20
Arab(ian) Jews 55, 56, 57, 58, 59, 60,
    62–4, 65
Arabian Judaism 59, 60
Arabian Peninsula 2, 6, 12, 55, 56, 57,
    58, 59, 60–63, 67, 68, 100, 124

Aslan, Reza 93
Association for Jewish Studies (AJS)
    39, 48
authenticity 18, 19, 66, 72, 88, 101
Awfa, Yosi b. 65
Axum (Ethiopian kingdom of) 64
Ayoub, Mahmoud 93

Baḥīrā 12, 13
Ben-Gurion, David 58
Bible Code, The 123
Boko Haram 14
Bowersock, Glen W. 66
Boyarin, Daniel 147
Boycott, Divest, Sanctions (BDS)
    movement 37, 46, 48, 49
Bulliet, Richard W. 133–5

Cairo Geniza 133, 139, 143
Campus Watch 118
Canadian Journal of Theology 155, 158–61
Case Western Reserve University, 46–7
Chokr, Melhem 86
Christopher Newport University 43–4
cognitive science of religion (CSR) 18,
    148, 165
comparison 3, 22, 37, 40–42, 55, 60, 62,
    67, 69, 76, 129, 131, 137–8
cosmopolitanism 119–20
COVID-19 5
Crone, Patricia 78, 142

Daneshgar, Majid 18, 25–8, 29
David, Larry 39
Day, Matthew 28
Dearborn (Michigan) 111
decoloniality 151–2
    see also cosmopolitanism
Dedan 63
Denny, Frederick Mathewson 94–5
description 5, 44, 74, 91, 108, 149, 152
dhimmi 74, 77
Dubuisson, Daniel 151
Dylan, Bob 117–18

Edmonton (Alberta) 111–12, 149
El-Badawi, Emran 142
Eliade, Mircea 148
engaged scholarship 13
Ernst, Carl 120, 123
Establishment Clause 154
Ewing, Katherine Pratt 120

Fairweather, Eugene R. 161
al-Faruqi, Ismail 159
Feyzbakhsh, Mohsen 29
Fort Simpson (NWT) 111

Geiger, Abraham 36, 61, 67, 141, 142
al-Ghazālī 20
Gleave, Ron 99
Goldziher, Ignác 2, 98, 101
Goitein, Shlomo Dov 41, 42, 61, 66, 107, 142
Graetz, Heinrich 60–61
Grewal, Zareena 17

ḥadīth 27, 78, 79–80, 81, 82, 86, 87, 108
ḥadīth folk see ḥadīth
Hammer, Juliane 23–4, 26, 103
heresiology 90, 101–2, 148
heterodoxy 55, 70–71, 72, 92, 94, 98, 99, 108
    see also orthodoxy

Ḥijāz 57, 64, 67
    see also Mecca, Medina, Yathrib
Hillel International 42–3, 44–5, 46, 47
Ḥimyar (Jewish kingdom of) 57, 58, 59, 64–6, 67
Hodgson, Marshall G. S. 107
Horovitz, Josef 2, 142
the humanities 4, 21, 23–4, 34, 47, 103, 120
Huntington, Samuel 133

Ibn Arabi 143
Ibn Muqaffaʿ 82–3
Ibn Warraq 125
identity politics 2, 4, 11, 16, 18, 20, 37, 51, 115, 120, 166
insider/outsider problem 27, 29
ISIS 14, 124
Islamic studies 1, 2, 4, 5, 6, 8, 11–32, 33, 34, 35, 39, 43, 48, 50–51, 56–7, 59, 67, 90, 91, 92, 96, 97, 99, 100–101, 102, 103, 104–5, 108, 113–14, 115, 118, 119, 121, 125, 152, 167
    and apologetics 7, 13
    and back-projection 6, 90–108
    and critical religion 18
    and gender justice 13, 24
    and ideological baggage 22
    impact of 9/11 on 16–8
    and normativity 23, 24, 26, 103
    North American context 11
    and study of Jews and Judaism in 100–101
    and Sunnī benefactors 98
    and Sunnī-centrism 6, 90–108
    see also identity politics; Jewish studies; religious studies; September 11, 2001 (9/11)
Islamic theological colleges (Germany) 31–2
Islamicate 107

Ismāʿīlīs 104
Ismāʿīlī studies 99
Israel 2, 3–4, 34, 37, 39, 45, 46, 47, 49–51, 58, 67, 97, 118, 123

Jerusalem 58, 63, 64, 84, 123,
Jewish Arabs 55, 65
Jewish Federations 45–7, 49
    and hiring committees 46
    Jewish Federation of Cleveland 47
    "Stand with Israel" 49
the "Jewish Question" 30
Jewish studies 1, 2, 4, 5, 6, 8, 33–51, 55, 56, 57, 59, 66, 67, 68–9, 96, 99, 105, 112, 121, 167
    and apologetics 4, 6, 33
    and BDS 37, 48
    centripetal v. centrifugal forces in 33–4, 36
    and community engagement 42–8
    and comparison 40–42
    and cultural Judaism 34, 39, 42
    and donor funding of 36–7, 39
    as ethnic studies 4
    and *hasbara* (pro-Israeli propaganda) 46
    and Israel 49–51
    and Jewish continuity 6, 56
    and non-Jews 55
    and particularism 33–4, 40
    and Six Day War 37
    see also Islamic studies; Neusner, Jacob; religious studies; Wissenschaft des Judentums
John of Damascus 12
Judeo-Arabic 4, 96
Judeo-Christian 130

Kaʿb al-Aḥbār 12
kāfir (pl. *kāfirūn*; "unbeliever") 77, 81, 82
kalām ("theology") 88, 106, 108

Kelsey, John 28–9
Khazars 57, 67
Kraus, Paul 2

Late Antiquity 6, 58, 60–62, 70, 124
Lentin, Ronit 49
Lewis, Bernard 55–6
Lincoln, Bruce 8, 19, 20, 21, 114, 119

al-Mahdī (caliph) 73, 78, 82, 83–7, 88
Maimonides 39
al-Maʾmūn (caliph) 74–5, 76, 84–5, 87
Manicheans 6, 72, 73–6, 77, 78
Marracci, Ludovico 1
Martin, Richard C. 29, 120, 123
Mas, Ruth 29
Masjid al-Rashid (Edmonton, AB) 112
Masuzawa, Tomoko 150
McCutcheon, Russell T. 8, 19, 20, 23
Mecca 57, 63, 64, 81, 84
Meddeb, Abdelwahab 30
Medina 57, 63, 64, 94
    see also Yathrib
Melchert, Christopher 80, 86
Method and Theory in the Study of Religion (*MTSR*) 18, 28
Middle Eastern studies 13
Middle Eastern Studies Association (MESA) 118
miḥna ("inquisition") 80, 83–7
Mishnah 56, 58, 62, 65, 66
Moltmann, Jürgen 131, 132
"monotheistic religions" 127
Morgenson, Eric B. 49
Muʿāwiya 85
Muhammad 6, 12, 55, 56, 59, 62, 63, 67, 68, 71, 80, 82, 83, 85, 86, 87, 88, 94, 96, 104, 108, 121, 122, 142
"Muslim Ban" (Executive Order 13769) 118–19
the "Muslim Question" 30
Mutual Street Arena (Toronto) 156

al-Najdi, Muhammad Ali ibn Khalil
111–12, 124–5
Nasr, Seyyed Hossein 98–9
Neusner, Jacob 37–40, 42, 43, 45, 51, 152
  and Jewish Theological Seminary (JTS) 38
  and religious studies 38–9
Nöldeke, Theodor 98
Nongbri, Brent 150
normativity 23, 24, 26, 42, 55, 60, 66, 91, 92, 93, 103, 104, 106, 108

Official Languages Act/Loi sur les langues officielles 160
Orientalism 1, 2, 5, 12, 13, 15, 17, 26, 30, 31, 61, 97–9, 100, 101, 117, 119, 120, 121, 123, 142
  criticism of 2
  German-Jewish tradition of 2, 3, 35
  handmaiden of colonialism 12
  "neo-Orientalism" 17
  positive aspects of 26
orthodoxy 6, 59, 70–72, 72, 75, 76, 78, 80, 81, 83–4, 87, 88–9, 91, 92, 94, 102, 108
  see also heterodoxy
Oslo Accords 50
Ottoman Empire 3
Oxford Center for Islamic Studies 31
Oxford Handbook of Abrahamic Religions 134, 135

Palestine 3, 46, 57
Pearson, Lester B. 159
Pines, Shlomo 142
Pipes, Daniel 118

Qurʾān 25–6, 27, 31, 36, 48, 56, 68, 70, 72, 73, 75, 76, 79, 81, 82, 83, 86, 87, 88, 93, 98, 108, 121–2, 141

Rabbinic Judaism 55, 59, 65, 68
Rabin, Yitzhak 123
Raḥmānān 64–5, 66
Ramadan, Tariq 92–3
Ramey, Steven 28
al-Rashīd, Hārūn 87
Reform Judaism 36
"religions of the West" 127
religious studies 1, 3, 5, 8, 11, 13, 14, 15, 17, 18, 20, 22, 24, 25, 28, 29, 33, 34, 38, 40, 47, 48, 103, 120, 124, 128, 129, 131, 132, 135, 138, 140–141, 143, 145, 148, 149, 150, 151, 153, 154, 161, 162, 165–7
  and Canadian context 154–5
  and the category "religion" 147–8, 150, 152, 165
  and construction of "good" religion 3
  decolonizing 151–2
  and experience 34
  inherent generalism of 140
  and "lived religion" 165
  and the modern nation state 152–5
  Protestant categories of 17, 32
  and reverence 21
  rigidity of 2–3
  and the sacred 34
  and scholarly activism 15
  and theology 22, 24
  theory and method 28
  and "world religions" 150
  see also Islamic studies, Jewish studies
Rippin, Andrew 29, 95
Robin, Christian J. 63, 65, 66
Roubekas, Nickolas 18–19
Royal Commission on Bilingualism and Biculturalism 158

Sabians 75
de Sacy, Antoine Isaac Silvestre 1

Safi, Omid 19, 20, 28
Said, Edward W. 25, 26, 30, 113, 142
Sarna, Jonathan 49–50
Schmidtke, Sabine 106
scholarly activism 13, 15, 24
School District of Abington Township, PA v. Schempp, 154
Schubel, Vernon 17
Second Temple 34, 57, 58, 59, 63, 67, 135
September 11, 2001 (9/11) 13–8, 28, 31, 130, 133
    see also Abrahamic religions; Islamic studies; religious studies
Shaben, Larry 112
Sheedy, Matt 20–22
Shiʿism 27, 71, 83, 88, 92–7, 98, 99, 104, 106, 107, 149
Shiʿī studies 99
Shoemaker, Stephen J. 96
Sira 121
Smith, Jonathan Z. 8, 20
Smith, Wilfred Cantwell 27
South Arabia 56, 57, 58, 64, 65, 68
Speyer, Heinrich 2, 142
State University of New York at Buffalo 44–5
Steinschneider, Moritz 36
Stewart, Devin J. 17, 20–22, 24
Stora, Benjamin 30
Stroumsa, Guy 129, 147
Stroumsa, Sarah 78
Studies in Religion/sciences religieuses 155, 158, 161–2
Sunna 78, 79, 80, 85, 86, 87, 93, 95
Sunnism 71, 95, 97, 102
Swidler, Leonard 130, 132
Sykes–Picot Agreement 116
symbiosis 41–2

al-Ṭabarī 86
Talmud 34, 56, 58, 65, 66
Tannous, Jack 96
Theodosian Code 70–71, 77
Tikvah Fund 50
Trudeau, Pierre Elliot 160
Trump, Donald J. 118–19
Turner, John P. 85–6

United Church of Canada 22, 155–7
    Basis of Union 156–7
    ecumenicism of 157
United Nations (UN) 4
United States Institute of Peace 131
Usha 62

Wansbrough, John 102
Wasserstrom Steven M. 107, 147
Watt, W. Montgomery 93–4
Weber, Max 3
Wisse, Ruth 50–51, 57
Wissenschaft des Judentums 35–7, 41, 55, 60
    see also Jewish studies
Wolfson, Elliot R. 142
Wolfson, Harry Austryn 141–2

xenophobia 7

Yathrib 63, 64
    see also Medina
Yavneh 62

Zindīq ("heretic") 6, 70–89, 96
    definition of 71
    as generic category 71–2
    and "ḥadīth folk" 79–81
    non-quranic term 71, 73
    typology of 77–9
Zionism 4, 45, 50, 122
Zohar 143
Zunz, Leopold 36

www.ingramcontent.com/pod-product-compliance
Lightning Source LLC
Chambersburg PA
CBHW062037220426
43662CB00010B/1530